*Feminine
Psychology*

KAREN HORNEY, M.D.

Feminine Psychology

○○○

Edited and with an Introduction by
HAROLD KELMAN, M.D.

W · W · NORTON & COMPANY
New York · London

W. W. Norton & Company, Inc., 500 Fifth Avenue,
New York, N.Y. 10110

EDITORIAL COMMITTEE

Harold Kelman, M.D.
Edward R. Clemmens, M.D.   John M. Meth, M.D.
Edward Schattner, M.D.   Gerda F. Willner, M.D.

First published in the Norton Library 1973

Published simultaneously in Canada by
Penguin Books Canada Ltd,
2801 John Street, Markham, Ontario L3R 1B4.

W.W. Norton & Company, Inc. is also the publisher of the works of Erik H.
Erikson, Otto Fenichel, Karen Horney, Harry Stack Sullivan, and The
Standard Edition of the Complete Psychological Works of Sigmund Freud.

Library of Congress Cataloging in Publication Data
Horney, Karen, 1885–1952.
   Feminine psychology.
   (The Norton library)
   "Sponsored by the Association for the Advancement of
Psychoanalysis."
   Includes bibliographical references.
   1. Woman—Psychology. 2. Sex (Psychology)
I. Association for the Advancement of Psychoanalysis.
II. Title. [DNLM: 1. Sex behavior. 2. Women.
HQ 1206 H816f 1967a]
[HQ1206.H6   1973]   155.6'33   72-13142

ISBN 0-393-00686-7

Printed in the United States of America

56789

CONTENTS

INTRODUCTION

○○○

*I*N 1935 FREUD STATED that he had reached the very climax of his psychoanalytic work in 1912.[1] He added, "since I put forward my hypothesis of the existence of two kinds of instinct [Eros and the death instinct] and since I proposed a division of the mental personality into an ego, a super-ego, and an id (in 1923), I have made no further decisive contributions to psychoanalysis."

By 1913 Karen Horney had received her medical degree in Berlin and had completed her psychiatric and psychoanalytic training there. In 1917 she wrote her first psychoanalytic paper[2] and by 1920 she had become a valued member of the teaching staff of the newly founded Berlin Psychoanalytic Institute. In 1923 she published the first of a series[*] of papers on feminine psychology—"On the Genesis of the Castration Complex in Women," which appears in this volume.

Freud was almost thirty years Horney's senior. During the per-

1. Sigmund Freud, "An Autobiographical Study," in *Collected Papers*, Vol. XX (London. The Hogarth Press, 1936; also published New York, W. W. Norton & Co., Inc., 1952).

2. Karen Horney, "The Technique of Psychoanalytic Therapy" ("Die Technik der psychoanalytischen Therapie"), *Zeitschr. f. Sexualwissenschaft*, IV (1917).

* The following papers on feminine psychology by Horney are not included in this volume: "The Masculinity Complex of Women" (Der Männlichkeitskomplex der Frau), *Arch. f. Frauenkunde*, XII (1927), pp. 141–54; "Psychological Suitability and Unsuitability for Marriage" ("Psychische Eignung und Nichteignung zur Ehe"), "On the Psychological Conditions of the Choice of a Marriage Partner" ("Über die psychischen Bestimmungen der Gattenwahl"), "On the Psychological Roots of Some Typical Marriage Conflicts" ("Über die psychischen Wurzeln einiger typischer Ehekonflikte"). In: *Ein biologisches Ehebuch*, by Max Marcuse (Berlin and Köln, A. Marcus and E. Weber, 1927); "The Distrust Between the Sexes" ("Das Misstrauen zwischen den Geschlechtern"), *Psychoanal. Bewegung*, II (1930), pp. 521–37.

iod when she was acquiring training for the most productive period of her life, Freud had passed the peak of his greatest creative
powers. Freud's self-evaluation, made in 1935, was partly contributed to by the pain of "a malignant disease" that had begun to
interfere with his life and work. After 1923, Freud's interests
were coming full circle, culminating in his last book, *Moses and
Monotheism* (1939). "My interest, after making a life-long detour
through the natural sciences, medicine, psychotherapy, returned
to the cultural problems which had fascinated me long before,
when I was a youth scarcely old enough for thinking".[3]

Scientific and cultural theories, like human beings, have their
rhythms. Their cycles and changing interests are reflected in the
successive generations who contribute to them. Similarly, in reviewing the history of the psychoanalytic movement, we see the
emergence of different ways of explaining behavior.[4] In this introduction particular emphasis will be placed on the emergence
of Freud's and Horney's ideas on feminine psychology.

There are limits to which a genius can transcend the *Weltanschauung* in which he was reared. It takes another generation to
make that radical leap to a new paradigm in science,[5] to a new
unitive world view of cosmos.

Freud was a product of the nineteenth century. The Age of
Enlightenment had fostered the dignity of the individual and the
primacy of reason. The methodology of the scientific outlook had
produced significant advances in the natural sciences. While Western man was still having difficulty accepting the idea of a helio-
centric universe, he was further bombarded by Darwin's concept
of evolution. Soon he would be confronted with Freud's ideas
about the unconscious.

Naturally, certain aspects of his more immediate milieu also
affected Freud's outlook. He was born in Freiberg, Moravia, a
province of Austria, into an ostracized minority group and
brought up in a traditionally Jewish household, where man was

3. Freud, *op. cit.*
4. Harold Kelman and J. W. Vollmerhausen, "On Horney's Psychoanalytic Techniques, Developments and Perspectives," in *Psychoanalytic
Techniques*, ed. B. B. Wolman (New York, Basic Books, 1967).
5. Thomas S. Kuhn, *The Structure of Scientific Revolutions* (Chicago,
The University of Chicago Press, First Phoenix Edition, 1964), p. 159.

lord and master and woman a lesser being. The importance of this patriarchy must have been further confirmed by the very obvious favoritism his mother showed toward him. The decaying Austro-Hungarian empire and Catholic Vienna left their impress on him, as did the prudish, puritanical, and hypocritical sexual mores of the Victorian era in which he was reared. As a male genius, Freud evolved a male-oriented psychology, which he based on anatomic immutables—"anatomy is destiny"—buttressed by the canons and methodologies of nineteenth-century science.

"Psychoanalysis," said Freud, "is a branch of science and can subscribe to the scientific *Weltanschauung*"; [6] facts were considered as the data relevant to scientific experimentation. Facts could be observed, measured, and objectified. They could be controlled in repeatable experiments with predictable outcomes. These experiments would test hypotheses that, when publicly verified, might be referred to as laws.

Nineteenth-century science concerned itself with isolated closed systems based on the notion of strict determinism. In the psychoanalytic treatment situation influenced by this system of thinking, the psychoanalyst and the environment in which the patient lived were considered to be fixed coordinates. Thus the patient was regarded as the only variable in Freud's experimental investigative structure and was treated as an isolated object, consistent with the methodologies of the natural sciences.

The natural sciences in the twentieth century became much less tightly structured and allowed for varying degrees of determinism. Similarly, in the psychoanalytic situation the environment as well as the patient became increasingly important as interdependent factors. Also aesthetic, moral, and spiritual values, which were not considered the concern of science in the nineteenth century and therefore not participant in psychoanalytic methodologies of investigation, were assuming a central place in twentieth-century science.

Karen Horney was born in Hamburg into an upper-middle-class Protestant family. Her father was a devout Bible reader and her mother a free-thinker. In her early teens Karen Horney went

6. Sigmund Freud, *New Introductory Lectures* (New York, W. W. Norton & Co., Inc., 1965), p. 181.

through a period of religious enthusiasm, which at that time was a common occurrence among adolescent girls. Her family was economically and socially secure. Her father (Berndt Henrik Wackels Danielsen) was a Norwegian sea captain, who became a German citizen and later Commodore of the North German Lloyd shipping company. In her youth Horney made long sea voyages with her father, and thus began her life-long passion for travel and interest in strange and far-away places. Her mother (Clothilde Marie van Ronzelen) was Dutch.

The contrast between the milieus into which Freud and Horney were born is striking. Freud's parents lived in restricted circumstances when he was born, and their social situation was made worse by the rising Czech nationalism opposed to Austrian rule, and by the Czech hostility toward the German-speaking Jewish minority. The declining textile industry, on which his father depended as a wool merchant, forced the family to move to Vienna when Freud was three. When he was only twelve, Freud experienced his father's "spiritless resignation and lack of courage" [7] when humiliated by a Gentile. This situation disturbed Freud, and he was middle-aged before he outgrew the need to replace his destroyed father ideal.

Although Horney spent much time with her father on long sea voyages, it was her mother who had the larger influence on her. Because of her father's long and frequent absences, she spent much more time with her dynamic, intelligent, and beautiful mother, who favored Berndt, Karen's older brother. Karen looked up to and was very much attached to him, though after her middle teens he played a limited role in her life.

At the end of the nineteenth century it was still unusual for a woman to decide to become a physician, which Karen Horney did with the encouragement of her mother. She went to Berlin for medical, psychiatric, and psychoanalytic training. Her reasons for choosing a career as a psychoanalyst have never been stated in her writings. She was an excellent student and was usually first in her class. Her ability and personality won the respect of her professors as well as that of her male colleagues.

7. F. G. Alexander and S. T. Selesnick, *The History of Psychiatry* (New York, Harper & Row, Publishers, 1966), pp. 186–87.

In 1909, at the age of twenty-four, she married Oscar Horney, a Berlin lawyer, and with him she had three daughters. Because of differing interests and Dr. Horney's increasing involvement in the psychoanalytic movement, she divorced him in 1937. The problems of being a mother and a career woman, and of dissolving a marriage she felt was no longer meaningful may have contributed to her growing interest in feminine psychology. I feel, however, that her interest was much more determined by her commitment to psychoanalysis, her enthusiasm for investigation, and the acuity of her clinical observations. As a therapist she was also motivated by her discovery of a discrepancy between the theories of Freudian psychoanalysis and what she found to be the therapeutic results of the application of these theories.

Horney spent most of her life in Berlin; this was at the time of the rise and fall of the Second Reich and of the Kaiser's dominion. Although surely influenced by these events, she had a limited interest in politics. And though she was certainly aware of the unequal status of women, I do not feel that her interest in feminine psychology was greatly affected by her observations on the sociological position of women. Nor was the rise of Hitler a determining factor in her departure for the United States in 1932. Despite the fact that Karen Horney was not moved to social action, she was well-informed about social issues and the world situation, and she generously supported relief organizations and liberal causes. In 1941 she made her position quite clear as an anti-Fascist and expressed her belief "that democratic principles, in sharp contrast to Fascist ideology, uphold the independence and strength of the individual and assert his right to happiness." [8]

Horney was analyzed first by Karl Abraham, whom Freud regarded as one of his ablest pupils, and then by Hanns Sachs, whose attitude toward Freud was a worshipful one. Analysis by such loyal disciples would seem likely to foster adherence to Freud's views rather than deviation.

However, Karen Horney's origins and early life experiences prepared her for wider perspectives. She was greatly interested in the emergence of twentieth-century science, and this interest cer-

8. Karen Horney, Biography, in *Current Biography*, Vol. II, No. 8 (New York, H. W. Wilson Co., August 1941), pp. 27-29.

tainly contributed to her becoming a physician and a psychoanalyst. She was also stimulated by the cosmopolitan atmosphere
of Berlin during her student days, especially the vitality of the
theater and the work of director Max Reinhardt.

She became a student of psychoanalysis when its foundations
had already been established and gradually accepted on a world-
wide basis. There was a youthfulness and competence about the
men and women gathered in Berlin immediately after World War
I, and with the founding of the Berlin Psychoanalytic Institute in
1920, a great time in psychoanalysis began. Many of those who
taught and were trained there created the basic tenets that psychoanalysis was to follow for the next fifty years.

By 1923 "the classical psychoanalytic approach" had been outlined—a psychology "characterized by five distinct points of
view." The topographical one asserts that "psychoanalysis is a
depth psychology and gives special significance to preconscious
and unconscious psychic activities." Secondly, "present behavior can only be understood in terms of the past." This genetic
orientation implies that mental phenomena are the outcome of
the interplay "of environmental experiences and of the biological
development," of the psycho-sexual structure. "The dynamic
point of view [the third] refers to the proposition that human behavior can be understood as the result of the interaction of instinctual impulses and counterinstinctual forces." The fourth,
"the economic point of view is based on the hypothesis that the
organism has a given quantity of energy at its disposal. . . ."

The structural point of view, the fifth, "is a working hypothesis which divides the mental apparatus into three separate struc-
tures. . . . The id is the instinctual reservoir of man and has its
basis in anatomy and physiology. . . . The id is under the dom-
ination of the primary process, which means that it operates in
accordance with the pleasure principle. . . . The ego is the control apparatus of the psychic structure. . . . It organizes and syn-
thesizes. . . . The conscious functions of the ego, as well as the
preconscious, are under the influence of the secondary process.
. . . The super-ego is the latest structure of the psychic apparatus
to develop. It results from the resolution of the Oedipus complex. As a consequence, a new agency is instituted in the ego, con-

taining the rewarding and punishing qualities and values of the parents. The ego-ideal and the conscience are different aspects of the super-ego. . . .

"All neurotic phenomena are the result of an insufficiency of the ego's normal function of control, which leads either to symptom-formation or to characterological change or both. . . . A neurotic conflict can best be explained structurally as a conflict between the forces of the ego on the one hand and the id on the other. . . . The decisive neurotic conflicts occur in the first years of childhood. . . . The . . . ultimate aim . . . of psychoanalytic therapy . . . is to resolve the infantile neurosis which is the nucleus of the adult neurosis and thereby to do away with the neurotic conflicts." [9]

In 1917, six years before Freud's formulation of the principles of psychoanalytic technique and before the publication of *The Ego and the Id*, Karen Horney stated in her paper on psychoanalytic technique, "Psychoanalysis can free a human being who has been tied hands and feet. It cannot give him new arms or legs. Psychoanalysis, however, has shown us that much that we have regarded as constitutional merely represents a blockage of growth, a blockage which can be lifted." [10] Her growth-oriented, life-affirming, freedom-seeking philosophy was already evident. Constitution for her was not something fixed at birth and unchanging throughout life, but represented plastic possibilities to be shaped by organismal environmental interactions. Thus by 1917 Karen Horney had defined her holistic concept of blockage [11] in contrast to Freud's mechanistic notion of resistance.

What she formulated in these early years was bound to cause a confrontation with the psychoanalysts who supported the Freudian approach to the treatment of psychoneuroses. Although Horney recognized the significance of unconscious forces, she believed that their dimension and meaning were quite different. For instance, she did not consider the term "dynamic" to mean the in-

9. R. R. Greenson, "The Classic Psychoanalytic Approach," in *The American Handbook of Psychiatry*, ed. S. Arieti (New York, Basic Books, 1959). This paper contains an authoritative, concise, recent presentation of Freudian psychoanalysis.

10. Horney, "The Technique of Psychoanalytic Therapy," *op. cit.*

11. Kelman and Vollmerhausen, *op. cit.*

teraction between instinct and counter instinct, but rather she viewed the conflict between the spontaneous forces of growth and the perversions of those healthy energies as sickness. The economic concept that there is a fixed quantity of energy available in the organism was an assumption of nineteenth-century science, which Freud considered applicable to psychoanalytic theory. This notion applied to isolated closed systems in a Newtonian mechanistic universe. Horney's thinking was of the open-system variety, similar to that of the field theories of twentieth-century physics. In spite of his assertions, Freud's orientation was not biological but based on a materialistic philosophy. Horney's was rooted in holistic and organismic philosophies expressed in a language of field relationships that defines environment and organism as a unitary process, each influencing the other.

Horney's position of 1917 sharply confronted a tripartite mental apparatus. Her assumption of human spontaneity rooted in anatomy and physiology questioned the primacy of the id and the destructive instincts. Her freedom-seeking philosophy cast doubt on the pleasure-pain principle based on the notion of absolute determinism. Horney asserted that man becomes destructive because of a blockage in growth. Freud saw sublimation as a secondary process, while Horney regarded it as a primary unobstructed manifestation of growth. The functions of what Freud subsumed under his ego and superego consequently had new meanings in Horney's theoretical structure.

The genetic point of view, which claimed that a given piece of behavior could only be understood in terms of the past, was questioned by Horney's concept of the "actual situation," [12, 13, 14] which involves "actually existing conflicts and the neurotic's attempts to solve them" and "his actually existing anxieties and the defenses he has built up against them".[15] The "actual situation" gives place and space for the exaggerating and mitigating influences of the ongoing present which is left out in the genetic

12. Kelman and Vollmerhausen, *op. cit.*

13. Karen Horney, *The Neurotic Personality of Our Time*, (New York, W. W. Norton & Co., Inc., 1937), chap. VII.

14. Karen Horney, *New Ways in Psychoanalysis*, (New York, W. W. Norton & Co., Inc., 1939), chap. X.

15. *Ibid.*, chap. VII.

focus.

Horney's early views contained many points of difference with Freud's basic theories. How divergent her theories were became evident only in her later formulations. Horney's earliest concerns were with Freud's libido theory and his theories of psychosexual development. The papers in this book contain her detailed confrontation of these theories. Just as we can only speculate about the factors in Horney's own development that contributed to the direction her thinking took in 1917, so we can only summarize the events that led her to begin an examination of Freud's theories and especially his genetic point of view reflected in the libido theory.

After the publication of her 1917 paper, Dr. Horney may have decided to wait before developing the ideas expressed in that paper, which were so much at variance with Freud's philosophy. She was still a newcomer to the field of psychoanalysis and her ideas needed a few years to mature sufficiently. Freud's libido theory was subject to much critical study by psychoanalysts at that time; and by 1923 Freud had developed it further by the inclusion of a dual-instinct theory.

"In some of his latest works Freud has drawn attention with increasing urgency to a certain one-sidedness in our analytic researches." Horney adds, "I refer to the fact that till quite recently the minds of boys and men only were taken as the objects of investigation. The reason for this is obvious. Psychoanalysis is the creation of a male genius, and almost all of those who have developed his ideas have been men. It is only right and reasonable that they should evolve more easily a masculine psychology and understand more of the development of men than of women".•

Dr. Horney's early interest in feminine psychology was also stimulated by clinical observations that seemed to contradict the libido theory. Her interest in the writings of social philosopher Georg Simmel and in anthropological works may have further contributed to her interest in feminine psychology. Clearly so-called masculine and feminine psychologies had to be formulated to prepare the way for her whole person philosophy.

What were the Freudian theories of sexuality that Horney

• "Flight from Womanhood," p. 54 in this volume.

learned and worked with during and after her analytic training? Freud's earliest theory (1895) was the premise that sexual frustration was the direct cause of neurosis. He asserted that the sexual instinct which becomes manifest in infancy has as its aim the discharge of tension, and as its object the person or substitute who gratifies this discharge. According to Freud, the neurotic does in fantasy what the pervert does in actuality, and the child is polymorphous-perverse. Freud extended the concept of sexuality to include all bodily pleasure, feelings of tenderness and affection, as well as the desire for genital gratification.

According to Freud the sex life of man is divided into three periods. The first is infantile sexuality,[16] which is further subdivided into the oral, anal, and phallic phases, and culminates in the Oedipus complex. The second, encompassing the years between seven and twelve, is the latency period. It begins with the resolution of the Oedipus complex and the establishment of a superego. Puberty is the third period, occurring approximately between the ages of twelve to fourteen, leading to mature genitality, heterosexual object choice, and sexual intercourse.

Freud later assumed that libido was the major source of psychic energy, not only for sexuality, but for the aggressive drive (1923), and furthermore, that there is a developmental process consisting of various libidinal stages. He also postulated that object choice results from transformations of libido, that the libidinal drives can be gratified, repressed, and handled by reaction formation, or sublimated. Character structure is determined by the ways in which biologically determined instincts are handled. Still further he assumed that neurosis is a fixation or regression to some phase of infantile sexuality.

Freud had not completely formulated "the phase of *primacy of the phallus*" until 1923.[17] Because it was such an important starting point for Dr. Horney's papers on feminine psychology, I shall quote this rather essential notion of the phallic phase as it is stated by Greenson in *The American Handbook of Psychiatry*.

16. Reuben Fine, *Freud: A Critical Re-evaluation of His Theories* (New York, David McKay Co., Inc., 1962).

17. Sigmund Freud, "The Infantile Genital Organization of the Libido" (1923), in *Collected Papers*, Vol. II (London, The Hogarth Press, 1933).

The phallic phase occurs about the third to seventh year. Here the development of boys and girls differs. In the boy the discovery of the sensitivity of the penis leads to masturbation. Usually, sexual fantasies concerning the mother enter the masturbation activity. Simultaneously the boy feels rivalry and hostility to the father. The coexistence of sexual love to the mother and hostile rivalry to the father, Freud called the Oedipus complex. The boy's discovery of the girl's lack of a penis at this time usually is interpreted by him to mean that she has lost this precious organ. The guilt for his sexual fantasies to the mother and death wishes toward the father continue to stir up in him castration anxiety. As a consequence, he usually renounces masturbation and thus eventually enters the latency period. In the girl the discovery that the boy has a penis and she has not, leads her to envy the boy and to blame her mother for this lack. As a consequence she renounces the mother as her primary love object and turns to the father. The clitoris is her main zone of masturbatory activities; the vagina is undiscovered. The girl fantasies getting a penis or a baby from her father and has hostile feelings of rivalry about her mother. As a general rule, she slowly gives up her oedipal strivings and enters latency owing to her fear of losing the love of her parents.[18]

Though Freud's clinical observations have always been highly regarded and seldom questioned, the theoretical constructions based on them have become the center of much controversy. He often stated that his primary interest was investigation and that only secondarily was he interested in therapy. Karen Horney's primary interest was therapy, and for this reason she was highly regarded as a teacher [19] and supervising analyst. Her talents for teaching and training expressed her natural ability for clinical research.

In his discussion of Horney's paper "Maternal Conflicts" *

18. Greenson, *Op. cit.*

19. C. P. Oberndorf, "Obituary, Karen Horney," *Int. J. Psycho-Anal.*, Part II, 1953.

* Zilboorg's discussion is contained in the *American Journal of Orthopsychiatry*, Vol. III (1933), pp. 461–63.

Gregory Zilboorg states that one of its features "requires further emphasis," namely, that it is "clinical psychoanalysis . . . It counteracts, I hope, the unusually strong and undeservedly popular trend toward technical problems and theoretical considerations which all too frequently obscure instead of illuminate the phenomena of human behavior." He emphasizes the need for "clinical observation, of clinical phenomena, in clinical circumstances." Thereby "we come again to the perennial clinical truth, according to which the study of the normal and the mildly neurotic individual is made possible only in the light of our knowledge which is acquired from the deeper analysis of severely pathological individuals, not only so-called border-line, but frankly psychotic ones."

All these early papers reveal Karen Horney's interest in clinical observation, her careful collection of data, and the rigorous testing of hypotheses formulated both by Freud and by herself. In her first paper written in 1917 she said, "The analytical theories have grown out of observations and experiences which were made in applying this method. The theories, in turn, later exerted their influence on the practice." [20] First came clinical observation and then the hypothesis based on the data. These hypotheses, while being further tested in the therapeutic situation, were influencing that very process. Horney's interest in careful investigation and clinical research never deviated. She never lost this spirit of searching, testing, revising, changing, dropping, and adding new hypotheses.

Always beginning with clinical data, she might start with a clinical construct, move on to a molar hypothesis, and then on to one of a higher order of abstraction. Unconnected smaller hypotheses were joined into one of a higher order of generality. Data that did not support one particular formulation were further tested and explained by new theories. In "The Problem of Feminine Masochism," a most closely reasoned paper, Horney comments on the data Freud provided for the hypothesis of the penis envy. She says, "The foregoing observations are sufficient to build a working hypothesis. . . . It must be realized, however, that this hypothesis is an hypothesis, not a fact; and that it is not

20. Horney, "The Technique of Psychoanalytic Therapy," *op. cit.*

even indisputably useful as an hypothesis."

All of the aspects of Dr. Horney's positive approach to psycho-analysis were present and operating as she evolved her theories of feminine psychology. In "The Flight from Womanhood" she was already referring to "my theory of feminine development." In "The Denial of the Vagina" she uses the expression "feminine psychology as a whole," and takes sharp issue with Freud and Helene Deutsch. In this paper she repeatedly refers to "my theory," and supports it with her clinical data. Although her purpose in "The Problem of Feminine Masochism" is a critical evaluation of the classical interpretation of masochism, she develops her ideas into an extensive clinical description of this term. She also speculates about the effect of cultural conditions in the problem of masochism. With these new perspectives, which included her own psychodynamic, phenomenological, and cultural approach, she was already working toward the theme developed in *The Neurotic Personality of Our Time* [21]—the consequences of the impact of culture on people, regardless of their sex.

In the first paper in this volume, "On the Genesis of the Castration Complex in Women," Horney questions Freud's claim that penis envy alone is responsible for women's castration fantasies. Using clinical evidence as data, Dr. Horney goes on to explain that both men and women, in their attempts to master the Oedipus complex, often develop a castration complex or move toward homosexuality.

In "The Flight from Womanhood" Horney comments on the extension of the penis-envy concept in a postulated phallic phase. This concept, which considers one genital organ, the male, conceives of the clitoris as a phallus. Horney, quoting social philosopher Georg Simmel on the "essentially masculine" orientation of our society, states that having assumed a primary penis envy, by "*a-posteriori*" reasoning, the logic for its "enormous dynamic power" is arrived at.

Freud's male-oriented theory leads Horney "as a woman" to "ask, in amazement, and what about motherhood? and the blissful consciousness of bearing a new life within oneself, the ineffable happiness of the increasing expectation of the appearance

21. Horney, *The Neurotic Personality of Our Time, op. cit.*

of this new being? and the joy when it finally makes it appearance? . . ." The penis envy concept attempts to deny and detract from all this, possibly because of male fear and envy.
Horney saw penis envy not as an unnatural phenomenon, but
as an expression of the mutual envy and attraction of the sexes
for each other. Penis envy becomes a pathological phenomenon
as a later development, due to problems in connection with the
resolution of the Oedipus complex.

Dr. Horney discusses in "The Dread of Women" the fears
men have of women, which may have contributed to the male-
oriented penis envy concept. Throughout history man has seen
woman as a sinister and mysterious being, particularly dangerous when she is menstruating. Man attempts to deal with his
dread by denial and defense. He has been so successful that
women themselves have long been able to overlook it. Men deny
their dread by love and adoration and defend themselves from
it by conquering, debasing, and diminishing the self-respect of
women.

In this same paper Dr. Horney emphasizes that there is no
reason to assume that the little boy's phallic desires to penetrate
his mother's genital are naturally sadistic. Therefore it is inad-
missable, in the absence of specific evidence in each case, to
equate the term "male" with "sadistic," and on similar lines
"female" with "masochistic." Horney is again emphasizing the
necessity for "specific evidence," and she is also exposing the
havoc that loose theorizing can perpetrate. Even among experienced analysts there is a tendency to accept as natural the theory
that women are passive and masochistic and that men are active
and sadistic. Such notions have come into common parlance on
the basis of such unsubstantiated theories.

Dr. Horney also considers the notion that the penis envy
concept might also have roots in male envy of the female. When
Horney began analyzing men, after years of working with women,
she was struck by the intensity of male "envy of pregnancy, childbirth, and motherhood, as well as of breasts and of the act of
suckling." *

Gregory Zilboorg, a psychoanalyst and contemporary of

* "The Flight from Womanhood," in this volume.

Karen Horney, speaks of the "woman envy on the part of man, that is psychogenetically older and therefore more fundamental" than penis envy. He adds, "there is no doubt that the further and deeper studies of man's psyche will yield a great deal of enlightening data, as soon as one learns to discount the androcentric veil which has heretofore covered a number of important psychological data." [22]

Dr. Bose, psychoanalyst, a Bengali from Calcutta and founder of the Indian Psychoanalytic Society (1922), wrote to Freud "that my Indian patients do not exhibit castration symptoms to such a marked degree as my European cases. The desire to be female is more easily unearthed in Indian male patients than European . . . . The Oedipus mother is very often a combined parental image." [23] Hindu philosophical, historical, and cultural patterns produce different attitudes toward woman, as a modern reflection of an ancient time (circa 5000 B.C.) when Indian culture was matriarchal, when women practiced polyandry and were able to establish their rights in many areas of everyday life.

Margaret Mead feels that many male initiation rites in preliterate groups are attempts to take over the functions of women. Among such cultures the elaborate ritual of couvade is almost universal, through which the male acquires the status of a postpartum female without all the attendant discomforts. [24]

In history there have been periods of harmony or submission under both matriarchies and patriarchies. Comparative cultural studies reveal instances of the healthy and pathological envy felt by each sex toward the other's functions and anatomical attributes. Bruno Bettelheim has found from his work with healthy and schizophrenic children and his study of puberty rites among pre-literate groups, that they function "to integrate, rather than to discharge, asocial instinctual tendencies." His premise is that *"one sex feels envy in regard to the sexual organs and functions of the other."* In addition to being critical of the male-oriented

22. Gregory Zilboorg, "Male and Female," *Psychiatry*, VII (1944).
23. G. Bose, "Bose-Freud Correspondence: Letter of April 11, 1929," *Samiksa*, 10 (1935). See also Bose Special Number, *Samiksa* (1955).
24. Margaret Mead, *Male and Female* (New York, William Morrow & Co., Inc., 1949).

negative emphasis on castration anxiety, in the interpretation of puberty rites, he questions Freud's supposed value-free concept of the "child's predisposition to being polymorphous-perverse." He prefers Jung's polyvalent notion, which is neutral and multipotential.[25]

"Inhibited Femininity" contains Dr. Horney's reasons for regarding "frigidity as illness" and not "the normal sexual attitude of civilized woman." She felt that its frequency was due rather to "supra-individual, cultural factors"—our male-oriented culture is "not favorable to the unfolding of woman, and her individuality."

In "The Problem of the Monogamous Ideal" Horney confronts "the tendentious confabulation in favor of men" that men naturally have "a more polygamous disposition," which she feels is an assertion without substantiation. There is no data on the psychological significance of the possibility of pregnancy following coitus; nor is there sufficient evidence to support the theory that a woman's urge to have intercourse is determined by a "possible reproductive instinct," with this urge diminishing once she becomes pregnant.

In "Premenstrual Tension" Dr. Horney offers the hypothesis that the varieties of tension felt by women are directly released by the physiological processes of preparation for pregnancy. Whenever such tensions are present, she anticipates finding "conflicts involving the wish for a child." Dr. Horney states further that the presence of premenstrual tension is not an expression of woman's basic weakness, but of the conflicts aroused about her need to have a child at this time. Horney contends that the desire for a child is a primary drive and that "motherhood represents a more vital problem than Freud assumes."

In "The Distrust Between the Sexes" Horney focuses on the attitude of distrust rather than the more usual concept of hatred and hostility, and she distinguishes between the origins of man's dread of woman as opposed to his distrust and resentment. She cites instances from the cultural patterns of various civilizations, from periods in history and literature, of a male-oriented bias

25. Bruno Bettelheim, *Symbolic Wounds, Puberty Rites, and the Envious Male* (New York, Collier Books, 1962), p. 10.

toward women and how it stimulates distrust.

This paper also reflects Dr. Horney's shift from focusing on so-called male and female psychologies to formulating her theory of neurotic character structure, and the patterns of dominance and submission. She explained and illustrated this theory as the "expansive" and the "self-effacing" solutions in *Neurosis and Human Growth.*" [26]

In "Problems of Marriage" she makes use of Freud's theories about the Oedipus complex and about unconscious processes and neurotic conflicts, and she points up some of the inevitable conflicts that a male-oriented psychology contributes to marriage. The husband brings to marriage many residual attitudes about his mother as the forbidding and saintly woman, whom he has never been able to satisfy. The wife brings to marriage her frigidity, her rejection of the male and her anxiety about being a woman, wife, and mother and her "flight into a desired or imagined *masculine* role. . . .

"Problems in marriage are not solved by admonitions regarding duty and renunciation nor by the recommendation of unlimited freedom for the instincts." What is required is "emotional stability acquired by both partners before marriage." Past and current literature on marriage is filled with the need for give and take. Dr. Horney emphasizes the need for "an inner renunciation of claims on the partner . . . . I mean claims in the sense of demands and not wishes." This is an exact definition of "neurotic claims," which she defined more carefully in her last book, *Neurosis and Human Growth.*

Although Dr. Horney discussed man's dread of the vagina in her paper "The Dread of Woman," she begins her criticism of the literature on the so-called "undiscovered vagina" in "The Denial of the Vagina." Freud thought that a little girl was unaware of her vagina and that her first genital sensations were centered first on the clitoris and only later in the vagina. Dr. Horney argues, with evidence from her own observations and those of other clinicians, that spontaneous vaginal sensations are present in little girls and that vaginal masturbation is common.

26. Karen Horney, *Neurosis and Human Growth* (New York, W. W. Norton & Co., Inc., 1950).

Clitoral masturbation is a later development. Because of anxieties generated in the little girl, her vagina, previously discovered, is denied.

In his paper "Some Psychological Consequences of the Anatomical Distinction Between the Sexes" (1925), Freud states that women are not what they are—women—but males who lack a penis. They "refuse to accept the fact of being castrated" and have the "hope of someday obtaining a penis in spite of everything . . . . I cannot escape the notion (though I hesitate to give it expression) that for woman the level of what is ethically normal is different from what it is in men . . . . We must not allow ourselves to be deflected from such conclusions by the denials of the feminists, who are anxious to force us to regard the two sexes as completely equal in position and worth." [27]

Freud concluded this paper with the statement: "In the valuable and comprehensive studies upon the masculinity and castration complex in women by Abraham (1921), Horney (1923), and Helene Deutsch (1925), there is much that touches closely upon what I have written but nothing that coincides completely, so that here again I feel justified in publishing this paper." For Freud to respond at all and to be critical—though indirectly— was unusual. It suggests that Horney's viewpoint was being taken seriously.

In "Female Sexuality" (1931) Freud said, referring to the pre-Oedipus phase in the little girl's development, "Everything connected with this first mother attachment has in analysis seemed to me so elusive. . . . It would in fact appear that women-analysts—for instance, Jeanne Lampl de Groot and Helene Deutsch—had been able to apprehend the facts with greater ease and clearness because they had the advantage of being suitable mother-substitutes in the transference-situation with the patients who they were studying." But what Karen Horney found (1923) as a mother-substitute "in the transference situation" Freud said did not completely coincide with his view. "Some authors are inclined to disparage the importance of the child's

27. Sigmund Freud, "Some Psychological Consequences of the Anatomical Distinction Between the Sexes" (1925), in *Collected Papers*, Vol. V (London, The Hogarth Press, 1956), pp. 186–97.

first, most primal libidinal impulses, laying stress rather on later developmental processes, so that—putting this view in its extreme form—all that the former can be said to do is to indicate certain 'trends, while the amounts of energy [*Intensitäten*] with which these trends are pursued are drawn from later regressions and reaction-formations. Thus, for example, K. Horney (1926) is of the opinion that we greatly over-estimate the girl's primary penis-envy and that the strength of her subsequent striving towards masculinity is to be attributed to a *secondary* penis-envy, which is used to ward off her feminine impulses, especially those connected with her attachment to her father. This does not agree with the impression that I myself have formed." [28]

Such an extensive and critical response suggests the importance Freud gave to Horney's views. Even with his qualifying disclaimer—"putting this view in its extreme form"—I feel two of Freud's statements are questionable. Horney did not "disparage the importance of the child's first, most primal impulses," and secondly she did not infer or state that all that could be said for them was that they indicated "certain trends" and that "later regressions and reaction formations" were more powerful.

After the publication of "Female Sexuality," until his death in 1939, Freud wrote little on the subject. In "Analysis Terminable and Interminable" (1937) he gives some of his final views on neurosis and therapy. He discusses "the wish for a penis in women, and in men, the struggle against passivity." He said, "Ferenczi was asking a very great deal" when "in 1927 he laid it down as a principle that in every successful analysis these two complexes must be resolved . . . . When we have reached the wish for a penis and the masculine protest, we have penetrated all the psychological strata and reached 'bedrock' and our task is accomplished. . . . The repudiation of femininity must surely be a biological fact, part of the great riddle of sex." [29] And there the matter rested for Freud, as it did for most of his followers.

In the "Introductory Note" to his unfinished *An Outline of*

28. Sigmund Freud, "Female Sexuality" (1931), *Collected Papers*, Vol. V (London, The Hogarth Press, 1956), pp. 252–72.

29. Sigmund Freud, "Analysis Terminable and Interminable," in *Collected Papers*, Vol. V (London, The Hogarth Press, 1956), pp. 355–57.

Psychoanalysis," Freud says, "The aim of this brief work is to bring together the doctrines of psychoanalysis and to state them, as it were, dogmatically . . . no one who has not repeated those observations upon himself or upon others is in a position to arrive at an independent judgment of it." [30] All these qualifications Karen Horney fulfilled, coming to "an independent judgment" at variance with Freud's on feminine psychology and on an increasing number of aspects of the theory and practice of psychoanalysis.

In his discussion of the development of sexual functions in the *Outline,* Freud says, "The third phase is the so-called phallic one . . . . What comes into question at this stage is not the genitals of both sexes but only those of the male (the phallus). The female genitals long remain unknown." In a footnote he adds, "The occurrence of early vaginal excitations is often asserted. But it is most probably a question of excitation in the clitoris, that is, in an organ analogous to the penis, so that this fact would not preclude us from describing the phase as phallic."

Freud's statement regarding early vaginal excitations could have been a direct response to Horney's paper "The Denial of the Vagina" in which she took issue with the notion of the undiscovered vagina, the primacy of clitoral sensations, the notion of a phallic phase, and the whole concept of penis envy. Even more specifically directed to her might have been another comment he made when discussing "the lack of agreement among analysts . . . We shall not be so very surprised if a woman analyst who has not been sufficiently convinced of her own desire for a penis also fails to assign adequate importance to that factor in her patients." [31] Freud's admonition in a footnote in "Female Sexuality" [32] seems pertinent here: "The use of analysis as a weapon of controversy obviously leads to no decision."

In her paper "Psychogenic Factors in Functional Female Disorders," Dr. Horney cites the "coincidence of disturbed psy-

30. Sigmund Freud, "An Outline of Psychoanalysis," in *Collected Papers,* Vol. XXIII (London, The Hogarth Press, 1956; also published New York, W. W. Norton & Co., Inc.).

31. *Ibid.*

32. Freud, "Female Sexuality," *op. cit.*

chosexual life on the one hand and functional female disorders on the other" and then asks whether this coincidence exists regularly. According to her observations, there was no regular coexistence of these bodily factors and emotional changes. She then moves to a third question: Is there a specific correlation between certain mental attitudes in the psychosexual life and certain genital disturbances?

Horney continued to be guided by some of Freud's concepts, giving them, however, her own interpretation. This is evident in "Maternal Conflicts" (1933) in which she said, "One of our basic analytic conceptions is that sexuality does not start at puberty but at birth, and consequently our early love feelings always have a sexual character. As we see it in the whole animal kingdom, sexuality means attraction between the different sexes. . . . The factors of competition and jealousy with regard to the parent of the same sex are responsible for conflicts arising from this source." Attraction is biological and natural, wholesome and spontaneous in Horney's holistic approach.

Dr. Horney's increasing interest in cultural factors is especially evident in "Maternal Conflicts," written in 1933. Having just arrived in the United States, she was acutely aware of the contrast with her experiences in Europe regarding similar problems. "Parents [in the United States] . . . are in terror of being disapproved of by their children . . . . Or they worry about whether they are giving the children the proper education and training."

True scientific investigation can be characterized by a movement back and forth, from the particularities, the observed data, to the hypothesis, each constantly checked and tested against the other. Different categories of data are isolated from each other by their similarities and differences; and the recurrence of groups of similar data are referred to in medicine as syndromes and complexes. When a particular cause can be definitely connected with a particular group of recurrent findings, the effect is called a disease entity. Both in the physical sciences and the humanities there is a category of recurrent similarities referred to as a type. The methodology of typologies is a highly developed one.

In "The Overevaluation of Love: A Study of a Common Present-Day Feminine Type" Horney made explicit use of anthropological and sociological methodologies as well as typologies. She saw individual and environment mutually and reciprocally influencing each other, as a single moving field. In short the "feminine type" of woman she describes in this paper is shaped as much by cultural factors as by certain instinctual demands. Horney further asserted that the "patriarchal ideal of womanhood" is culturally determined, not an immutable given.

In "Feminine Masochism" Dr. Horney confronts some unsubstantiated hypotheses derived from Freud's theories—namely, that "masochistic phenomena are more frequent in woman than in man," because they "are inherent in, or akin to, the very essence of female nature" and that feminine masochism is "one psychic consequence of anatomical sex differences." This paper reveals Horney's detailed knowledge of the literature on the subject, the closeness and clarity of her reasoning, as well as her understanding of clinical research and anthropological investigation. After commenting on some reasons for the failure of psychoanalysis to answer many question regarding feminine psychology, she offers guidelines for anthropologists to follow in seeking data about the presence of masochistic tendencies in men and women.

She again questions Freud's hypothesis that there is no fundamental difference between pathologic and "normal" phenomena and "that pathologic phenomena merely show more distinctly as through a magnifying glass the processes going on in all human beings." On Freud's premises of id (destructive) instincts as being basic, natural, normal, it follows that pathologic phenomena are merely quantifiably different from the normal. But for Horney pathology is not an exaggeration of health, but a transformation into something radically different in kind—namely, sickness. Freud considered his theory of human nature to be universal and the only explanation for behavior—what held true for his small sample of middle-class Viennese would hold for all of mankind across time and place. The same methodological error would occur in Freud's contention that the Oedipus complex was a ubiquitous human phenomenon when anthropological studies showed that it "is nonexistent under widely different cultural conditions." In answer to Freud's assumption that women generally are more jealous than men, Horney responded according to her premises that "the statement probably is correct so far as the present German and Austrian cultures are concerned."

In the paper "Personality Changes in Female Adolescents" Dr. Horney discusses some observations from her analysis of adult women. She says that "although in all cases the determining conflicts had arisen in early childhood, the first personality changes had taken place in adolescence," and that "the onset of these changes coincided approximately with the beginning of menstruation." She then goes on to distinguish four types of women and to explain the psychodynamics involved in the similarities and differences observed in them.

In "The Neurotic Need for Love" Dr. Horney distinguishes between normal, neurotic, and spontaneous love, and delineates the nature of compulsiveness as differentiated from spontaneity. Although the neurotic need for love could be seen as "an expression of a 'mother fixation,'" Dr. Horney felt that Freud's concept did not clarify the fundamental question regarding the dynamic factors that maintain, in later life, an attitude acquired in childhood, or that make it impossible to let go of an infantile one. Already in "The Problem of Feminine Masochism" Dr. Horney said, "It is one of the great scientific merits of Freud to have vigorously stressed the tenacity of childhood impressions; yet psychoanalytic experience shows also that an emotional reaction that has once occurred in childhood is maintained throughout life only if it continues to be supported by various dynamically important drives." This clear and rigorous delineation of her position regarding the influences of the past and the present, are of course at variance with Freud's statements in "Female Sexuality."

Again in "The Neurotic Need for Love" she questions Freud's libido theory, where he considers "the increased need for love" as "a libidinal phenomenon." Horney felt this concept to be unproven. "The neurotic need for love," she adds, "could represent . . . an expression of an oral fixation or a 'regression.' This concept presupposes a willingness to reduce complex psychological phenomena to physiological factors. I believe this assumption is not only untenable but that it makes the understanding of psychological phenomena even more difficult."

By questioning Freud's libido theory and his notions about fixation and regression, and by postulating the importance of life and human spontaneity as therapeutic, Dr. Horney was disputing Freud's theory of the repetition compulsion. The very notion of "blockages of development" instead of "resistance," "fixation," and "regression" is in direct opposition to Freud's notion of repetition compulsion and of strict determinism.

In these early papers Dr. Horney shows herself to have been a phenomenologist and existentialist. The ontological differentiation between *being* and *having* and *doing* is made in "The Dread of Woman": "Now one of the exigencies of the biological differences between the sexes is this—that the man is actually obliged to go on proving his manhood to the woman. There is no analogous necessity for her; even if she is frigid, she can engage in sexual intercourse and conceive and bear a child. She performs her part by merely *being*, without any *doing*—a fact that has always filled men with admiration and resentment. The man, on the other hand, has to *do* something in order to fulfill himself. The ideal of 'efficiency' is a typical masculine ideal" in the male-dominated western world, oriented toward the materialistic, the mechanistic, toward action based on a universe divided into subjects and objects in opposition.

Existentially, there is a meeting, *Begegnung*, confrontation in an I-Thou relationship. There is meeting in all forms of intercourse, including sexual, the primacy of personhood in meeting is alien to our western outlook. In this book and in Horney's subsequent publications, the existential viewpoint becomes more developed and explicit.

Existential notions of being have deep roots. In the Yin-Yang philosophy of ancient China, the male and female principles are seen as natural and complementary, not opposed, and that life can be harmonious only when they are in balance. Differentness as an expression of the natural state was accepted and regarded as essential to joining, union, and enrichment through similarity and difference. This orientation is in opposition to Freud's western male orientation that saw penis envy and male resistance to passive feelings as biologically determined.

In "The Neurotic Need for Love" creature anxiety (*Angst der Kreatur*), a general human phenomenon and an explicit existential notion, forms the core of Dr. Horney's concept of basic anxiety, which is made up of feelings of helplessness and isolation in a world considered to be potentially hostile. The difference between the healthy person and the neurotic is that in the latter the amount of basic anxiety is increased. The neurotic may be unaware of his anxiety, but it will manifest itself in a variety of ways and he will attempt to avoid his feelings.

This volume presents Dr. Horney's evolving ideas on feminine psychology as well as her differences with Freud. After confronting Freud's male-oriented psychology with her own so-called female psychology, she prepared the way for a philosophy, psychology, and psychoanalysis of whole people living and interacting with their changing environments.

In reading these early papers of Dr. Horney's we see a woman of wisdom and experience at work searching for better ways to alleviate human suffering. The closing sentences of Dr. Horney's *Neurosis and Human Growth* fittingly convey the spirit, the method, and the efforts displayed not only in the papers in this volume, but in her whole life's work: "Albert Schweitzer uses the terms 'optimistic' and 'pessimistic' in the sense of 'world and life affirmation' and 'world and life negation.' Freud's philosophy, in this deep sense, is a pessimistic one. Ours, with all its cognizance of the tragic element in neurosis, is an optimistic one."

HAROLD KELMAN

New York City
1966

ACKNOWLEDGMENTS

*T*HIS BOOK is sponsored by the Association for the Advancement of Psychoanalysis. Acknowledgment and thanks are due to Dr. Horney's daughters, Brigitte Swarzenski, Doctor Marianne Eckardt, and Renate Mintz. They gave permission for the publication of the book and waived all financial remuneration.

Special thanks are due to the members of the committee responsible for the production of this volume, Doctors Edward R. Clemmens, John M. Meth, Edward Schattner, and Gerda F. Willner. The papers were selected by their mutual agreement and translated from the German as a joint effort. The prevailing spirit of cooperation and responsibility with which each carried out the many tasks involved made for a fulfilling and enjoyable experience.

To our literary editor, Miss Lee Metcalfe, we are all deeply indebted. She suggested the idea for this book and contributed greatly to making it a reality.

Feminine
Psychology

ON THE GENESIS OF THE CASTRATION

COMPLEX IN WOMEN*

WHILE OUR KNOWLEDGE of the forms that the castration complex may assume in women has become more and more comprehensive,[1] our insight into the nature of the complex as a whole has made no corresponding advance. The very abundance of the material collected, which is now familiar to us, brings to our minds more strongly than ever the remarkable character of the whole phenomenon, so that the phenomenon in itself becomes a problem. A survey of the forms assumed by the castration complex in women that have hitherto been observed and of the inferences tacitly drawn from them shows that, so far, the prevailing conception is based on a certain fundamental notion, which may be briefly formulated as follows (I quote in part *verbatim* from Abraham's work on the subject): Many females, both children and adults, suffer either temporarily or permanently from the fact of their sex. The manifestations in the mental life of women that spring from the objection to being a woman are traceable to their coveting a penis when they were little girls. The unwelcome idea of being fundamentally lacking in this respect gives rise to passive castration fantasies, while active fantasies spring from a revengeful attitude against the favored male.

* Paper delivered at the Seventh International Psycho-Analytical Congress, Berlin, September 1922, "Zur Genese des weiblichen Kastrationskomplexes." *Intern. Zeitschr. f. Psychoanal.*, IX (1923), pp. 12-26; *Int. J. Psycho-Anal.*, V, Part 1 (1924), pp. 50-65. Reprinted with the permission of *The International Journal of Psycho-Analysis.*

1. Cf. in particular Abraham, "Manifestations of the Female Castration Complex" (1921), *Int. J. Psycho-Anal.*, Vol. III, p. 1.

In this formulation we have assumed as an axiomatic fact that females feel at a disadvantage because of their genital organs, without this being regarded as constituting a problem in itself— possibly because to masculine narcissism this has seemed too self-evident to need explanation. Nevertheless, the conclusion so far drawn from the investigations—amounting as it does to an assertion that one half of the human race is discontented with the sex assigned to it and can overcome this discontent only in favorable circumstances—is decidedly unsatisfying, not only to feminine narcissism but also to biological science. The question arises, therefore: Is it really the case that the forms of the castration complex met with in women, pregnant with consequences as they are, not only for the development of neurosis but also for the character-formation and destiny of women who for all practical purposes are normal, are based solely on a dissatisfaction due to her coveting a penis? Or is this possibly but a pretext (at any rate, for the most part) put forward by other forces, the dynamic power of which we know already from our study of the formation of neurosis?

I think that this problem can be attacked from several sides. Here I merely wish to put forward from the purely ontogenetic standpoint, in the hope that they may contribute to a solution, certain considerations that have gradually forced themselves upon me in the course of a practice extending over many years, amongst patients, the great majority of whom were women and in whom on the whole the castration complex was very marked.

According to the prevailing conception, the castration complex in females is entirely centered in the penis-envy complex; in fact the term masculinity complex is used as practically synonymous. The first question which then presents itself is: How is it that we can observe this penis envy occurring as an almost invariable typical phenomenon, even when the subject has not a masculine way of life, where there is no favored brother to make envy of this sort comprehensible and where no "accidental disasters"[2] in the woman's experience have caused the masculine role to seem the more desirable?

2. Cf. Freud, "Tabu der Virginität," *Sammlung kleiner Schriften*, Vierte Folge.

The more important point here seems to be the fact of raising the question; once it has been put, answers suggest themselves almost spontaneously from the material with which we are sufficiently familiar. For supposing we take as our starting point the form in which penis envy probably most frequently directly manifests itself, namely, in the desire to urinate like a man, a critical sifting of the material soon shows that this desire is made up of three component parts, of which sometimes one and sometimes another is the more important.

The part about which I can speak most briefly is that of *urethral erotism* itself, for sufficient stress has already been laid on this factor, as it is the most obvious one. If we want to appraise in all its intensity the envy springing from this source, we must above all make ourselves realize the narcissistic over-estimation[3] in which the excretory processes are held by children. Fantasies of omnipotence, especially those of a sadistic character, are as a matter of fact more easily associated with the jet of urine passed by the male. As an instance of this idea—and it is only one instance among many—I can quote something I was told of a class in a boys' school: When two boys, they said, urinate to make a cross, the person of whom they think at the moment will die.*

Now even though it is certain that a strong feeling of being at a disadvantage must arise in little girls in connection with urethral erotism, yet it is exaggerating the part played by this factor if, as has hitherto been done in many quarters, we straightway attribute to it every symptom and every fantasy whose content is the desire to urinate like a man. On the contrary, the motive force that originates and maintains this wish is often to

3. Cf. Abraham, "Zur narzisstischen Überwertung der Excretionsvorgänge in Traum und Neurose," *Intern. Zeitschr. f. Psychoanal.*, 1920.

* EDITOR'S NOTE: This game was more often played earlier in the century by pre- and early-adolescent boys of European parents. Standing at right angles, they would make a cross on the ground with their respective urinary streams while concentrating their thoughts on a specific person and wishing hard that this person would die. The atmosphere of the experience was laden with much magic and power, derived from the magic of thought and the power of the phallus, and enhanced by the extension of the penis as the urinary stream. The significance of the cross was heightened by its religious connotation and by the importance of the notion that X marks the spot.

be found in quite other instinct components—above all, in active and passive scoptophilia. This connection is due to the circumstance that it is just in the act of urinating that a boy can display his genital and look at himself and is even permitted to do so, and that he can thus in a certain sense satisfy his sexual curiosity, at least as far as his own body is concerned, every time he passes urine.

This factor, which is rooted in the scoptophilic instinct, was particularly evident in a patient of mine in whom the desire to urinate like a male dominated the whole clinical picture for a time. During this period she seldom came to the analysis without declaring that she had seen a man urinating in the street, and once she exclaimed quite spontaneously: "If I might ask a gift of Providence it would be to be able just for once to urinate like a man." Her associations completed this thought beyond all possibility of doubt: "For then I should know how I really am made." The fact that men can see themselves when urinating, while women cannot, was in this patient, whose development was to a great extent arrested at a pregenital stage, actually one of the principal roots of her very marked penis envy.

Just as woman, because her genital organs are hidden, is ever the great riddle for man, so man is an object of lively jealousy for woman precisely on account of the ready visibility of his organ.

The close connection between urethral erotism and the scoptophilic instinct was obvious in yet another patient, a woman whom I will call Y. She practiced masturbation in a very peculiar way, which stood for urinating like her father. In the obsessional neurosis from which this patient suffered, the chief agent was the scoptophilic instinct; she had the most acute feelings of anxiety consequent on the idea of being seen by others while practicing masturbation. She was therefore giving expression to the far-back wish of the little girl: I wish I had a genital too, which I could show, like father, every time I pass urine.

I think, moreover, that this factor plays a leading part in every case of exaggerated embarrassment and prudery in girls, and I further conjecture that the difference in the dress of men and women, at least in our civilized races, may be traced to this very circumstance—that the girl cannot exhibit her genital organs and that therefore in respect of her exhibitionistic tendencies she regresses to a stage at which this desire to display herself still applied to her whole body. This puts us on the track of the reason why a woman wears a low neck, while a man wears a dress coat. I think too that this connection explains to some extent the criterion that is always mentioned first when the points of difference between men and women are under discussion—namely, the greater subjectivity of women as compared with the greater objectivity of men. The explanation would be that the man's impulse to investigate finds satisfaction in the examination of his own body and may, or must, subsequently be directed to external objects; while the woman, on the other hand, can arrive at no clear knowledge about her own person, and therefore finds it far harder to become free of herself.

Finally, the wish that I have assumed to be the prototype of penis envy has in it a third element, namely, suppressed onanistic wishes, as a rule deeply hidden but nonetheless important on that account. This element may be traced to a connection of ideas (mostly unconscious) by which the fact that boys are permitted to take hold of their genital when urinating is construed as a permission to masturbate.

Thus a patient who had witnessed a father reproving his little daughter for touching that part of her body with her tiny hands said to me quite indignantly: "He forbids her to do that and yet does it himself five or six times a day." You will easily recognize the same connection of ideas in the case of the patient Y, in whom the male way of urinating became the decisive factor in the form of masturbation that she practiced. Moreover, in this case it became clear that she could not become completely free from the compulsion to masturbate so long as she unconsciously maintained the claim that she should be a man. The conclusion I drew from my observation of this case is, I think, quite a typical one: girls have a very special difficulty in overcoming masturbation because they feel that they are unjustly forbidden something that boys are allowed to do on account of their different bodily formation. Or, in terms of the problem before us, we may put it in another way and say that the difference in bodily formation may easily give rise to a bitter feeling of injury, so that the argument that is used later to account for the repudiation of womanhood, namely, that men have greater freedom in their sexual life, is really based upon actual experiences to that effect in early childhood. Van Ophuijsen, at the conclusion of his work on the masculinity complex in women, lays stress on the strong impression he received in analysis of the existence of an intimate connection between the masculinity complex, infantile masturbation of the clitoris, and urethral erotism. The connecting link would probably be found in the considerations I have just put before you.

These considerations, which constitute the answer to our initial question about the reason why penis envy is of typical occurrence, may be summarized shortly as follows: The little girl's sense of inferiority is (as Abraham has also pointed out in one passage) by no means primary. But it seems to her that, in comparison with boys, she is subject to restrictions as regards the possibility of gratifying certain instinct-components that are of the greatest importance in the pregenital period. Indeed, I think I would put the matter even more accurately if I said that *as an actual fact,* from the point of view of a child at this stage of development, little girls *are* at a disadvantage compared with boys in respect of certain possibilities of gratification. For unless we are quite clear about the *reality* of this disadvantage we shall not understand that penis envy is an almost inevitable phenomenon in the life of female children, and one that cannot but complicate female development. The fact that later, when she reaches maturity, a great part in sexual life (as regards creative power perhaps even a greater part than that of men) devolves upon a woman—I mean when she becomes a mother—cannot be any compensation to the little girl at this early stage, for it still lies outside her potentialities of direct gratification.

I shall here break off this line of thought, for I now come to the second, more comprehensive, problem: Does the complex we are discussing really rest on penis envy and is the latter to be regarded as the ultimate force behind it?

Taking this question as our starting point, we have to consider what factors determine whether the penis complex is more or less successfully overcome or whether it becomes regressively reinforced so that fixation occurs. A consideration of these possibilities compels us to examine more closely *the form of object libido* in such cases. We then find that the girls and women whose desire to be men is often so glaringly evident have at the very outset of life passed through a phase of extremely strong father fixation. In ouser words: They tried first of all to master the Oedipus complex in the normal way by retaining their original identification with the mother, and like the mother, taking the father as love object.

We know that at this stage there are two possible ways in which a girl may overcome the penis envy complex without detriment to herself. She may pass from the autoerotic narcissistic desire for the penis to the woman's desire for the man (or the father), precisely in virtue of her identification of herself with her mother; or to the material desire for a child (by the father). With regard to the subsequent love life of healthy as well as abnormal women, it is illuminating to reflect that (even in the most favorable instances) the origin, or at any rate one origin, of either attitude was narcissistic in character and of the nature of a desire for possession.

Now in the cases under consideration it is evident that this womanly and maternal development has taken place to a very marked degree. Thus in the patient Y, whose neurosis, like all those which I shall cite here, bore throughout the stamp of the castration complex, many fantasies of rape occurred, which were indicative of this phase. The men whom she thought of as committing rape upon her were one and all unmistakably father images; hence these fantasies had necessarily to be construed as the compulsive repetition of a primal fantasy in which the patient, who till late in life felt herself one with her mother, had experienced with her the father's act of complete sexual appropriation. It is noteworthy that this patient, who in other respects was perfectly clear in her mind, was at the beginning of the analysis strongly inclined to regard these fantasies of rape as actual fact.

Other cases also manifest—in another form—a similar clinging to the fiction that this primal feminine fantasy is real. From another patient, whom I will call X, I heard innumerable remarks constituting direct proof of how very real this love-relation with the father had seemed to her. Once, for instance, she recollected how her father had sung a love song to her, and with the recollection there broke from her a cry of disillusion and despair: "And yet it was all a lie!" The same thought was expressed in one of her symptoms, which I should like to cite here as typical of a whole similar group: at times she was under a compulsion to eat quantities of salt. Her mother had been obliged to eat salt on account of hemorrhages of the lungs, which had occurred in the patient's early childhood; she had unconsciously construed them as the result of her parents' intercourse. This symptom therefore stood for her unconscious claim to have suffered the same experience from her father as her mother had undergone. It was the same claim that made her regard herself as a prostitute (actually she was a virgin) and that made her feel a compelling need to make a confession of some kind to any new love object.

The numerous unmistakable observations of this kind show us how important it is to realize that at this early stage—as an ontogenetic repetition of a phylogenetic experience—the child constructs, on the basis of a (hostile or loving) identification with its mother, a fantasy that it has suffered full sexual appropriation by the father; and further, that in fantasy this experience presents itself as having actually taken place—as much a fact as it must have been at that distant time when all women were primarily the property of the father.

We know that the natural fate of this love-fantasy is a denial of it by reality. In cases that are subsequently dominated by the castration complex, this frustration often changes into a profound *disappointment*, deep traces of which remain in the neurosis. Thus there arises a more or less extensive disturbance in the development of the sense of reality. One often receives the impression that the emotional intensity of this attachment to the father is too strong to admit of a recognition of the essential unreality of the relation; in other cases again it seems as though from the outset there had been an excessive power of fantasy, making it difficult to grasp actuality correctly; finally the real relations with the parents are often so unhappy as to account for a clinging to fantasy.

These patients feel as if their fathers had actually once been their lovers and had afterward been false to them or deserted them. Sometimes this again is the starting point of doubt: Did I only imagine the whole thing, or was it true? In a patient whom I will call Z, of whom I shall have to speak in a moment, this doubting attitude betrayed itself in a repetition compulsion, which took the form of anxiety whenever a man appeared attracted to her, lest she might only be imagining this liking on his part. Even when she was actually engaged to be married she had to be constantly reassuring herself that she had not simply imagined the whole thing. In a daydream she pictured herself as assailed by a man whom she knocked down with a blow on the nose, treading upon his penis with her foot. Continuing the fantasy, she wished to bring him up on charges but refrained because she was afraid he might declare she had imagined the scene. When speaking of the patient Y, I mentioned the doubt she felt as to the actuality of her fantasies of rape, and that this doubt had reference to the original experience with the father. In her it was possible to trace out the way in which the doubt from this source extended to every occurrence in her life and so actually became the basis of her obsessional neurosis. In her case, as in many others, the course of the analysis made it probable that this origin of the doubt had deeper roots than that uncertainty, with which we are familiar, about the subject's own sex.[4]

In the patient X, who used to revel in numerous recollections of that earliest period of her life, which she called her childhood's paradise, this disappointment was closely connected in her memory with an unjust punishment inflicted on her by her father when she was five or six years old. It transpired that at this time a sister had been born and that she had felt herself supplanted by this sister in her father's affections. As deeper strata were revealed, it became clear that behind the jealousy of her sister there lay a furious jealousy of her mother, which related in the first instance to her mother's many pregnancies. "Mother *always* had the babies," she once said indignantly. More strongly repressed were two further roots (by no means equally important) of her feeling that her father was faithless to her. The one was sexual jealousy of her mother dating from her witnessing parental

---

4. Cf. the explanation Freud gives of doubt as doubt of the subject's capacity for love (hate).

coitus; at that time her sense of reality made it impossible for her to incorporate what she saw in the fantasy of herself as the father's lover. It was a mishearing on her part that put me on the track of this last source of her feeling. Once as I was speaking of a time "nach *der Enttäuschung*" (after the disappointment), she understood me to say "Nacht *der Enttäuschung*" (the night of the disappointment) and gave the association of Brangäne keeping vigil during Tristan and Isolde's love night.

A repetition compulsion in this patient spoke in language no less clear: The typical experience of her love life was that she first of all fell in love with a father-substitute and then found him faithless. In connection with occurrences of this sort the final root of the complex became plainly evident; I allude to her feelings of guilt. Certainly a great part of these feelings was to be construed as reproaches originally directed against her father and then turned upon herself. But it was possible to trace very clearly the way in which the feelings of guilt, especially those that resulted from strong impulses to do away with her mother (to the patient this identification had the special significance of "doing away with her" and "replacing her"), had produced in her an expectation of calamity, which of course referred above all to the relation with her father.

I wish especially to emphasize the strong impression I received in this case of the importance of *the desire to have a child* (from the father).[5] My reason for laying stress upon it is that I think we are inclined to underestimate the unconscious power of this wish and in particular its libidinal character, because it is a wish to which the ego can later more easily assent than to many other sexual impulses. Its relation to the penis-envy complex is twofold. On the one hand it is well-known that the maternal instinct receives an "unconscious libidinal reinforcement"[6] from the desire for a penis, a desire that comes earlier in point of time because it belongs to the autoerotic period. Then when the little girl experiences the disappointment described in relation to her

---

5. Cf. O. Rank's paper "Perversion and Neurosis," *Int. J. Psycho-Anal.*, Vol. IV, Part 3.

6. Cf. Freud, "Über Triebumsetzungen insbesondere der Analerotik," *Sammlung kleiner Schriften*. Vierte Folge.

father, she renounces not only her claim upon him but also the desire for a child. This is regressively succeeded (in accordance with the familiar equation) by ideas belonging to the anal phase and by the old demand for the penis. When this takes place, that demand is not simply revived, but is reinforced with all the energy of the girl-child's desire for a child.

I could see this connection particularly clearly in the case of the patient Z, who after several symptoms of the obsessional neurosis had vanished, retained as the final and most obstinate symptom a lively dread of pregnancy and childbirth. The experience that had determined this symptom proved to be her mother's pregnancy and the birth of a brother when the patient was two years old, while observations of parental coitus, continued after she was no longer an infant, contributed to the same result. For a long time it seemed that this case was singularly well-calculated to illustrate the central importance of the penis envy complex. Her coveting of the penis (her brother's) and her violent anger against him as the intruder who had ousted her from her position of only child, when once revealed by analysis, entered consciousness heavily charged with affect. The envy was, moreover, accompanied by all the manifestations that we are accustomed to trace to it: first and foremost the attitude of revenge against men, with very intense castration fantasies; repudiation of feminine tasks and functions, especially that of pregnancy; and further, a strong unconscious homosexual tendency. It was only when the analysis penetrated into deeper strata under the greatest resistance imaginable that it became evident that the source of the penis envy was her envy on account of the child that her mother and not she had received from her father, whereupon by a process of displacement the penis had become the object of envy in place of the child. In the same way her vehement anger against her brother proved really to have reference to her father, who she felt had deceived her, and to her mother, who instead of the patient herself, had received the child. Only when this displacement was canceled did she really become free from penis envy and from the longing to be a man, and was she able to be a true woman and even to wish to have children herself.

Now what process had taken place? Quite roughly it may be

outlined as follows: (1) the envy relating to the child was displaced to the brother and his genital; (2) there clearly ensued the
mechanism discovered by Freud, by which the father as love
object is given up and the object relation to him is regressively
replaced by an identification with him.

The latter process manifested itself in those pretensions to
manhood on her part of which I have already spoken. It was
easy to prove that her desire to be a man was by no means to
be understood in a general sense, but that the real meaning of
her claims was to act her father's part. Thus she adopted the
same profession as her father, and after his death her attitude to
her mother was that of a husband who makes demands upon his
wife and issues orders. Once when a noisy eructation escaped her
she could not help thinking with satisfaction: "Just like Papa."
Yet she did not reach the point of a completely homosexual
object choice: the development of the object libido seemed rather
to be altogether disturbed, and the result was an obvious regression to an autoerotic narcissistic stage. To sum up: displacement
of the envy that had reference to children on to the brother and
his penis, identification with the father and regression to a pregenital phase all operated in the same direction—to stir up a
powerful penis envy, which then remained in the foreground and
seemed to dominate the whole picture.

Now in my opinion this kind of development of the Œdipus
complex is typical of those cases in which the castration complex
is predominant. What happens is that a phase of identification
with the mother gives way to a very large extent to one of identification with the father, and at the same time there is regression
to a pregenital stage. This process of identification with the father
I believe to be one root of the castration complex in women.

At this point I should like to answer at once two possible
objections. One of them might run like this: Such an oscillation
between father and mother is surely nothing peculiar. On the
contrary, it is to be seen in every child, and we know that, according to Freud, the libido of each one of us oscillates throughout
life between male and female objects. The second objection
relates to the connection with homosexuality, and may be expressed thus: In his paper on the psychogenesis of a case of homo-

sexuality in a woman, Freud has convinced us that such a development in the direction of identification with the father is one of the bases of manifest homosexuality; yet now I am depicting the same process as resulting in the castration complex. In answer, I would emphasize the fact that it was just this paper of Freud which helped me to understand the castration complex in women. It is exactly in these cases that, on the one hand, the extent to which the libido normally oscillates is considerably exceeded from a quantitative point of view, while on the other hand, the repression of the love attitude toward the father and the identification with him are not so completely successful as in cases of homosexuality. And so the similarity in the two courses of development is no argument against its significance for the castration complex in women; on the contrary, this view makes homosexuality much less of an isolated phenomenon.

We know that in every case in which the castration complex predominates there is without exception a more or less marked tendency to homosexuality. To play the father's part always amounts also to desiring the mother in some sense. There may be every possible degree of closeness in the relation between narcissistic regression and homosexual object cathexis, so that we have an unbroken series culminating in manifest homosexuality.

A third criticism that suggests itself here relates to the temporal and causal connection with penis envy and runs as follows: Is not the relation of the penis envy complex to the process of identification with the father just the opposite of that depicted here? May it not be that in order to establish this sort of permanent identification with the father there has first to be an unusually strong penis envy? I think we cannot fail to recognize that a specially powerful penis envy (whether it is constitutional or the result of personal experience) does help to prepare the way for the changeover by which the patient identifies herself with the father; nevertheless, the history of the cases I have described, and of other cases as well, shows that notwithstanding the penis envy, a strong and wholly womanly love relation to the father had been formed, and that it was only when this love was disappointed that the feminine role was abandoned. This abandonment and the consequent identification with the father then revives the penis envy, and only when it derives nourishment from such powerful sources as these can that feeling operate in its full strength.

For this revulsion to an identification with the father to take place, it is essential that the sense of reality should be at least to some extent awakened; hence it is inevitable that the little girl should no longer be able to content herself, as she formerly did, simply with a fantasied fulfillment of her desire for the penis, but should now begin to brood upon her lack of that organ or ponder over its possible existence. The trend of these speculations is determined by the girl's whole affective disposition; it is characterized by the following typical attitudes: a feminine love attachment, not yet wholly subdued, to her father, feelings of vehement anger and of revenge directed against him because of the disappointment suffered through him, and last but not least, feelings of guilt (relating to incestuous fantasies concerning him) that are violently aroused under the pressure of the privation. Thus it is that these broodings invariably have reference to the father.

I saw this very clearly in the patient Y, whom I have already mentioned more than once. I told you that this patient produced fantasies of rape—fantasies that she regarded as fact—and that ultimately these related to her father. She too had reached the point of identifying herself to a very great extent with him; for instance, her attitude to her mother was exactly that of a son. Thus, she had dreams in which her father was attacked by a snake or wild beasts, whereupon she rescued him.

Her castration fantasies took the familiar form of imagining that she was not normally made in the genital region, and besides this she had a feeling as though she had suffered some injury to the genitals. On both these points she had evolved many ideas, chiefly to the effect that these peculiarities were the result of acts of rape. Indeed, it became plain that her obstinate insistence upon these sensations and ideas in connection with her genital organs was actually designed to prove the reality of these acts of violence, and so, ultimately, the reality of her love relation with her father. The clearest light is thrown upon the importance of this fantasy and the strength of the repetition compulsion under which she labored, by the fact that before analysis she had insisted on under-

going six laparotomy operations, several of which had been performed simply on account of her pains. In another patient, whose
coveting of the penis took an absolutely grotesque form, this
feeling of having sustained a wound was displaced on to other
organs, so that when her obsessional symptoms had been resolved,
the clinical picture was markedly hypochondriacal. At this point
her resistance took the following form: "It is obviously absurd
for me to be analyzed, seeing that my heart, my lungs, my stomach,
and my intestines are evidently organically diseased." Here again
the insistence on the reality of her fantasies was so strong that
on one occasion she had almost compelled performance of an
intestinal operation. Her associations constantly brought the idea
that she had been struck down (*geschlagen*) with illness by her
father. As a matter of fact, when these hypochondriacal symptoms
cleared up, fantasies of being *struck* (*Schlagephantasien*) became
the most prominent feature in her neurosis. It seems to me quite
impossible to account satisfactorily for these manifestations simply
by the penis-envy complex. But their main features become perfectly clear if we regard them as an effect of the impulse to experience anew, after a compulsive fashion, the suffering undergone at
the hands of the father and to prove to herself the reality of the
painful experience.

This array of material might be multiplied indefinitely, but
it would only repeatedly go to show that we encounter under
totally different guises this basic fantasy of having suffered castration through the love relation with the father. My observations
have led me to believe that this fantasy, whose existence has
indeed long been familiar to us in individual cases, is of such
typical and fundamental importance that I am inclined to call
it the second root of the whole castration complex in women.

The great significance of this combination is that a highly
important piece of repressed womanhood is most intimately
bound up with the castration fantasies. Or, to look at it from
the point of view of succession in time, that it is wounded womanhood which gives rise to the castration complex, and that it
is this complex which injures (not *primarily*, however) feminine
development.

Here we probably have the most fundamental basis of the

revengeful attitude toward men that is so often a prominent feature in women in whom the castration complex is marked;
attempts to explain this attitude as resulting from penis envy
and the disappointment of the little girl's expectation that her
father would give her the penis as a present, do not satisfactorily
account for the mass of facts brought to light by an analysis of
deeper strata of the mind. Of course in psychoanalysis the penis
envy is more readily exposed than is the far more deeply repressed
fantasy, which ascribes the loss of the male genital to a sexual
act with the father as partner. That this is so, follows from the
fact that no feelings of guilt at all are attached to penis envy
in itself.

It is specially frequent for this attitude of revenge against men
to be directed with particular vehemence against the man who
performs the act of defloration. The explanation is natural—
namely, that it is precisely the father with whom, according to
the fantasy, the patient mated for the first time. Hence in the
subsequent actual love life, the first mate stands in a quite peculiar way for the father. This idea is expressed in the customs
described by Freud in his essay on the taboo of virginity; according to these the performance of the act of defloration is actually
entrusted to a father-substitute. To the unconscious mind, defloration is the repetition of the fantasied sexual act performed with
the father, and therefore when defloration takes place all those
affects belonging to the fantasied act are reproduced—strong feelings of attachment combined with the abhorrence of incest, and
finally the attitude described above of revenge on account of disappointed love and of the castration supposedly suffered through
this act.

This brings me to the end of my remarks. My problem was
the question of whether that dissatisfaction with the female sexual role that results from penis envy is really the alpha and omega
of the castration complex in women. We have seen that the anatomical structure of the female genitals is indeed of great significance in the mental development of women. Also, it is indisputable
that penis envy does essentially condition the *forms* in which the
castration complex manifests itself in them. But the deduction
that therefore repudiation of their womanhood is based on that

envy seems inadmissible. On the contrary, we can see that penis envy by no means precludes a deep and wholly womanly love attachment to the father and that it is only when this relation comes to grief over the Oedipus complex (exactly as in the corresponding male neuroses) that the envy leads to a revulsion from the subject's own sexual role.

The male neurotic who identifies himself with the mother, and the female who identifies herself with the father, repudiate, both in the same way, their respective sexual roles. And from this point of view the castration fear of the male neurotic (behind which there lurks a castration wish upon which, to my mind, sufficient stress is never laid) corresponds exactly to the female neurotic's desire for the penis. This symmetry would be much more striking were it not that the man's inner attitude toward identification with the mother is diametrically opposed to that of the woman toward identification with the father. And this in two respects: In a man this wish to be a woman is not merely at variance with his conscious narcissism, but is rejected for a second reason, namely, because the notion of being a woman implies at the same time the realization of all his fears of punishment, centered as they are in the genital region. In a woman, on the other hand, the identification with the father is confirmed by old wishes tending in the same direction, and it does not carry with it any sort of feelings of guilt but rather a sense of acquittal. For there ensues, from the connection I have described as existing between the ideas of castration and the incest fantasies relating to the father, the fateful result, opposite to that in men, that being a woman is in itself felt to be culpable.

In his papers entitled "Trauer und Melancholie"[7] (Grief and Melancholia) and "The Psychogenesis of a Case of Female Homosexuality,"[8] and in his *Group Psychology and Analysis of the Ego,* Freud has shown more and more fully how large the process of identification looms in human mentality. It is just this identification with the parent of the opposite sex that seems to me to be the point from which in either sex both homosexuality and the castration complex are evolved.

7. *Sammlung kleiner Schriften.* Vierte Folge.
8. *Int. J. Psycho-Anal.,* Vol. I, p. 125.

THE FLIGHT FROM WOMANHOOD*

The Masculinity-Complex in Women
as Viewed by Men and by Women

○○○

*I*N SOME OF HIS LATEST WORKS Freud has drawn attention with increasing urgency to a certain one-sidedness in our analytical researches. I refer to the fact that till quite recently the minds of boys and men only were taken as objects of investigation.

The reason for this is obvious. Psychoanalysis is the creation of a male genius, and almost all those who have developed his ideas have been men. It is only right and reasonable that they should evolve more easily a masculine psychology and understand more of the development of men than of women.

A momentous step toward the understanding of the specifically feminine was made by Freud himself in discovering the existence of penis envy, and soon after, the work of van Ophuijsen and Abraham showed how large a part this factor plays in the development of women and in the formation of their neuroses. The significance of penis envy has been extended quite recently by the hypothesis of the phallic phase. By this we mean that in the infantile genital organization in both sexes only one genital organ, namely the male, plays any part, and that it is just this that distinguishes the infantile organization from the final genital organization of the adult.[1] According to this theory, the clitoris

● "Flucht aus der Weiblichkeit," *Intern. Zeitschr. f. Psychoanal.*, XII (1926), pp. 360-74; *Int. J. Psycho-Anal.*, VII (1926), pp. 324-39. Reprinted with the permission of *The International Journal of Psycho-Analysis*.

1. Freud, "The Infantile Genital Organization of the Libido." *Collected Papers*, Vol. II, No. XX. [Horney's references to Freud are usually to editions prior to the Standard one (*The Complete Psychological Works of Sigmund Freud* and the *Collected Papers*, published by the Hogarth Press, London).]

is conceived of as a phallus, and we assume that little girls as well as boys attach to the clitoris in the first instance exactly the same value as to the penis.[2]

The effect of this phase is partly to inhibit and partly to promote the subsequent development. Helene Deutsch has demonstrated principally the inhibiting effects. She is of the opinion that at the beginning of every new sexual function e.g., at the beginning of puberty, of sexual intercourse, of pregnancy and childbirth), this phase is reactivated and has to be overcome every time before a feminine attitude can be attained. Freud has elaborated her exposition on the positive side, for he believes that it is only penis envy and the overcoming of it which gives rise to the desire for a child and thus forms the love bond to the father.[3]

The question now arises as to whether these hypotheses have helped to make our insight into feminine development (insight that Freud himself has stated to be unsatisfactory and incomplete) more satisfactory and clear.

Science has often found it fruitful to look at long-familiar facts from a fresh point of view. Otherwise there is a danger that we shall involuntarily continue to classify all new observations among the same clearly defined groups of ideas.

The new point of view of which I wish to speak came to me by way of philosophy, in some essays by Georg Simmel.[4] The point that Simmel makes there and that has been in many ways elaborated since, especially from the feminine side,[5] is this: Our whole civilization is a masculine civilization. The State, the laws, morality, religion, and the sciences are the creation of men. Simmel by no means deduces from these facts, as is commonly done by other writers, an inferiority in women, but he first of all gives considerable breadth and depth to this conception of a masculine civilization: "The requirements of art, patriotism, morality in general and social ideas in particular, correctness in practical judgment and objectivity in theoretical knowledge, the energy

2. H. Deutsch, *Psychoanalyse der weiblichen Sexualfunktionen* (1925).

3. Freud, "Einige psychische Folgen der anatomischen Geschlechtsunterschiede," *Intern. Zeitschr. f. Psychoanal.,* XI (1925).

4. Georg Simmel, *Philosophische Kultur.*

5. Cf. in particular Vaerting, *Männliche Eigenart im Frauenstaat und Weibliche Eigenart im Männerstaat.*

and the profundity of life—all these are categories which belong as it were in their form and their claims to humanity in general, but in their actual historical configuration they are masculine throughout. Supposing that we describe these things, viewed as absolute ideas, by the single word 'objective,' we then find that in the history of our race the equation objective = masculine is a valid one."

Now Simmel thinks that the reason why it is so difficult to recognize these historical facts is that the very standards by which mankind has estimated the values of male and female nature are "not neutral, arising out of the differences of the sexes, but in themselves essentially masculine. . . . We do not believe in a purely 'human' civilization, into which the question of sex does not enter, for the very reason that prevents any such civilization from in fact existing, namely, the (so to speak) naïve identification of the concept 'human being'[6] and the concept 'man,'[7] which in many languages even causes the same word to be used for the two concepts. For the moment I will leave it undetermined whether this masculine character of the fundamentals of our civilization has its origin in the essential nature of the sexes or only in a certain preponderance of force in men, which is not really bound up with the question of civilization. In any case this is the reason why, in the most varying fields, inadequate achievements are contemptuously called 'feminine,' while distinguished achievements on the part of women are called 'masculine' as an expression of praise."

Like all sciences and all valuations, the psychology of women has hitherto been considered only from the point of view of men. It is inevitable that the man's position of advantage should cause objective validity to be attributed to his subjective, affective relations to the woman, and according to Delius[8] the psychology of women hitherto actually represents a deposit of the desires and disappointments of men.

An additional and very important factor in the situation is that women have adapted themselves to the wishes of men and

6. German *Mensch*.
7. German *Mann*.
8. Delius, *Vom Erwachen der Frau*.

felt as if their adaptation were their true nature. That is, they see or saw themselves in the way that their men's wishes demanded of them; unconsciously they yielded to the suggestion of masculine thought.

If we are clear about the extent to which all our being, thinking, and doing conform to these masculine standards, we can see how difficult it is for the individual man and also for the individual woman really to shake off this mode of thought.

The question then is how far analytical psychology also, when its researches have women for their object, is under the spell of this way of thinking, insofar as it has not yet wholly left behind the stage in which frankly and as a matter of course masculine development only was considered. In other words, how far has the evolution of women, as depicted to us today by analysis, been measured by masculine standards and how far therefore does this picture fail to present quite accurately the real nature of women.

If we look at the matter from this point of view our first impression is a surprising one. The present analytical picture of feminine development (whether that picture be correct or not) differs in no case by a hair's breadth from the typical ideas that the boy has of the girl.

We are familiar with the ideas that the boy entertains. I will therefore only sketch them in a few succinct phrases, and for the sake of comparison will place in a parallel column our ideas of the development of women.

THE BOY'S IDEAS	OUR IDEAS OF FEMININE DEVELOPMENT
Naïve assumption that girls as well as boys possess a penis	*For both sexes it is only the male genital which plays any part*
Realization of the absence of the penis	*Sad discovery of the absence of the penis*
Idea that the girl is a castrated, mutilated boy	*Belief of the girl that she once possessed a penis and lost it by castration*
Belief that the girl has suffered punishment that also threatens him	*Castration is conceived of as the infliction of punishment*

THE BOY'S IDEAS	OUR IDEAS OF FEMININE DEVELOPMENT
The girl is regarded as inferior	*The girl regards herself as inferior. Penis envy*
The boy is unable to imagine how the girl can ever get over this loss or envy	*The girl never gets over the sense of deficiency and inferiority and has constantly to master afresh her desire to be a man*
The boy dreads her envy	*The girl desires throughout life to avenge herself on the man for possessing something which she lacks*

The existence of this over-exact agreement is certainly no criterion of its objective correctness. It is quite possible that the infantile genital organization of the little girl might bear as striking a resemblance to that of the boy as has up till now been assumed.

But it is surely calculated to make us think and take other possibilities into consideration. For instance, we might follow Georg Simmel's train of thought and reflect whether it is likely that female adaptation to the male structure should take place at so early a period and in so high a degree that the specific nature of a little girl is overwhelmed by it. Later I will return for a moment to the point at which it does actually seem to me probable that this infection with a masculine point of view occurs in childhood. But it does not seem to me clear offhand how everything bestowed by nature could be thus absorbed into it and leave no trace. And so we must return to the question I have already raised—whether the remarkable parallelism I have indicated may not perhaps be the expression of a one-sidedness in our observations, due to their being made from the man's point of view.

Such a suggestion immediately encounters an inner protest, for we remind ourselves of the sure ground of experience upon which analytical research has always been founded. But at the same time our theoretical scientific knowledge tells us that this ground is not altogether trustworthy, but that all experience by its very nature contains a subjective factor. Thus, even our analytical experience is derived from direct observation of the material that our patients bring to analysis in free associations, dreams, and symptoms and from the interpretations we make or the conclusions we draw from this material. Therefore, even when the technique is correctly applied, there is in theory the possibility of variations in this experience.

Now, if we try to free our minds from this masculine mode of thought, nearly all the problems of feminine psychology take on a different appearance.

The first thing that strikes us is that it is always, or principally, the genital difference between the sexes which has been made the cardinal point in the analytical conception and that we have left out of consideration the other great biological difference, namely, the different parts played by men and by women in the function of reproduction.

The influence of the man's point of view in the conception of motherhood is most clearly revealed in Ferenczi's extremely brilliant genital theory.[9] His view is that the real incitement to coitus, its true, ultimate meaning for both sexes, is to be sought in the desire to return to the mother's womb. During a period of contest man acquired the privilege of really penetrating once more, by means of his genital organ, into a uterus. The woman, who was formerly in the subordinate position, was obliged to adapt her organization to this organic situation and was provided with certain compensations. She had to "content herself" with substitutes in the nature of fantasy and above all with harboring the child, whose bliss she shares. At the most, it is only in the act of birth that she perhaps has potentialities of pleasure denied to the man.[10]

According to this view the psychic situation of a woman would certainly not be a very pleasurable one. She lacks any real primal impulse to coitus, or at least she is debarred from all direct—even if only partial—fulfillment. If this is so, the impulse

9. Ferenczi, *Versuch einer Genitaltheorie* (1924).
10. Cf. also Helene Deutsch, *Psychoanalyse der Weiblichen Sexualfunktionen;* and Groddeck, *Das Buch vom Es.*

toward coitus and pleasure in it must undoubtedly be less for her than for the man. For it is only indirectly, by circuitous ways, that she attains to a certain fulfillment of the primal longing— i.e., partly by the roundabout way of masochistic conversion and partly by identification with the child she may conceive. These, however, are merely "compensatory devices." The only thing in which she ultimately has the advantage over the man is the, surely very questionable, pleasure in the act of birth.

At this point I, as a woman, ask in amazement, and what about motherhood? And the blissful consciousness of bearing a new life within oneself? And the ineffable happiness of the increasing expectation of the appearance of this new being? And the joy when it finally makes its appearance and one holds it for the first time in one's arms? And the deep pleasurable feeling of satisfaction in suckling it and the happiness of the whole period when the infant needs her care?

Ferenczi has expressed the opinion in conversation that in the primal period of conflict which ended so grievously for the female, the male as victor imposed upon her the burden of motherhood and all it involves.

Certainly, regarded from the standpoint of the social struggle, motherhood *may* be a handicap. It is certainly so at the present time, but it is much less certain that it was so in times when human beings were closer to nature.

Moreover, we explain penis envy itself by its biological relations and not by social factors; on the contrary, we are accustomed without more ado to construe the woman's sense of being at a disadvantage socially as the rationalization of her penis envy.

But from the biological point of view woman has in motherhood, or in the capacity for motherhood, a quite indisputable and by no means negligible physiological superiority. This is most clearly reflected in the unconscious of the male psyche in the boy's intense envy of motherhood. We are familiar with this envy as such, but it has hardly received due consideration as a dynamic factor. When one begins, as I did, to analyze men only after a fairly long experience of analyzing women, one receives a most surprising impression of the intensity of this envy of pregnancy, childbirth, and motherhood, as well as of the breasts and of the act of suckling.

In the light of this impression derived from analysis, one must naturally inquire whether an unconscious masculine tendency to depreciation is not expressing itself intellectually in the above-mentioned view of motherhood. This depreciation would run as follows: In reality women do simply desire the penis; when all is said and done motherhood is only a burden that makes the struggle for existence harder, and men may be glad that they have not to bear it.

When Helene Deutsch writes that the masculinity complex in women plays a much greater part than the femininity complex in man, she would seem to overlook the fact that the masculine envy is clearly capable of more successful sublimation than the penis envy of the girl, and that it certainly serves as one, if not as the essential, driving force in the setting up of cultural values.

Language itself points to this origin of cultural productivity. In the historic times that are known to us, this productivity has undoubtedly been incomparably greater in men than in women. Is not the tremendous strength in men of the impulse to creative work in every field precisely due to their feeling of playing a relatively small part in the creation of living beings, which constantly impels them to an overcompensation in achievement?

If we are right in making this connection, we are confronted with the problem of why no corresponding impulse to compensate herself for her penis envy is found in woman. There are two possibilities: Either the envy of the woman is absolutely less than that of the man; or it is less successfully worked off in some other way. We could bring forward facts in support of either supposition.

In favor of the greater intensity of the man's envy we might point out that an actual anatomical disadvantage on the side of the woman exists only from the point of view of the pregenital levels of organization.[11] From that of the genital organization of adult women there is no disadvantage, for obviously the capacity of women for coitus is not less but simply other than that of men. On the other hand, the part of the man in reproduction is ulti-

11. K. Horney, "On the Genesis of the Castration Complex in Women," *Int. J. Psycho-Anal.*, Vol. V (1924) [in this volume, p. 37].

mately less than that of the woman.

Further, we observe that men are evidently under a greater necessity to depreciate women than conversely. The realization that the dogma of the inferiority of women had its origin in an unconscious male tendency could only dawn upon us after a doubt had arisen whether in fact this view were justified in reality. But if there actually are in men tendencies to depreciate women behind this conviction of feminine inferiority, we must infer that this unconscious impulse to depreciation is a very powerful one.

Further, there is much to be said in favor of the view that women work off their penis envy less successfully than men, from a cultural point of view. We know that in the most favorable case this envy is transmuted into the desire for a husband and child, and probably by this very transmutation it forfeits the greater part of its power as an incentive to sublimation. In unfavorable cases, however, as I shall presently show in greater detail, it is burdened with a sense of guilt instead of being able to be employed fruitfully, while the man's incapacity for motherhood is probably felt simply as an inferiority and can develop its full driving power without inhibition.

In this discussion I have already touched on a problem that Freud has recently brought into the foreground of interest:[12] namely, the question of the origin and operation of the desire for a child. In the course of the last decade our attitude toward this problem has changed. I may therefore be permitted to describe briefly the beginning and the end of this historical evolution.

The original hypothesis[13] was that penis envy gave a libidinal reinforcement both to the wish for a child and the wish for the man, but that the latter wish arose independently of the former. Subsequently the accent became more and more displaced on to the penis envy, till in his most recent work on this problem, Freud expressed the conjecture that the wish for the child arose only through penis envy and the disappointment over the lack

12. Freud, *"Über einige psychische Folgen der anatomischen Geschlechts-unterschiede."*

13. Freud, "On the Transformation of Instincts with Special Reference to Anal Erotism," *Collected Papers,* Vol. II, No. XVI.

of the penis in general, and that the tender attachment to the father came into existence only by this circuitous route—by way of the desire for the penis and the desire for the child.

This latter hypothesis obviously originated in the need to explain psychologically the biological principle of heterosexual attraction. This corresponds to the problem formulated by Groddeck, who says that it is natural that the boy should retain the mother as a love object, "but how is it that the little girl becomes attached to the opposite sex?"[14]

In order to approach this problem we must first of all realize that our empirical material with regard to the masculinity complex in women is derived from two sources of very different importance. The first is the direct observation of children, in which the subjective factor plays a relatively insignificant part. Every little girl who has not been intimidated displays penis envy frankly and without embarrassment. We see that the presence of this envy is typical and understand quite well why this is so; we understand how the narcissistic mortification of possessing less than the boy is reinforced by a series of disadvantages arising out of the different pregenital cathexes: the manifest privileges of the boy in connection with urethral erotism, the scoptophilic instinct, and onanism.[15]

I should like to suggest that we should apply the term *primary* to the little girl's penis envy, which is obviously based simply on the anatomical difference.

The second source upon which our experience draws is to be found in the analytical material produced by adult women. Naturally it is more difficult to form a judgment on this, and there is therefore more scope for the subjective element. We see here in the first instance that penis envy operates as a factor of enormous dynamic power. We see patients rejecting their female functions, their unconscious motive in so doing being the desire to be male. We meet with fantasies of which the content is: "I once had a penis; I am a man who has been castrated and mutilated," from which proceed feelings of inferiority that have for after-effect all

14. Groddeck, *Das Buch vom Es.*
15. I have dealt with this subject in greater detail in my paper "On the Genesis of the Castration Complex in Women."

manner of obstinate hypochondriacal ideas. We see a marked attitude of hostility toward men, sometimes taking the form of depreciation and sometimes of a desire to castrate or maim them, and we see how the whole destinies of certain women are determined by this factor.

It was natural to conclude—and especially natural because of the male orientation of our thinking—that we could link these impressions on to the primary penis envy and to reason _a posteriori_ that this envy must possess an enormous intensity, an enormous dynamic power, seeing that it evidently gave rise to such effects. Here we overlooked the fact, more in our general estimation of the situation than in details, that this desire to be a man, so familiar to us from the analyses of adult women, had only very little to do with that early, infantile, primary penis envy, but that it is a secondary formation embodying all that has miscarried in the development toward womanhood.

From beginning to end, my experience has proved to me with unchanging clearness that the Oedipus complex in women leads (not only in extreme cases where the subject has come to grief, but _regularly_) to a regression to penis envy, naturally in every possible degree and shade. The difference between the outcome of the male and the female Oedipus complexes seems to me in average cases to be as follows. In boys the mother as a sexual object is renounced owing to the fear of castration, but the male role itself is not only affirmed in further development but is actually overemphasized in the reaction to the fear of castration. We see this clearly in the latency and prepubertal period in boys and generally in later life as well. Girls, on the other hand, not only renounce the father as a sexual object but simultaneously recoil from the feminine role altogether.

In order to understand this flight from womanhood we must consider the facts relating to early infantile onanism, which is the physical expression of the excitations due to the Œdipus complex.

Here again the situation is much clearer in boys, or perhaps we simply know more about it. Are these facts so mysterious to us in girls only because we have always looked at them through the eyes of men? It seems rather like it when we do not even concede to little girls a specific form of onanism but without more ado describe their autoerotic activities as male; and when we conceive of the difference, which surely must exist, as being that of a negative to a positive, i.e., in the case of anxiety about onanism, that the difference is that between a castration threatened and castration that has actually taken place! My analytical experience makes it most decidedly possible that little girls have a specific feminine form of onanism (which incidentally differs in technique from that of boys), even if we assume that the little girl practices exclusively clitoral masturbation, an assumption that seems to me by no means certain. And I do not see why, in spite of its past evolution, it should not be conceded that the clitoris legitimately belongs to and forms an integral part of the female genital apparatus.

Whether in the early phase of the girl's genital development she has organic vaginal sensations is a matter remarkably difficult to determine from the analytical material produced by adult women. In a whole series of cases I have been inclined to conclude that this is so, and later I shall quote the material upon which I base this conclusion. That such sensations should occur seems to me theoretically very probable for the following reasons. Undoubtedly the familiar fantasies that an excessively large penis is effecting forcible penetration, producing pain and hemorrhage, and threatening to destroy something, go to show that the little girl bases her Oedipus fantasies most realistically (in accordance with the plastic concrete thinking of childhood) on the disproportion in size between father and child. I think too that both the Oedipus fantasies and also the logically ensuing dread of an internal—i.e., vaginal—injury go to show that the vagina as well as the clitoris must be assumed to play a part in the early infantile genital organization of women.[16] One might even infer from the later phenomena of frigidity that the vaginal zone has actually a stronger cathexis (arising out of anxiety and attempts at defence) than the clitoris, and this because the incestuous wishes

16. Since the possibility of such a connection occurred to me, I have learned to construe in this sense—i.e., as representing the dread of vaginal injury—many phenomena that I was previously content to interpret as castration fantasies in the male sense.

are referred to the vagina with the unerring accuracy of the unconscious. From this point of view frigidity must be regarded as an attempt to ward off the fantasies so full of danger to the ego. And this would also throw a new light on the unconscious pleasurable feelings that, as various authors have maintained, occur at parturition, or alternatively, on the dread of childbirth. For (just because of the disproportion between the vagina and the baby and because of the pain to which this gives rise) parturition would be calculated to a far greater extent than subsequent sexual intercourse to stand to the unconscious for a realization of those early incest fantasies, a realization to which no guilt is attached. The female genital anxiety, like the castration dread of boys, invariably bears the impress of feelings of guilt and it is to them that it owes its lasting influence.

A further factor in the situation, and one that works in the same direction, is a certain consequence of the anatomical difference between the sexes. I mean that the boy can inspect his genital to see whether the dreaded consequences of onanism are taking place; the girl, on the other hand, is literally in the dark on this point and remains in complete uncertainty. Naturally this possibility of a reality test does not weigh with boys in cases where the castration anxiety is acute, but in the slighter cases of fear, which are practically more important because they are more frequent, I think that this difference is very important. At any rate, the analytical material that has come to light in women whom I have analyzed has led me to conclude that this factor plays a considerable part in feminine mental life and that it contributes to the peculiar inner uncertainty so often met with in women.

Under the pressure of this anxiety the girl now takes refuge in a fictitious male role.

What is the economic gain of this flight? Here I would refer to an experience that all analysts have probably had: They find that the desire to be a man is generally admitted comparatively willingly and that when once it is accepted, it is clung to tenaciously, the reason being the desire to avoid the realization of libidinal wishes and fantasies in connection with the father. Thus the wish to be a man subserves the repression of these feminine wishes or the resistance against their being brought to light. This constantly recurring, typical experience compels us, if we are true to analytical principles, to conclude that the fantasies of being a man were at an earlier period devised for the very purpose of securing the subject against libidinal wishes in connection with the father. The fiction of maleness enabled the girl to escape from the female role now burdened with guilt and anxiety. It is true that this attempt to deviate from her own line to that of the male inevitably brings about a sense of inferiority, for the girl begins to measure herself by pretensions and values that are foreign to her specific biological nature and confronted with which she cannot but feel herself inadequate.

Although this sense of inferiority is very tormenting, analytical experience emphatically shows us that the ego can tolerate it more easily than the sense of guilt associated with the feminine attitude, and hence it is undoubtedly a gain for the ego when the girl flees from the Scylla of the sense of guilt to the Charybdis of the sense of inferiority.

For the sake of completeness I will add a reference to the other gain that, as we know, accrues to women from the process of identification with the father, which takes place at the same time. I know of nothing with reference to the importance of this process itself to add to what I have already said in my earlier work.

We know that this very process of identification with the father is one answer to the question of why the flight from feminine wishes in regard to the father always leads to the adoption of a masculine attitude. Some reflections connected with what has already been said reveal another point of view that throws some light on this question.

We know that whenever the libido encounters a barrier in its development an earlier phase of organization is regressively activated. Now, according to Freud's latest work, penis envy forms the preliminary stage to the true object love for the father. And so this train of thought suggested by Freud helps us to some comprehension of the inner necessity by which the libido flows back precisely to this preliminary stage whenever and insofar as it is driven back by the incest barrier.

I agree in principle with Freud's notion that the girl develops toward object love by way of penis envy, but I think that the nature of this evolution might also be pictured differently.

For when we see how large a part of the strength of primary penis envy is accrued only by retrogression from the Œdipus complex, we must resist the temptation to interpret in the light of penis envy the manifestations of so elementary a principle of nature as that of the mutual attraction of the sexes.

Whereupon, being confronted with the question of how we should conceive psychologically of this primal, biological principle, we would again have to confess ignorance. Indeed, in this respect the conjecture forces itself more and more strongly upon me that perhaps the causal connection may be the exact converse and that it is just the attraction to the opposite sex, operating from a very early period, which draws the libidinal interest of the little girl to the penis. This interest, in accordance with the level of development reached, acts at first in an autoerotic and narcissistic manner, as I have described before. If we view these relations thus, fresh problems would logically present themselves with regard to the origin of the male Oedipus complex, but I wish to postpone these for a later paper. But, if penis envy were the first expression of that mysterious attraction of the sexes, there would be nothing to wonder at when analysis discloses its existence in a yet deeper layer than that in which the desire for a child and the tender attachment to the father occur. The way to this tender attitude toward the father would be prepared not simply by disappointment in regard to the penis but in another way as well. We should then instead have to conceive of the libidinal interest in the penis as a kind of "partial love," to use Abraham's term.[17] Such love, he says, always forms a preliminary stage to true object love. We might explain the process too by an analogy from later life: I refer to the fact that admiring envy is specially calculated to lead to an attitude of love.

With regard to the extraordinary ease with which this regression takes place, I must mention the analytical discovery [18] that in the associations of female patients the narcissistic desire to possess the penis and the object libidinal longing for it are often so interwoven that one hesitates as to the sense in which the words

17. Abraham, *Versuch einer Entwicklungsgeschichte der Libido* (1924).
18. Freud referred to this in *The Taboo of Virginity*.

"desire for it" [19] are meant.

One word more about the castration fantasies proper, which have given their name to the whole complex because they are the most striking part of it. According to my theory of feminine development, I am obliged to regard these fantasies also as a secondary formation. I picture their origin as follows: When the woman takes refuge in the fictitious male role, her feminine genital anxiety is to some extent translated into male terms—the fear of vaginal injury becomes a fantasy of castration. The girl gains by this conversion, for she exchanges the uncertainty of her expectation of punishment (an uncertainty conditioned by her anatomical formation) for a concrete idea. Moreover, the castration fantasy, too, is under the shadow of the old sense of guilt—and the penis is desired as a proof of guiltlessness.

Now these typical motives for flight into the male role—motives whose origin is the Oedipus complex—are reinforced and supported by the actual disadvantage under which women labor in social life. Of course we must recognize that the desire to be a man, when it springs from this last source, is a peculiarly suitable form of rationalization of those unconscious motives. But we must not forget that this disadvantage is actually a piece of reality and that it is immensely greater than most women are aware of.

Georg Simmel says in this connection that "the greater importance attaching to the male sociologically is probably due to his position of superior strength," and that historically the relation of the sexes may be crudely described as that of master and slave. Here, as always, it is "one of the privileges of the master that he has not constantly to think that he is master, while the position of the slave is such that he can never forget it."

Here we probably have the explanation also of the underestimation of this factor in analytical literature. In actual fact a girl is exposed from birth onward to the suggestion—inevitable, whether conveyed brutally or delicately—of her inferiority, an experience that constantly stimulates her masculinity complex.

There is one further consideration. Owing to the hitherto purely masculine character of our civilization, it has been much

19. German, *Haben-Wollen*.

harder for women to achieve any sublimation that would really satisfy their nature, for all the ordinary professions have been filled by men. This again must have exercised an influence upon women's feelings of inferiority, for naturally they could not accomplish the same as men in these masculine professions and so it appeared that there was a basis in fact for their inferiority. It seems to me impossible to judge to how great a degree the unconscious motives for the flight from womanhood are reinforced by the actual social subordination of women. One might conceive of the connection as an interaction of psychic and social factors. But I can only indicate these problems here, for they are so grave and so important that they require a separate investigation.

The same factors must have quite a different effect on the man's development. On the one hand they lead to a much stronger repression of his feminine wishes, in that these bear the stigma of inferiority; on the other hand it is far easier for him successfully to sublimate them.

In the foregoing discussion I have put a construction upon certain problems of feminine psychology, which in many points differs from current views. It is possible and even probable that the picture I have drawn is one-sided from the opposite point of view. But my primary intention in this paper was to indicate a possible source of error arising out of the sex of the observer, and by so doing to make a step forward toward the goal that we are all striving to reach: to get beyond the subjectivity of the masculine or the feminine standpoint and to obtain a picture of the mental development of woman that will be more true to the facts of her nature—with its specific qualities and its differences from that of man—than any we have hitherto achieved.

INHIBITED FEMININITY*

Psychoanalytical Contribution
to the Problem of Frigidity

○○○

THE TREMENDOUS PREVALENCE of feminine frigidity has, curiously, led physicians and sexologists to two diametrically opposed views.

One group compares frigidity, in its importance for the individual, to potency disturbances in the male. They claim, therefore, that the former phenomenon is just as much an illness as is the latter. This position points to the importance of dealing even more seriously with the etiology and therapy of frigidity, particularly because of the frequency of its occurrence.

On the other hand, this very frequency has led to the notion that one cannot consider so common a phenomenon as an illness, that frigidity in all its gradations should rather be considered as the normal sexual attitude of civilized woman. Whatever scientific hypotheses were formulated to prove this concept,[1] they all conclude that the physician has neither a reason for, nor a chance of success through his therapeutic intervention.

One gets the impression that the general arguments, both pro and con, whether they emphasize social or constitutional factors, are based on strong subjective convictions, and hence are not helpful in leading us to a general, factual clarification of the problem in question. The science of psychoanalysis, from its inception, has

---

* "Gehemmte Weiblichkeit: Psychoanalytischer Beitrag zum Problem der Frigidität," *Zeitschr. f. Sexualwissenschaft,* Vol. 13 (1926–27), pp. 67-77. Reprinted in translation with the permission of the Karen Horney Estate.

1. For references on this subject see "Neuropathia Sexualis" by Max Marcuse in Moll's *Handbook of Sexual Sciences,* 3rd Edition, Vol. II, 1926.

taken a different direction, which, by its very nature, it had to follow. It is the medico-psychological observation of the individual
and his development.

If we consider how much closer this road can take us to a solution of the problems, it seems as if we might finally expect answers
to the following two questions:

(1) What developmental processes, according to our experience, lead to the formation of the symptom of frigidity in a
particular woman?

(2) What significance is to be attributed to this phenomenon
in the libidinal economy of the woman?

The same questions can be expressed less theoretically in the
following way: Is it only an isolated symptom, and as such, rather
unimportant? Or is it closely connected with real disturbances of
psychological or physical health?

Permit me to illustrate the meaning or possible value of these
questions by a crude—and therefore in many ways poor—comparison. If we were to imagine that we knew nothing about the
pathological processes that produce the symptom of coughing, we
could certainly envision the possibility of a discussion on whether
coughing is, in all cases, a sign of sickness or merely represents a
subjective annoyance, since obviously many people cough without
really being sick. However, differences of opinion about this could
only exist as long as we remained in ignorance of the connection
of coughing with factual deeper disturbances.

The basis for my making such a comparison, despite its evident shortcomings, is that a particular perspective is opened to us.
Is it possible that frigidity—like coughing—is only a signal, indi-
cating that deep inside something is wrong?

A doubt, however, immediately emerges. We know of many
women who are frigid, yet healthy and efficient. But this objection
is not as convincing as it appears at first glance for two reasons.
First of all, only a detailed and careful investigation of an individual case can show whether there might not exist disturbances
that are hard to recognize or to connect with frigidity. I am thinking here, for example, of character difficulties or failures in plan-
ning one's life, which are wrongly attributed to external factors.
Secondly, one has to consider that our psychological structure is

not rigid like a machine, which must fail as a whole if there is a fault or an inherent weakness at just one point. Rather we have considerable ability to transform sexual forces into nonsexual ones, thus perhaps sublimating them successfully in a culturally valuable way.

Before I go into the individual genesis of frigidity, I would like to take a look at the phenomena we actually and frequently find associated with it. I want to limit myself to the phenomena that lie more or less within the limits of normalcy.

Whether or not we conceive of frigidity as being organically or psychologically conditioned, it is an inhibition of female sexual functioning. Therefore it is not surprising to find frigidity connected with the impairment of other specifically female functions. We see in many cases the most diverse functional disturbances of menstruation.[2] They include irregularities of the cycle, dysmenorrhea, or—remaining entirely within the psychological sphere—states of tension, irritability or weakness, frequently setting in eight to fourteen days prior to menstruation, every time causing a rather severe impairment of the psychic equilibrium.

In other cases the difficulty lies in the woman's attitude toward motherhood. In some instances pregnancy is rejected outright—with some form of rationalization being given. In others, miscarriages occur without demonstrable organic conditions. In still others we encounter those numerous well-known complaints of pregnancy.[3] Disturbances such as neurotic anxiety or functional weakness of labor may set in during delivery. In other women, nursing becomes difficult, from the extremes of complete failure of breast feeding to nervous exhaustion. Or we may not find the proper motherly attitude toward the child. We may see instead those irritated or overanxious mothers who cannot give the child real warmth and are inclined to leave him with a governess.

Something similar often happens regarding the woman's household chores. Either housework is overrated and turned into

2. I am excluding here, as well as in the following considerations, disorders due to definite organic causes.

3. We quite evidently cannot blame the physiological-chemical changes in metabolism for these disturbances, because when a favorable psychic attitude exists, they alone cannot bring about these difficulties.

a torture for the family, or it tires her excessively, just as every task that is done unwillingly becomes a strain.

However, even where all these disturbances of female functions are absent, *one* relationship will regularly be impaired or incomplete—namely, the attitude toward the male. I shall come back to the nature of these disturbances in another context. Here I want to say only this much: Whether they reveal themselves in indifference or morbid jealousy, in distrust or irritability, in claims or feelings of inferiority, in a need for lovers or for intimate friendships with women, they have one thing in common—the incapacity for a full (that is, including both body and soul) love relationship with a heterosexual love object.

If during analysis we gain a deeper insight into the unconscious psychic life of these women, we meet, as a rule, with a very determined rejection of the female role. This is the more remarkable, since the conscious ego of these women often does not contain evidence of such an active rejection of femininity. On the contrary, the general appearance as well as the conscious attitude can be altogether feminine. It has been correctly pointed out that frigid women can be even erotically responsive and sexually demanding, an observation that warns us against equating frigidity with the rejection of sex. As a matter of fact we do not meet, at deeper levels, with sexual rejection in general, but rather with a reluctance to assume the specifically female role. To the extent that this aversion reaches awareness, it usually is rationalized as due to such factors as social discrimination against women or by accusations against the husband or men in general. However, at a deeper level is another clearly discernible motivation—a more or less intensive wish for, or fantasies of, masculinity. I want to emphasize that we are here already within the realm of the unconscious. Although such wishes can be partially conscious, the woman is generally unconscious of their extent and deeper instinctive motivation.

The entire complex of feelings and fantasies that have for their content the woman's feeling of being discriminated against, her envy of the male, her wish to be a man and to discard the female role, we call the *masculinity complex of woman*. Its effects in the life of the more or less healthy as well as of the neurotic woman are so tremendously manifold that I must content myself with sketching the main directions in a rather schematic way.[4]

To the extent that the envy of the male is in the foreground, these wishes express themselves in resentment against the male, in an inner bitterness against the male as the privileged one—similar to the concealed hostility of the worker against his employer and his efforts to defeat the employer or to weaken him psychologically by the thousand means of daily guerilla warfare. In brief, we recognize at first glance the picture, for it appears in innumerable marriages.

Simultaneously, however, we see how the same woman who disparages all men, nevertheless regards them as very much her superior. She has no faith in women's capacity for any real achievement and is rather inclined to identify with the masculine disregard for women. Though herself not a male, she at least aspires to share his judgment of women. Frequently this attitude alternates with definite depreciatory tendencies toward the male, so that one is reminded of the story of the fox and the sour grapes.

Furthermore, such an unconscious attitude of envy renders the woman blind to her own virtues. Even motherhood appears only as a burden to her. Everything is measured against the masculine —that is, by a yardstick intrinsically alien to her—and therefore she easily perceives herself as insufficient. Thus we find nowadays a considerable degree of uncertainty even in gifted women whose achievements are both positive and recognized. This arises from the depth of their masculinity complex and may express itself in excessive sensitivity to criticism or in timidity.

On the other hand, the feeling of having been basically damaged and discriminated against by fate, can also result in unconscious claims against life for compensation because of these wrongs done her. It is consistent with the origin of these claims that they can never actually be satisfied. One is accustomed to explain the picture of the perpetually demanding, perpetually discontented woman as deriving from general sexual dissatisfaction. But deeper insights clearly demonstrate that the dissatisfaction can already be

4. Abraham, "Manifestations of the Female Castration Complex," *Int. J. Psycho-Anal.*, Vol. 4 (1921). Freud, "The Taboo of Virginity," (*The Standard Edition*, Vol. XI), p. 191.

a consequence of the masculinity complex. It is easily understandable, as well as proven by experience, that strong unconscious
claims for masculinity are unfavorable to a feminine attitude. Because of their inner logic these claims must lead to frigidity, if the
male is not rejected altogether as a sex partner. Frigidity, in turn,
is likely to intensify the above-mentioned inferiority feelings, since
at a deeper level it unerringly is experienced as an incapacity for
love. Often this is in complete opposition to the conscious moral
evaluation of frigidity as a manifestation of decency or chastity.
In turn, this unerring unconscious feeling of a lack in the sexual
sphere leads easily to a neurotically reinforced jealousy of other
women.

Other consequences of the masculinity complex are more
deeply rooted in the unconscious and are not likely to be understood without an exact knowledge of the unconscious mechanisms.
The dreams and symptoms of many women clearly demonstrate
that basically they have not come to terms with their femininity.
On the contrary, in their unconscious fantasy lives they have
maintained the fiction of having actually been created as males.
They believe that through some influences they have been mutilated, injured, or wounded. In keeping with such fantasies, the
female genital is conceived of as a sick and damaged organ, a concept that later can be confirmed and activated again and again
through the evidence of menstruation—their conscious and better
knowledge notwithstanding. The connection with unconscious
fantasies of such a nature can easily lead to the above-mentioned
menstrual difficulties, as well as to pains during sexual intercourse,
and to gynecological difficulties.[5]

In other cases these ideas, and the complaints and hypochondriacal fears, associated with them, are not attached to the genital
itself, but are transferred to all other possible organs. Only the detailed examination of psychoanalytic material, such as would ex-
ceed the framework of an orientation paper, could furnish us with
insight into the processes that take place in the individual case.
One can only gain an impression regarding the tenacity of these
unconscious masculinity wishes through the process of analysis
itself.

5. Even where actual organic changes, such as ectopias, are present, the
subjective complaints frequently derive from such psychic factors.

If one searches for the origin of this curious complex in the psychological development of these women, one can often identify and directly observe a childhood stage, during which little girls do in fact envy boys their genitals. This is a well-established finding that can easily be checked by direct observation. Analytic interpretations, which after all are subjective, have added nothing to these observations, and yet even at the point of direct confirmation one meets with firm disbelief. Wherever critics cannot dispute the fact that children may express such ideas, they attempt at the least to deny their developmental significance. They state that such a wish or even envy may be observable in some girls, but that it means no more than the envy similar to that shown for another child's toys or sweets.

Permit me, therefore, to refer to a factor that perhaps will make us wonder about such an opinion—i.e., the greater role that the meaning of the body plays in the life of young children before the development into a psychological differentiation has taken place. Such a primitive attitude toward the physical strikes us adult Europeans as strange. We see, however, that other groups who think more naïvely and thus less repressedly in sexual matters, quite openly practice cults involving worship of the physical emblems of sexuality, especially the phallus, to which they attribute divine rank and miraculous power. The pattern of thought underlying these phallic cults is in fact so closely related to a child's that it is clearly intelligible to anyone familiar with the child's way of being. Conversely, it can help us to better understand the child's world.

If we now accept the stage of penis envy as an empirical fact, an objection easily arises that can hardly be refuted in the light of rational thinking; it says that the girl has no reason at all to envy the boy. In her capacity for motherhood she has such indubitable biological advantages that one could rather think of the reverse, an envy of motherhood in the boy's mind. I want to indicate briefly that such a phenomenon really exists and that from it a powerful stimulus arises that drives the male to his productivity in the cultural area.[6] On the other hand, the little girl at that early stage has not yet understood that she has a prospective ad-

---

6. Cf. the linguistic equivalence of such words as "child" and "work" (German *Werk* = productions), "create" and "give birth," etc.

vantage over the boy, and therefore it does not prevent her from feeling at a disadvantage at this time. Nevertheless, there is some validity in the criticism leveled against us for overrating penis envy. Because in effect, the masculinity complex of later life, with its frequent catastrophic consequences, is not a direct offspring of this early developmental period, but arises only after a complicated detour.

For an understanding of these conditions, one has to realize that the attitude of penis envy is a narcissistic one, being directed toward one's own ego and not toward the object. In the case of a favorable feminine development, this narcissistic penis envy becomes almost completely submerged in the object-libidinal desire for a man and for a child.[7] This experience fits in well with the observation that women who rest securely in their femininity show no traces worth mentioning of the above expressions of masculinity claims.

Psychoanalytic insights, however, have shown that many conditions must be fulfilled in order to guarantee such a normal development and that there are just as many possibilities for blockages or disturbances in the development. The decisive phase for further psychosexual development is the one in which the first object relationships within the family take place.[8] During this phase, which reaches its peak between the third and fifth year of life, different factors may enter, causing the girl to shrink back from her female role. Gross favoritism of a brother, for instance, can often contribute a great deal toward establishing strong masculinity wishes in the little girl. Early sexual observations have a still more lasting influence in this direction. This is particularly true in a milieu where sexual matters are otherwise concealed from the child, so that they take on, just by this very contrast, the character of the uncanny and the forbidden. Sexual intercourse by the parents, so frequently observed during the first years of childhood, is typically conceived of by the child as the mother's being

7. I assume a knowledge of the psychoanalytic investigations of this stage, which we summarize under the collective term of the Oedipal situation. About its relationship to the masculinity complex, see Horney, "On the Genesis of the Castration Complex in Women," *Int. J. Psycho-Anal.* (1924).

8. Sigmund Freud, "On the Transformation of Instincts with Special Reference to Anal Erotism," *Collected Papers*, Vol. II, pp. 164-171.

raped, injured, wounded, or made ill. Observation of traces of the mother's menstrual blood reinforce the child's opinion. Accidental impressions, like real brutality on the part of the father and sickness of the mother may increase in the child the notion that the woman's position is precarious and one of danger.

All this affects the little girl, particularly since it occurs at the stage of her first sexual developmental surge, during which she unconsciously identifies her own instinctual claims with those of her mother. From these unconscious instinctual claims originate another impulse that may operate in the same direction. That is, the more intensive this early feminine love attitude toward the father, the greater is the danger that it will fail due to disappointments in the father, or due to guilt feelings toward the mother. Furthermore, these affects remain inseparably linked with the feminine role. Such a linkage with guilt feelings can especially follow intimidations on account of masturbation, which, as is known, is the physical expression of sexual stimulation during this period.

Because of these anxieties and guilt feelings, the girl may turn away altogether from the female role and take refuge in a fictitious masculinity for the sake of security. The masculinity wishes that originally had arisen from a naïve envy, which by its own nature was destined to disappear early, now become overcathected by these powerful impulses and can, at this point, unfold the tremendous effects that I have indicated above.

The non-analytic mind will be more inclined to think first of disappointments in later love life. We do sometimes observe that a man, after having been disappointed by a woman, may turn to homosexual love objects. We certainly should not underrate these later events, but our experiences remind us that these later misfortunes in love life may already be the result of an attitude acquired in childhood. On the other hand, all these consequences may happen without such later experiences.

Once these unconscious masculinity claims have taken hold, the woman has fallen into a fatal, vicious circle. Whereas she originally had fled from the female role into the fiction of the male one, the latter, once established, contributes in turn to her rejection of the female role even further and now with an added tinge of the contemptible. A woman who has built her life on

such unconscious pretenses is basically endangered from two sides:
by her masculinity wishes on the one hand, since they shake her
feeling of self, and by her repressed femininity on the other, in
that some experience inevitably reminds her of her feminine role.

Literature describes for us the fate of a woman who broke under such a conflict. We recognize her in the figure of Schiller's
Maid of Orleans, drawn in the grand and sweeping lines of history. The romanticized cloak of history presents the heroine as
breaking under her guilt feelings, because for a brief moment she
loves an enemy of her country. Yet this motivation seems insufficient for such profound guilt feelings and such a severe breakdown; the correlation between the crime and the punishment is
incorrect and unjust. A meaning of profound psychological import, however, emerges, once we assume that poetic intuition has
pictured a conflict arising from the unconscious. Access to a psychological understanding of the drama would then have to be
sought in the prologue. Here the Maid hears God's voice forbidding her all womanly experiencing, but promising her male
honors instead. To quote:

> *With man's love thou shalt never be embraced*
> *Nor passion's sinful flame thy heart invest,*
> *Thy hair shall not by bridal wreath be graced,*
> *No lovely child may nestle at thy breast,*
> *But with war's honors I will make thee great*
> *Before all earthly women's fame and fate.*[9]

Let us suppose that God's voice is psychologically equivalent
to the father's, an assumption that is warranted through a thousand experiences. Thus at the core of the basic situation would be
the fact that the prohibition of feminine experiencing is connected with her feelings for her father; and that this prohibition,
projected to the father, pushes her into a masculine role. The
complete breakdown would therefore not arise because she loves
an enemy of the country, but because she loves at all, and because
the repressed femininity has broken through and is accompanied
by feelings of guilt. Incidentally, it is very characteristic that this

9. Friedrich Schiller. *Maid of Orleans*, translated by Charles E. Passage
(New York, Frederick Unger Publishing Company, 1961), p. 15.

conflict leads not only to an emotional depression, but also to failure in her "male" achievement.

Frequently enough in medical psychology, cases are observed that on a small scale are similar to those created by the intuitive genius of the poet. These are the cases of women who become neurotic or show character changes after their first sexual experience, be it merely after finding out about sex or after actual physical experience. Summarizing, one can say that these are the cases in which the road to the specific feminine role is barred through unconscious feelings of guilt or anxiety. Such a blockage must not necessarily lead to frigidity. It is only a question of the quantity of these resistances that determines to what extent feminine experiencing will be blocked. We can observe here a continuous sequence of symptoms, from women who reject the very thought of a sexual experience, to those in whom resistance becomes apparent only through the body language of frigidity. If the resistance is of a relatively minor degree, the frigidity is usually not a rigid, unchangeable mode of reaction. It can be given up under certain, for the most part unconscious, conditions. For some women the sexual experience has to occur within an atmosphere of the forbidden, for others it has to be accompanied by the suffering of some violence, and in still others it is only possible if all emotional involvement is excluded. In these last instances women may be frigid with a beloved man, and yet capable of complete physical surrender to a man who is merely sensually desired, but unloved.

From these different manifestations of frigidity one can correctly infer its psychogenic origin. Moreover, analytic insights into its development help us understand that its appearance or disappearance in certain psychological situations is strictly determined by the individual's developmental history. Stekel's statement that "the anesthetic woman is merely the woman who has not found the form of satisfaction adequate to her" is, from this point of view, a misunderstanding, inasmuch as the "adequate form" may be connected with unconscious conditions that are either not realizable at all or are unacceptable to the conscious ego.

The phenomenon of frigidity thus fits into a larger framework. It may indeed constitute an important symptom in its own right, inasmuch as an accumulation of libido, because of a lack of actual release, is poorly tolerated by many women. Yet it acquires its real significance only through the developmental disturbance that is at its base and of which it is merely an expression. From this insight, it is easily comprehensible why other female functions are also affected so frequently by frigidity and why there is rarely serious nervous disturbance in a woman that is not accompanied by frigidity and its underlying inhibitions.

Thus we return to the initial problem as to the *frequency* of these phenomena. It follows without further comment that according to this concept, the prevalence of frigidity is not reason enough to call it normal, especially since we can trace frigidity back to the developmental inhibitions that give rise to it. However, the question still remains open as to the cause of its frightening frequency.

This question is not to be answered by analytic means alone. Psychoanalysis can do no more than point the ways to, or better, the byways of the development through which frigidity comes about. Beyond this it permits us certain insights into the easy accessibility of these ways. But it can tell us nothing as to why these roads are actually traveled so often, or in any case, nothing that goes beyond speculation.

It seems to me that the explanation for this frequency has rather to do with supra-individual, cultural factors. Our culture, as is well known, is a male culture, and therefore by and large not favorable to the unfolding of woman and her individuality.[10] Among the manifold influences that this factor exercises on woman, I want to call special attention to only two.

Firstly, no matter how much the individual woman may be treasured as a mother or as a lover, it is always the male who will be considered more valuable on human and spiritual grounds. The little girl grows up under this general impression. If we realize that from her first years of childhood, the girl carries with her a reason for envy of the male, then we can easily grasp how much this social impression must contribute to justify her masculinity wishes on a conscious level, and how much it impedes an inner

10. Georg Simmel, "Philosophische Kultur," *Gesammelte Essays von Georg Simmel*, ed. Dr. Werner Klinkhardt (Leipzig, 1911).

affirmation of her female role.

An additional unfavorable factor lies in a certain peculiarity of contemporary male eroticism. The split into sensual and romantic components of the love life, which we find only occasionally in women, seems to be about as frequent in educated men as frigidity is in women.[11] Thus, on the one hand, man searches for his life's companion and friend who is close to him spiritually, but toward whom his sensuousness is inhibited, and who, deep down, he expects will reciprocate with a similar attitude. The effect on the woman is clear; it can very easily lead to frigidity, even if the inhibitions she has brought with her from her own development are not insurmountable. On the other hand, such a man will search for a woman, with whom he can have sexual relations only, a trend he manifests most clearly in his relationships with prostitutes. The repercussion of this attitude upon the woman, however, must also result in frigidity. Since in women the emotional life is, as a rule, much more closely and uniformly connected with sexuality, she cannot give herself completely when she does not love or is not loved. Let us take into consideration that because of the dominant position of the male, his subjective needs can be satisfied in reality. Let us also consider the influence that custom and education exercise upon the creation and maintenance of female inhibitions. Then these brief references will demonstrate what powerful forces are at work to restrict woman in the free unfolding of her femininity. On the other hand, psychoanalysis shows that in the female development there are many possibilities and tendencies that can lead, from within, to a rejection of the female role.

The extent to which the decisive effect rests with *exogenous* or *endogenous* factors will be different in each individual case. Yet fundamentally it is a question of the joint operation of both these factors. Perhaps we can surmise that a more accurate insight into the mode of their acting together might open up a real understanding of the frequency of feminine inhibitions.

11. Sigmund Freud, "Contributions to the Psychology of Love; A Special Type of Choice of Object Made by Men" (1910), Collected Papers, Vol. IV, pp. 192-202.

THE PROBLEM OF THE

MONOGAMOUS IDEAL*

ooooooooooooooooooooooooooooooooooooooooooooooo

F OR SOME TIME I have asked myself with growing astonishment why there has as yet been no thorough analytical exposition of the problems of marriage,[1] although assuredly every single analyst would have a great deal to say on the subject, and although both practical and theoretical considerations are necessitating some attack on these problems: practical considerations, because every day we are confronted with matrimonial conflicts; theoretical, because there is hardly another situation in life that is so intimately and so obviously related to the Œdipus situation as is marriage.

Perhaps (I said to myself) the whole question touches us too closely to form an attractive object of scientific curiosity and ambition. But it is also possible that it is not the problems but the conflicts that touch us too closely, lie too near to some of the deepest roots of our most intimate personal experience. And there is another difficulty: Marriage is a social institution, and our approach to its problems from the psychological standpoint is neces-

* Read at the Tenth International Psychoanalytical Congress, Innsbruck, September 3, 1927. Int. J. Psycho-Anal. Vol. IX (1928), pp. 318-31. Reprinted with the permission of The International Journal of Psycho-Analysis.

1. This does not imply that almost every aspect of these problems has not already been touched on in psychoanalytical literature. I have only to refer to Freud, " 'Civilized' Sexual Morality and Modern Nervousness" and "Contributions to the Psychology of Love"; Ferenczi, "Psycho-Analysis of Sexual Habits"; Reich, Die Funktion des Orgasmus; Schultz-Henke, Einführung in die Psycho-analyse; Flügel, The Psycho-Analytic Study of the Family. Again, in the Ehebuch (edited by Max Marcuse) we have papers by Róheim, "Urformen und Wandlungen der Ehe"; Horney, "Psychische Eignung und Nichteignung zur Ehe"; "Über die psychischen Bedingungen zur Gattenwahl"; "Über die psychischen Wurzeln einiger typischer Ehekonflikte."

sarily hampered; at the same time the practical importance of these problems obliges us at least to try to understand what is their psychological basis.

Though for the purposes of my present paper I have selected one particular problem, we must first of all try to form a conception (though but in broad outline) of the fundamental psychical situation implied by marriage. In his *Ehebuch* Keyserling has recently propounded a question that is as remarkable as it is obvious. What is it, he asks, that in spite of constant matrimonial unhappiness in all ages, continues to impel human beings into marriage? In order to answer this question we are fortunately neither driven to fall back on the notion of a "natural" desire for a husband and children, nor, as Keyserling does, on metaphysical explanations; we can assert with greater precision that what drives us into matrimony is clearly neither more nor less than the expectation that we shall find in it the fulfillment of all the old desires arising out of the Oedipus situation in childhood —the desire to be a wife to the father, to have him as one's exclusive possession, and to bear him children. In passing I may say that, knowing this, we are likely to be extremely skeptical when we hear it prophesied that the institution of marriage will soon come to an end, though we admit that at any given period the structure of society will affect the form of these undying wishes.

Hence, the initial situation in marriage is fraught with a perilously heavy load of unconscious wishes. This is more or less inevitable, for we know that there is no cure for the persistent recurrence of these desires and that neither conscious insight into the difficulties nor our experience of them in the lives of others really can help much. Now there are two reasons why this freight of unconscious wishes is dangerous. From the side of the id, the subject is threatened with disappointment not only because actually being a father or mother oneself does not in the least realize the picture left in our minds by our childish longings, but also because—as Freud says—the husband or the wife is always only a substitute. The bitterness of the disappointment depends on the one hand on the degree of fixation, and on the other, on the degree of discrepancy between the object found and the gratification achieved and the specific unconscious sexual desires.

From the other side the superego is menaced by the resuscitation of the old incest prohibition—this time in relation to the marriage partner, and the more complete the fulfillment of unconscious wishes, the greater is the danger. The revival of the incest prohibition in marriage is apparently very typical and leads *mutatis mutandis* to the same results as in the relation between child and parent; that is, the direct sexual aims give place to an affectionate attitude in which the sexual aim is inhibited. I know personally of only one case in which this development has not supervened, the wife remaining permanently in love with her husband as a sexual object, and in this case the woman had, at the age of twelve, enjoyed actual sexual gratification with her father.

Of course there is another reason why sexuality tends to develop on these lines in married life—the sexual tension is reduced as a result of the fulfillment of desire, and especially because it can always easily be gratified in relation to the one object. But the deeper motivation of this typical phenomenon, at any rate the rapidity of the process and particularly the degree to which it develops, are all traceable to some such repetition of the Oedipus development.[2] Apart from accidental factors, the manner and degree in which the influence of the early situation will show itself will depend on the extent to which the incest prohibition still makes itself felt as a living force in the mind of the individual concerned. The more profound effects, though their manifestations are so different in different persons, may be described by a common formula: They lead to certain limitations or conditions, given which the subject is still able to tolerate the marriage relation, despite the incest prohibition.

2. In his paper "On the Most Prevalent Form of Degradation in Erotic Life" (*Collected Papers*, Vol. IV, p. 203) Freud has attacked this problem in a similar form. He says there: "But is it true that the mental value of an instinct invariably sinks with gratification of it?" And he reminds us of what happens with an habitual drinker and his wine—how the mere passage of time causes him to become more and more strongly attached to his particular kind of drink. Freud's answer to the whole question is the same as is given here, insofar as he reminds us that in our erotic life the original object may be represented by an endless series of substitutes, "none of which is wholly satisfactory." I would only add to this explanation that not only is a search for the "true" love object continually being carried on, but there also has to be considered the recoil from the object of the moment due to the prohibition that so easily attaches itself to fulfillment of the wish.

As we know, such limitations may make themselves felt already in the type of husband or wife chosen. It may be that the woman selected as wife must in no way recall the mother; in race or social origin, intellectual calibre or appearance she must present a certain contrast to the mother. This helps to explain why marriages prompted by prudence or contracted through the intervention of a third party tend to turn out relatively better than genuine love matches. Though the similarity of the marriage situation to the desires arising out of the Oedipus complex automatically produces a repetition of the subject's early attitude and development, nevertheless this is less if the unconscious expectations have not all from the outset attached themselves to the future husband or wife. Moreover, when we take into account the unconscious tendency to protect marriage from the more violent forms of disaster, we can perceive that there was a certain psychological wisdom in the institution of an intermediary to arrange marriages, such as obtains among the Eastern Jews.

Within wedlock itself we see how such conditions as these may be created by all the psychic institutions in our minds. In regard to the id, there are genital inhibitions of all sorts, ranging from a simple sexual reserve toward the partner, which rules out variations in forepleasure or coitus, to complete impotence or frigidity. Further, we see on the part of the ego, attempts at reassurance or justification that may take very varied forms. One of these amounts to a kind of denial of the marriage, and frequently manifests itself in women as a merely external recognition of the fact of their being married, without any inner appreciation of it, accompanied by an inner feeling of being constantly amazed at it, by a tendency to sign their maiden names, behave in a girlish fashion, and so forth.

But impelled by the inner necessity to justify marriage to the conscience, the ego often adopts the opposite attitude toward wedlock, laying upon it an exaggerated stress, or more precisely, stressing in an exaggerated manner the love felt to husband or wife. One might coin the phrase "justification by love," and see an analogy in the more lenient verdicts passed by the tribunal of the law on criminals actuated by love. In his paper on a case of female homosexuality, Freud says that there is nothing about which our consciousness can be so incomplete or false as about the degrees of affection or dislike we feel for another human being. This is quite especially true of marriage, it being often the case that the degree of love felt is overestimated. I have long asked myself how we are to explain this. That one is liable to an illusion of this sort where the relation is a fleeting one is really not very surprising, but one would suppose that in marriage not only the permanence of the relation but also the more frequent gratification of sexual desire would be calculated to do away with sexual overestimation and the illusions bound up with it. The most obvious answer would be that people very naturally endeavor to account to themselves for the great demands on the psychic life involved in marriage by conceiving that they are due to a strong emotion, and therefore to hold tenaciously to the idea of such an emotion, even after it has ceased to be a living force. Nevertheless, it must be admitted that this explanation is rather superficial; it probably springs from the need for synthesis with which we are familiar in the ego and to which we may well ascribe a falsification of the facts for the sake of demonstrating a single-minded attitude in a relation so important in life.

Once again, the relation to the Oedipus complex provides a very much deeper explanation. For we see that the commandment and the vow to love and cleave to husband or wife with which one enters into matrimony are regarded by the unconscious as a renewal of the fourth commandment. Hence, not to love the partner in marriage becomes as great a sin to the unconscious as the failure to fulfill that commandment in relation to the parents, and in this respect also—the suppression of hate and the exaggeration of love—the earlier experiences are compulsorily repeated with exactness in every detail. I now think that in many cases we do not correctly appreciate this phenomenon unless we assume that love itself can be one of the conditions necessary to lend the semblance of justification to a relation prohibited by the superego. Naturally, then, the retention of love, or the illusion of it, serves an important economic function, and that is why it is so obstinately striven after.

Finally, we will not be surprised to find that suffering (as in a neurotic symptom) is one of the conditions under which marriage can hold its own against a very strong incest prohibition. Affliction may take on such manifold forms for this purpose that one cannot hope to do them justice in a short sketch. I will therefore only suggest a few of them. There are, for instance, conditions in the domestic or professional life of some people, which are engineered by unconscious arrangement, so that the subject is overworked or has to make undue sacrifices "for the sake of the family," which he or she regards as a burden. Or again, it is a matter of frequent observation that after marriage, people sacrifice a considerable part of their personal development, whether in the sphere of their professional life or in that of character or intellect. Finally, we must include the countless cases in which one partner becomes a slave to the demands of the other and endures this painful position willingly, probably through the conscious enjoyment of a strong sense of responsibility.

With regard to such marriages as these, one often asks oneself in amazement—what can be the reason that they are not dissolved, but are often, on the contrary, so stable? But reflection shows, as I have indicated, that it is just the fulfillment of the condition of affliction that guarantees the permanence of such unions.

Having arrived at this point, we realize that there is by no means a clear dividing line between these cases and those others in which marriage is purchased at the price of a neurosis. Into the latter, however, I do not wish to enter, because in this paper I wish principally to discuss only those situations that may be described as normal.

It seems almost superfluous to mention that in this survey I am doing a certain violence to the real facts, not only because every one of the conditions I have described may be otherwise determined, but also because in order to present them clearly, I have taken each one separately, whereas in reality they are generally intermingled. To give you an instance: We can perceive something of all these conditions, particularly in highly estimable women in whom a fundamentally *maternal* attitude is by no means uncommon—an attitude that alone seems to make marriage possible for them. It is as though they said: In my relations with my husband I must not play the part of the wife and mistress, but only that of the mother, with all that this implies of loving care and responsibility. Such an attitude is in one way a good safeguard for a marriage, but it is based on a limitation of love, and the inner life of husband and wife may be rendered arid by it.

Whatever in the individual case may be the outcome of this dilemma between too much and too little fulfillment, in all the cases where it is especially acute, these two factors—disillusionment and the incest prohibition—with all their consequences of secret hostility to husband or wife, will alienate the other partner and drive him or her involuntarily to seek for new love objects. This is the basic situation that gives rise to the *problem* of monogamy.

There are other channels open to the libido thus liberated—sublimation, repression, the regressive cathexis of former objects, and the outlet through children—but with these we will not concern ourselves today.

The possibility that other human beings may become the objects of our love is, we must admit, always there. For the impressions of our childhood and their secondary elaborations are so multifarious that normally they do in fact admit of the choice of widely differing objects.

Now this impulse to seek after fresh objects may (again, in quite normal people) acquire a great impetus from unconscious sources. For although marriage does represent a fulfillment of infantile desires, these can be fulfilled only insofar as the subject's development enables him or her to effect a real identification with the role of father or mother. Whenever the outcome of the Oedipus complex departs from this fictive norm, we find the same phenomenon: The person in question is clinging in some fundamental points to the role of child in the triad of mother, father, and child. When this is the case, the desires arising out of this instinctual attitude cannot be directly gratified through marriage.

These conditions of love carried over from childhood are familiar to us from Freud's works. I need therefore only recall them to your memory in order to show how the inner meaning of marriage prevents their fulfillment. For the child the love object is indissolubly connected with the idea of something forbidden; yet love for husband or wife is not merely permitted—there looms beyond this the portentous idea of conjugal duty. Rivalry (the condition of there being an injured third party concerned) is excluded by the very nature of monogamous marriage; indeed, monopoly is a privilege accorded by law. Again (and here we are genetically on a different level, for the above conditions have their origin in the Oedipus situation itself, whereas those I am about to mention may be traced to fixation to special situations in which the Oedipus conflict has terminated) there may be a compulsion repeatedly to demonstrate potency or erotic attraction, because of genital uncertainty and a corresponding weakness in the structure of the narcissism. Or where there is an unconscious tendency to homosexuality, there is the compulsion to seek for an object of the same sex as the subject. From the standpoint of the woman this may be achieved by a circuitous route; either the husband may be driven into relations with other women, or the wife herself may seek for relations in which another woman plays a part. Above all—and from the practical point of view, this is probably the most important thing—where a dissociation in the love life persists, the subject will be compelled to center tender feelings on objects other than those of sensual desires.

We can easily see that the retention of any of these infantile conditions is unfavorable to the principle of monogamy; rather, it must inevitably drive the husband or wife to seek other love objects.

These polygamous desires, then, come into conflict with the partner's demand for a monogamous relation and with the ideal of faithfulness that we have set up for ourselves in our own minds.

Let us begin by considering the first of these two claims, for obviously a claim for someone else to make a renunciation is a more primitive phenomenon than imposing a renunciation upon ourselves. The origin of this claim, broadly speaking, is clear; plainly it is a revival of the infantile wish to monopolize the father or mother. Now this claim to monopolize is by no means peculiar to married life (as we should expect, seeing that its source lies within every one of us); on the contrary, it is of the essence of every full love relation. Of course, in wedlock as well as in other relations, it may be a claim made purely out of love, but in its origin it is so indissolubly connected with destructive tendencies and hostility to the object that often nothing is left of the love that makes the claim but a screen behind which these hostile tendencies fulfill themselves.

In analysis this desire for monopoly reveals itself first of all as a derivative of the oral phase, when it takes the form of the desire to incorporate the object in order to have sole possession of it. Often, even to ordinary observation, it betrays its origin in the greed of possession that not only grudges the partner any other erotic experience, but is also jealous of his or her friends, work, or interests. These manifestations confirm the expectation derived from our theoretical knowledge, namely, that in this possessiveness, as in every orally-conditioned attitude, there is an admixture of ambivalence. Sometimes we have the impression that men have not only actually succeeded in enforcing the naïve and complete demand for monogamous fidelity upon their wives more energetically than women have upon their husbands, but that the instinct to claim monopoly is stronger in men, and there are important conscious reasons for this—e.g., men wish to make sure of their fatherhood—but it may well be that precisely the oral origin of the demand gives it a stronger impetus in the male, for when his mother suckled him he experienced at any rate a partial incorporation of the love object, whereas the girl cannot go back to any corresponding experience in her relation to her father.

Further destructive elements are closely welded with this desire in another connection. In earlier days the claim to monopolize the love of father or mother met with frustration and disappointment, and the result was a reaction of hate and jealousy. Hence there lurks always behind this demand a certain hatred, which can generally be detected by the manner in which the claim is enforced, and which often breaks out if the old disappointment is repeated.

Now the early frustration wounded not only our object love but also our self-regard in its tenderest spot, and we know that here every human being carries a narcissistic scar. For this reason it is largely our pride that later demands a monogamous relation and demands it with an imperiousness proportionate to the sensitiveness of the scar left by the early disappointment. In patriarchal society, where the claim to exclusive possession is made above all by the man, this narcissistic factor is plainly manifested in the ridicule attaching to the "cuckold." Here, again, the claim is not made out of love; it is a question of prestige. In a society dominated by males, it is especially bound to become more and more a matter of prestige, for as a rule men think more of their status with their fellows than of love.

Finally, the demand for monogamy is closely bound up with anal-sadistic instinctual elements, and it is these, which together with the narcissistic elements, impart a peculiar character to the claim for monogamy in marriage. For in contrast to free love-relations, in marriage questions of possession are in a twofold manner intimately connected with its historical significance. The fact that marriage as such represents an economic partnership is of less importance than the view according to which woman was regarded as a chattel of man. Hence, without any special individual stressing of anal characteristics, these elements come into force in wedlock and convert the claim of love into an anal-sadistic demand for possession. Elements of this origin are to be seen in their crudest form in the old penal judgments on unfaithful wives, but in marriage today they still often betray themselves in the means employed to enforce the claim: a more or less affectionate compulsion and an ever wakeful suspicion calculated to torment the partner—both familiar to us from analyses of the obsessional neurosis.

Thus the sources from which the ideal of monogamy derives its strength seem to be sufficiently primitive. In spite of this so-to-speak humble origin, it has grown to be an imperious ideal, and here it shares, as we know, the evolution of other ideals in which elementary instinctual impulses rejected by consciousness find their fulfillment. In this instance what contributes to the process is the fact that the fulfillment of certain of our most powerful repressed wishes represents at the same time a valuable achievement in various social and cultural respects. As Rado has shown in his paper "An Anxious Mother,"[3] this ideal-formation enables

3. *Int. J. Psycho-Anal.*, Vol. IX (1928).

the ego to restrain its critical function, which would otherwise teach it that this claim to permanent monopoly, while understandable as a *wish*, as a *demand* is not only difficult to enforce but also unjustifiable; and further, that it represents the fulfillment of narcissistic and sadistic impulses far more than it indicates the wishes of genuine love. As Rado puts it, the formation of this ideal provides the ego with a "narcissistic insurance," under cover of which it is free to give play to all these instincts that it would otherwise condemn, and at the same time is raised in its own estimation through the sense that the claim it advances is right and ideal.

Of course, the fact that these demands are sanctioned by law is of enormous importance. In proposals for reform that spring from the realization of the dangers to which marriage is exposed because of just this compulsion, special exception is commonly taken to this latter point. Nevertheless, this legal sanction is probably simply the outward and visible expression of the value that this demand has in the minds of human beings. And when we realize upon what a deeply rooted instinctual basis the claim to monopoly takes its stand, we also see that if the present ideal justification for it were taken from humanity, we would at all costs in some way or other find a fresh one. Moreover, so long as society attaches importance to monogamy, it has from the point of view of psychic economics an interest in permitting the gratification of the elementary instincts that underlie the demand, in order to compensate for the restriction of instinct it imposes.

The demand for monogamy, while it has this general basis, may in individual cases be reinforced from various quarters. Sometimes one of its constituent elements may play an overwhelmingly great part in the instinctual economy, or all those factors that we recognize as motive forces in jealousy in general may contribute. In fact we might describe the demand for monogamy as an insurance against the torments of jealousy.

Just like jealousy, it may on the other hand be repressed through the weight of feelings of guilt, which whisper that we have no right to the exclusive possession of the father. Or again, it may be submerged under other instinctual aims, as in the well-known manifestations of latent homosexuality.

Further, as I said, polygamous desires come into collision with our own ideal of faithfulness. Unlike the claim to monogamy in others, our own attitude toward fidelity has no direct prototype in our infantile experience. Its content represents a restriction of instinct; hence it is obviously nothing elementary, but is, even in its earliest beginnings, an instinctual transformation.

As a rule we have more opportunity with women than with men of studying this demand for monogamy, and we ask ourselves why this should be so. The question for us is not whether (as is so frequently asserted) men have naturally a more polygamous disposition; for one thing, we know so little with certainty on questions of natural disposition. But apart from that, this assertion is so obviously simply a tendentious confabulation in favor of the man. I think, however, that we are justified in asking what can be the psychological factors that make faithfulness in actual life so much rarer in men than in women.

This question admits of more than one answer, for it cannot be separated from historical and social factors. For instance, we may consider how far woman's greater faithfulness might be secondarily conditioned by the fact that men have enforced their demand for monogamy more effectively in every way. Here I am thinking not only of the economic dependence of women, nor of the draconic punishments decreed for feminine unfaithfulness; there are other more complicated factors in the question, which Freud has made plain in "The Taboo of Virginity"—mainly, the demand made by men that a woman enter matrimony as a virgin, in order to ensure some measure of "sexual thraldom" in her.

From the analytical standpoint two questions suggest themselves in connection with this problem. The first is this: Seeing that the possibility of conception makes coitus physiologically a more momentous matter for women than for men, is it not to be expected that this fact will have some psychological representation? Personally, I should be surprised if it were not so. We know so little on this subject that so far we have never been able to isolate a special reproductive instinct, but have always only succeeded in seeing it beneath its psychical superstructure. We know that the dissociation between "spiritual" and sensual love, which has so strong a bearing on the possibility of faithfulness, is pre-

dominantly—indeed, almost specifically—a masculine characteristic. Might it not be that here we have that for which we are
looking—the psychic correlative to the biological differences between the sexes?

The second question arises out of the following reflection. The
difference in the outcome of the Œdipus complex in men and
in women might be formulated thus: The boy makes a more
radical renunciation of the primal love object for the sake of his
genital pride, whereas the girl remains more strongly fixated to
the person of the father, but can obviously do so only on condition that she abandons to a greater extent her sexual role. The
question then would be whether we have not evidence in later
life of this difference between the sexes in the woman's fundamentally greater genital inhibition and whether it is not precisely
this that makes faithfulness easier for her, just as it is far more
common to meet with frigidity than with impotence, both of
which are manifestations of genital inhibition.

Thus we have arrived at one of the factors that we should be
inclined to regard quite generally as an essential condition of
faithfulness, namely, genital inhibition. Nevertheless, we have
only to look at the tendency to unfaithfulness characteristic of
frigid women or men of feeble potency to realize that, while it is
perhaps not incorrect thus to formulate the condition of faithfulness, yet a more precise statement is certainly necessary.

We advance a little further when we observe that people whose
faithfulness is of an obsessional character often conceal a sense of
sexual guilt behind conventional prohibitions.[4] All that is forbidden by convention—and this includes all sexual relations un-
sanctioned by marriage—becomes loaded with the whole burden
of unconscious prohibitions, and this is what gives such convention its great moral weight. As we should expect, this difficulty is
met with in these people who can only feel free to marry under
certain conditions.

Now these feelings of guilt are experienced especially in relation to the husband or wife. The partner not only assumes for
the unconscious the role of the parent whom the child coveted
and loved, but further, the old dread of prohibitions and punish-

4. This connection is very clearly shown by Sigrid Undset in *Kristin
Lavransdatter.*

ments may revive and be referred to him or her. In particular the old feelings of guilt on account of onanism now become reactivated, and so under pressure of the fourth commandment, create the same guilt-laden atmosphere of an exaggerated sense of duty, or else a reaction of irritability. Or in other cases, the atmosphere is one of insincerity, or else there is an anxiety reaction of dread of concealing anything at all from the partner. I am inclined to suppose that unfaithfulness and onanism are more directly connected than simply by way of the sense of guilt. It is true that originally in onanism the sexual wishes relating to the parents found physical expression. But as a rule, in the masturbation fantasies the parents are replaced by other objects at a very early age; hence these fantasies represent, as well as the primal wishes, the child's first unfaithfulness to the parents. The same applies to early erotic experiences with brothers and sisters, playmates, servants, and so on. Just as onanism represents the first unfaithfulness in the sphere of fantasy, it is represented in that of reality by these experiences. And in analysis we find that people who have retained a specially lively sense of guilt on account of these early incidents, whether fantasies or real, for that very reason shun with peculiar anxiety any unfaithfulness in wedlock, for this would signify a repetition of the old guilt.

Frequently it is this remnant of the old fixation that repeats itself in persons whose faithfulness is, as it were, obsessional, in spite of their vehement polygamous desires.

But faithfulness may also have a quite different psychological basis, which may either coexist in the same people with that which we have just been discussing or be entirely independent. The people in question, for one or other of the reasons I have mentioned, are especially sensitive about their claim to exclusive possession of the partner and also, in reaction, they make the same demand upon themselves. Consciously, it may seem to them only that they should themselves fulfill the claims that they make upon others, but in such cases the deeper reason lies in fantasies of omnipotence, according to which one's own renunciation of other relations is like a magic gesture compelling the partner likewise to renounce.

We have now seen what motives are at the back of the demand for monogamy and with what forces it comes into conflict. To use a simile from physical life, we might call these opposing impulses the centrifugal and the centripetal forces in matrimony, and we should have to say that here we have a trial of strength in which the opponents are equally matched. For both derive their motive power from the most elementary and direct desires arising from the Œdipus complex. It is inevitable that both sets of impulses should be mobilized in married life, though with every possible variation in the degree of their activity. This helps us to understand why it never has been and never will be possible to find any principle that will solve these conflicts of married life. Even in individual cases, although we can see tolerably clearly what motives are at work, it is only when we look back in the light of analytical experience that we can perceive which results have actually ensued from behavior of one sort or another.

In short, we observe that the elements of hate can find an outlet not only when the principle of monogamy is violated but when it is observed, and may vent themselves in very different ways; that the feelings of hate are directed against the partner in one form or another, and that on both sides they are at work to undermine the foundation upon which married life should be built up—the tender attachment between husband and wife. We must leave it to the moralist to decide what is then the right course.

Nevertheless, the insight thus gained does not leave us entirely helpless in the face of such matrimonial conflicts. The discovery of the unconscious sources that feed them may so weaken not only the ideal of monogamy but also the polygamous tendencies, that it may become possible for the conflicts to be fought out. And the knowledge we have acquired helps us in yet another way. When we see the conflicts in the married life of two people, we often involuntarily tend to think that the only solution is that they should separate. The deeper our understanding of the inevitability of these and other conflicts in every marriage, the more profound will be our conviction that our attitude toward such unchecked personal impressions must be one of complete reserve, and the greater will be our ability to control them in reality.

PREMENSTRUAL TENSION*

○○

*W*E CAN HARDLY BE SURPRISED to find that menstruation, being such a conspicuous occurrence, has become the starting point and the focus of fantasies beset with anxiety. This is particularly so, since we have become more enlightened regarding the extent to which anxiety is connected with everything sexual. Our experiences derive from the analyses of individual patients as well as from most impressive ethnological facts. This anxious fantasizing is engaged in by both sexes; the taboos of primitive people[1] bear eloquent testimony to man's deep fear of women, which centers precisely around menstruation. Every woman's analysis shows that with the appearance of menstrual blood, cruel impulses and fantasies of both an active and a passive nature are awakened in her. Although our understanding of these fantasies and their significance for the woman experiencing them is still insufficient, it has already furnished us with a practical, useful tool. It enables us to therapeutically influence the manifold psychological and functional disorders of menstruation. It is remarkable that so little attention has been paid to the fact that disturbances occur not only during menstruation but even more frequently, though less obtrusively, in the days before the onset of the menstrual flow. These disturbances are generally known; they consist of varying degrees of tension, ranging from

* "Die prämenstruellen Verstimmungen," *Zeitschr. f. psychoanalytische Pädagogik*, Vol. 5, No. 5/6 (1931), pp. 1-7. Reprinted in translation with the permission of the Karen Horney Estate.

1. At this point I shall not go into the causation of the taboos surrounding menstruation; I merely refer to the profound and informative papers by Daly, "Hindu Mythology and the Castration Complex, 1927" and "The Menstruation Complex, 1928," *Internationaler Psychoanalytischer Verlag.* [Cf. also the letter by C. D. Daly in *Zeitschr. f. psychoanalytische Pädagogik*, Vol. 5, No. 5/6.]

a feeling that everything is too much, a sense of listlessness or of being slowed down, and intensities of feelings of self-depreciation to the point of pronounced feelings of oppression and of being severely depressed. All these feelings are frequently intermingled with feelings of irritability or anxiousness. One gets the impression that these fluctuations of mood are generally closer to normal experiencing than are true menstrual disturbances. They frequently occur in otherwise healthy women and usually do not give the impression of a pathological process. Also, they are seldom connected with psychological disturbances or conversion hysteria.

They obviously have little to do with elaborations of fantasies about the menstrual flow. They may indeed change into actual menstrual disturbances, but usually they recede at the onset of the bleeding, with a concomitant feeling of relief. Some women are surprised every time on seeing the connection with their menstruation. They explain their feeling of relief with the onset of bleeding by insisting that this whole tormenting nightmare is nothing but a deception by an entirely physiological process. Another factor supporting the theory that these conditions really have nothing to do with the bleeding and its interpretation, is their frequent occurrence prior to the very first menstruation; that is, at a time when not even a subliminal connection could have existed with an anticipated bleeding. The psychological process is analogous to the physiological one, in that menstruation is more than bleeding.

These premenstrual tensions are of less concern to physiologically oriented physicians than they are to us. For they know that essential, and perhaps even the most essential, events of the total process take place before the onset of bleeding. They are more easily satisfied with the general notion of a psychological burden that is physically conditioned.

It might be useful to briefly review these events. About halfway between two periods an ovum matures in one of the ovaries, the surrounding membranes (follicle) rupture, and the ovum travels through the Fallopian tubes to the uterus to embed itself, if fertilization has taken place. For about two weeks the ovum remains viable and ready to be fertilized. In the meantime the ruptured membranes of the ovum have changed into the corpus luteum. This yellow body functionally is an endocrine gland— that is, it secretes a substance that recently has been isolated in pure form. It has been called the "estrogenic hormone" because of its ability to bring about an estrous cycle even in mice whose ovaries have been removed. This estrogenic hormone acts upon the uterus in such a way that the mucous membrane lining the inside of the uterus changes as if pregnancy were to ensue; that is, the entire mucous membrane turns spongy, becomes congested with blood, and the glands situated in it become replete with secretion. If no fertilization takes place, the superficial layers of the mucosa are cast off, the substances stored up for the growth of the embryo are expelled, and the dead ovum is flushed out by the subsequent bleeding. At the same time the regeneration of the mucous membrane commences.

The function of the estrogenic hormone is not exhausted with this one effect; the rest of the genitalia also become more congested, as do the breasts, in which one often can even demonstrate an actual growth of the glandular tissue prior to the onset of the period. Moreover, the hormone effects measurable changes in the blood, blood pressure, metabolism, and temperature. In view of the extent of these effects, we speak of a great rhythmic cycle in the life of women, the biological meaning of which is a monthly preparation for the process of procreation.

The knowledge of these biological events does not by itself give us any information about the particular psychological content of premenstrual tensions, but it is nevertheless indispensable to their understanding, because certain psychological processes parallel these physical events, or are caused by them.

This statement, in the main, is not new. It is an established biological fact that along with the described events, there occurs an increase in sexual libido. This parallel event can clearly be observed in animals and it is because of this connection that the hormone derives the name of estrogen. We agree with well-known researchers, such as Havelock Ellis, who assume the same psychological parallel process of an increase in libido in the human female. Thus women would be confronted with the problem, rendered difficult by cultural restrictions, of having to master this increase of libidinal tension within themselves. That is, if there are opportunities for the satisfaction of essential instinctual needs, then the task will easily succeed. It will become difficult only if such opportunities are not available, for external or internal reasons. This connection is confirmed in healthy women as well, that is in women with a relatively undisturbed psychosexual development. Their menstrual disturbances disappear completely during periods of fulfillment of their love life, and reappear during periods of external frustration or unsatisfying experiences. Observation of the mechanisms leading to the appearance of these tensions reveal that we are dealing here with women who for some reason take frustrations poorly, who react to them with rage,[2] but cannot deflect any or only some of this rage to the outside and who therefore turn it against themselves.

More serious symptoms and more complicated mechanisms are found in women who are dissatisfied for reasons of emotional inhibitions. Here we get the impression that they may still be able to maintain a precarious balance, though suffering some loss of vitality. However, when the libido increases, it is dammed up and can no longer be kept in balance. Hence regressive phenomena occur, different ones in every individual, expressed in the reappearance of infantile reactions as their symptomatology.

These reflections, which are supported by clinical observations, are hardly controversial. However, we will have to ask ourselves whether there are conditions that limit this causal connection, since premenstrual tensions, especially mild ones, occur frequently, yet not as frequently as we might expect. We do not even find them in every neurosis. In order to be able to answer this latter problem, we would now have to connect, in numerous neuroses, the characteristic accumulations and elaboration of genital libido with the presence or absence of premenstrual tension. This might perhaps make more comprehensible some aspects of individual conditions. First of all we must repeat the question: Is the increase of the libido as such really the specific agent for the tensions arising during this period?

Actually we have only considered the effect of a partial aspect

2. The form that such reactions take is irrelevant in this general clarification of the processes involved.

of a psychological event and have thus far neglected the effect of the other, biologically decisive, part. Let us keep in mind that the increase of the libido has as its biological meaning the preparation for conception, and the essential organic changes serve as a preparation for pregnancy.

We must therefore ask: Is it conceivable that woman has an unconscious awareness of these processes? Could it be that the physical readiness for pregnancy manifests itself this way in the psychic life?

Let us review our experience. My own observations definitely favor such a possibility. A patient T spontaneously reported that prior to her period her dreams were always sensuous and red, that she felt as though under the pressure of something wicked and sinful and that her body felt heavy and full. With the onset of menstruation she would immediately have a feeling of relief. She had often thought that the child had arrived. A few details from her life history: She is the oldest and has two younger sisters; the mother is domineering and quarrelsome; her father is devoted to the patient with a kind of chivalrous tenderness. On trips together, father and daughter are often taken for a married couple. At the age of eighteen, she married a man thirty years her senior who resembled her father in personality and appearance. For a few years she lived quite happily with this man without any sexual relations. During that period she had an intensive affective dislike for children. Later on, as she gradually became dissatisfied with her marital and life situations, a change took place in her attitude toward children. She then decided to have a career though she vacillated between becoming a nursery school teacher or a midwife, choosing the former. During her many years as a teacher she had had a particularly loving disposition toward children; then her profession became repugnant to her. She began to experience that these children were not hers but only other people's children. Sexually she remained rejecting except for a brief period when instead of conceiving a child in her uterus, she developed fibroids and had to undergo a hysterectomy. It seemed as though her sexual desire had made itself apparent only after her wish for a child had become unfulfillable. I hope that this extremely incomplete sketch will suffice to show one thing—that in this case what was most deeply repressed was the wish for a child. Her neurotic structure showed strong aspects of motherliness as well as of childishness and was in its totality an elaboration of this same central problem.

I do not want to go into the question of what, in this case, had reinforced the wish for a child and had led to such an intensive repression. Suggestive evidence may suffice to indicate that here, as in other cases of similar nature, the wish for a child was excessively cathected with anxiety or guilt feelings because of old connections with destructive impulses.

Such a repression, if extreme, leads to the complete, effective rejection of the wish for children of one's own. I have found without exception and completely independent of the rest of the neurotic structure, the appearance of premenstrual tension in those cases in which one can assume with relative certainty the particularly strong desire for a child, but where there is such a strong defense against it that its realization has never been even a remote possibility. This makes us wonder and leads us to the supposition that at a time when the organism is preparing to conceive a child, the repressed wish for a child is mobilized with all its counter-cathexes, leading to disturbances of the psychic equilibrium. Dreams that reveal this conflict occur with striking frequency in the period immediately preceding menstruation. However, more exact tests are necessary to check on the frequency of the temporal coincidence with dreams dealing in some form with problems of motherhood. For example, premenstrual tensions occurred regularly in a patient whose manifest wish for a child was very strong, but whose anxiety resulted from the fear of all the phases of its possible realization, beginning with the fear of the sex act and including infant care; likewise tensions occurred in a woman whose fear of dying during childbirth prevented any possible realization of her strong desire for a child.

It seems to me that premenstrual tension states develop less regularly in those cases in which the wish for a child is fraught with conflict, but in which, nevertheless, pregnancies and births occur. I am thinking here of a number of women for whom motherhood obviously held a place of crucial import in their lives, but in whom the associated unconscious conflicts expressed themselves in one form or another, such as in morning sickness, weakness of labor contractions, or overprotectiveness toward their children.

Here I can summarize my impressions, but only with a great deal of caution. Apparently these tensions may occur in cases in which the wish for a child has been enhanced by an actual experience, but real fulfillment has, for some reason, become impossible. The fact that the increase in libidinal tension is not alone responsible became obvious to me through the observation of a woman whose motherliness was strongly developed, yet full of conflicts. She suffered from particularly disturbing premenstrual tensions, despite the fact that at the time her sexual relations with a man were usually quite satisfying. For cogent reasons, however, there was no possibility of fulfilling her wish for a child, a wish which was especially strong just at that time. Prior to her period her breasts used to become enlarged. During this phase of her life, discussions came up regularly about the problems of having children, sometimes under the guise of thinking about prophylactics, their effect and possible harmfulness.

Still another phenomenon, which I have not gone into as yet, shows that, generally, the libidinal increase does indeed have a share in creating premenstrual tensions, but that it is not the specific agent. I refer to the marked relief with the onset of menstruation. Since the libidinal increase continues throughout the time of the menstrual period, the sudden drop of emotional tension cannot be understood from this point of view. The onset of bleeding, however, terminates the fantasies of pregnancy, as is expressed in the case of patient T, "Now the child has arrived." The individual psychological processes may be quite different. In one of the above-mentioned cases the idea of sacrifice was in the foreground. The woman in question would think at the onset of her period "God has accepted the sacrifice." Likewise, in individually differing ways, the relief of tension may depend sometimes on the unconscious fulfillment of fantasies as represented by bleeding, or on the relaxing of the superego, because strongly rejected fantasies have now come to an end. The essential fact is that they cease with the beginning of menstruation.

Briefly summarized, from all the impressions that have been reported here, the hypothesis arises that premenstrual tensions are directly released by the physiological processes of preparation for pregnancy. I have by now become so certain of this connection that in the presence of the disturbance, I anticipate finding conflicts involving the wish for a child at the core of the illness and the personality. And I believe I have never been mistaken in this expectation.

I want once more to mark the boundaries of this concept as against that of the gynecologists. We are not dealing with a basic weakness, a condition leading to the tendentious conclusion of the lesser efficiency of women. I rather hold that this particular time in women's cycle represents a burden only to those women in whom the idea of motherhood is fraught with great inner conflicts.

I do believe, though, that motherhood represents a more vital problem for women than Freud assumes. Freud repeatedly maintains that the wish for a child is something that "belongs absolutely to ego-psychology,"[3] that it comes into existence only secondarily because of the disappointment over the lack of a penis,[4] and therefore is not a primary instinct.

By contrast I feel that the wish for a child may indeed draw considerable secondary reinforcement from the wish for a penis, but that the desire is primary and instinctually anchored deeply in the biological sphere. Observations dealing with premenstrual tension seem to be understandable only on the basis of this fundamental concept. Indeed, I am of the opinion that just these observations are apt to show that the wish for a child fulfills all the conditions Freud himself has postulated for "drives." The drive toward motherhood therefore illustrates the "psychic representation of a continuously flowing innersomatic stimulus."[5]

3. Sigmund Freud, "On the Transformation of Instincts with Special Reference to Anal Erotism" (1916), Collected Papers, Vol. II, pp. 164-71.
4. Sigmund Freud, "Some Psychological Consequences of the Anatomical Differences Between the Sexes" (1925), Collected Papers, Vol. V, 1956, p. 175-80.
5. Freud, "Three Papers on the Theory of Sex," *Collected Papers*, Vol. V.

THE DISTRUST BETWEEN THE SEXES*

As I BEGIN TO TALK TO YOU TODAY about some problems in the relationship between the sexes, I must ask you not to be disappointed. I will not concern myself primarily with the aspect of the problem that is most important to the physician. Only at the end will I briefly deal with the question of therapy. I am far more concerned with pointing out to you several psychological reasons for the distrust between the sexes.

The relationship between men and women is quite similar to that between children and parents, in that we prefer to focus on the positive aspects of these relationships. We prefer to assume that love is the fundamentally given factor and that hostility is an accidental and avoidable occurrence. Although we are familiar with slogans such as "the battle of the sexes" and "hostility between the sexes," we must admit that they do not mean a great deal. They make us overfocus on sexual relations between men and women, which can very easily lead us to a too one-sided view. Actually, from our recollection of numerous case histories, we may conclude that love relationships are quite easily destroyed by overt or covert hostility. On the other hand we are only too ready to blame such difficulties on individual misfortune, on incompatibility of the partners, and on social or economic causes.

The individual factors, which we find causing poor relations between men and women, may be the pertinent ones. However, because of the great frequency, or better, the regular occurrence of disturbances in love relations, we have to ask ourselves whether the disturbances in the individual cases might not arise from a

* Read before the Berlin-Brandenburg Branch of the German Women's Medical Association on November 20, 1930, "Das Misstrauen zwischen den Geschlechtern." *Die Ärztin*, VII (1931), pp. 5-12. Reprinted in translation with the permission of the Karen Horney Estate.

common background; whether there are common denominators for this easily and frequently arising suspiciousness between the sexes?

It is almost impossible to attempt within the framework of a brief lecture to give you a complete survey of so large a field. I therefore will not even mention such factors as the origin and effects of such social institutions as marriage. I merely intend to select at random some of the factors that are psychologically understandable and pertain to the causes and effects of the hostility and tension between the sexes.

I would like to start with something very commonplace— namely, that a good deal of this atmosphere of suspiciousness is understandable and even justifiable. It apparently has nothing to do with the individual partner, but rather with the intensity of the affects and with the difficulty of taming them.

We know or may dimly sense, that these affects can lead to ecstasy, to being beside oneself, to surrendering oneself, which means a leap into the unlimited and the boundless. This is perhaps why real passion is so rare. For like a good businessman, we are loath to put all our eggs in one basket. We are inclined to be reserved and ever ready to retreat. Be that as it may, because of our instinct for self-preservation, we all have a natural fear of losing ourselves in another person. That is why what happens to love, happens to education and psychoanalysis; everybody thinks he knows all about them, but few do. One is inclined to overlook how little one gives of oneself, but one feels all the more this same deficiency in the partner, the feeling of "You never really loved me." A wife who harbors suicidal thoughts because her husband does not give her all his love, time, and interest, will not notice how much of her own hostility, hidden vindictiveness, and aggression are expressed through her attitude. She will feel only despair because of her abundant "love", while at the same time she will feel most intensely and see most clearly the lack of love in her partner. Even Strindberg [who was a mis-ogynist] defensively managed to say on occasion that he was no woman hater, but that women hated and tortured him.

Here we are not dealing with pathological phenomena at all. In pathological cases we merely see a distortion and exaggeration of a general and normal occurrence. Anybody, to a certain extent, will be inclined to overlook his own hostile impulses, but under pressure of his own guilty conscience, may project them onto the partner. This process must, of necessity, cause some overt or covert distrust of the partner's love, fidelity, sincerity, or kindness. This is the reason why I prefer to speak of distrust between the sexes and not of hatred; for in keeping with our own experience we are more familiar with the feeling of distrust.

A further, almost unavoidable, source of disappointment and distrust in our normal love life derives from the fact that the very intensity of our feelings of love stirs up all of our secret expectations and longings for happiness, which slumber deep inside us. All our unconscious wishes, contradictory in their nature and expanding boundlessly on all sides, are waiting here for their fulfillment. The partner is supposed to be strong, and at the same time helpless, to dominate us and be dominated by us, to be ascetic and to be sensuous. He should rape us and be tender, have time for us exclusively and also be intensely involved in creative work. As long as we assume that he could actually fulfill all these expectations, we invest him with the glitter of sexual overestimation. We take the magnitude of such overvaluation for the measure of our love, while in reality it merely expresses the magnitude of our expectations. The very nature of our claims makes their fulfillment impossible. Herein lies the origin of the disappointments with which we may cope in a more or less effective way. Under favorable circumstances we do not even have to become aware of the great number of our disappointments, just as we have not been aware of the extent of our secret expectations. Yet there remain traces of distrust in us, as in a child who discovers that his father cannot get him the stars from the sky after all.

Thus far, our reflections certainly have been neither new nor specifically analytical and have often been better formulated in the past. The analytical approach begins with the question: What special factors in human development lead to the discrepancy between expectations and fulfillment and what causes them to be of special significance in particular cases? Let us start with a general consideration. There is a basic difference between human and animal development—namely, the long period of

the infant's helplessness and dependency. The paradise of childhood is most often an illusion with which adults like to deceive
themselves. For the child, however, this paradise is inhabited
by too many dangerous monsters. Unpleasant experiences with
the opposite sex seem to be unavoidable. We need only recall
the capacity that children possess, even in their very early years,
for passionate and instinctive sexual desires similar to those of
adults and yet different from them. Children are different in the
aims of their drives, but above all, in the pristine integrity of
their demands. They find it hard to express their desires directly,
and where they do, they are not taken seriously. Their seriousness sometimes is looked upon as being cute, or it may be overlooked or rejected. In short, children will undergo painful and
humiliating experiences of being rebuffed, being betrayed, and
being told lies. They also may have to take second place to a
parent or sibling, and they are threatened and intimidated when
they seek, in playing with their own bodies, those pleasures that
are denied them by adults. The child is relatively powerless in
the face of all this. He is not able to ventilate his fury at all, or
only to a minor degree, nor can he come to grips with the experience by means of intellectual comprehension. Thus, anger and
aggression are pent up within him in the form of extravagant
fantasies, which hardly reach the daylight of awareness, fantasies
that are criminal when viewed from the standpoint of the adult,
fantasies that range from taking by force and stealing, to those
about killing, burning, cutting to pieces, and choking. Since the
child is vaguely aware of these destructive forces within him, he
feels, according to the talion law, equally threatened by the adults.
Here is the origin of those infantile anxieties of which no child
remains entirely free. This already enables us to understand better
the fear of love of which I have spoken before. Just here, in this
most irrational of all areas, the old childhood fears of a threatening father or mother are reawakened, putting us instinctively on
the defensive. In other words, the fear of love will always be
mixed with the fear of what we might do to the other person,
or what the other person might do to us. A lover in the Aru
Islands, for example, will never make a gift of a lock of hair to
his beloved, because should an argument arise, the beloved might

burn it, thus causing the partner to get sick.

I would like to sketch briefly how childhood conflicts may affect the relationship to the opposite sex in later life. Let us take as an example a typical situation: The little girl who was badly hurt through some great disappointment by her father, will transform her innate instinctual wish to receive from the man, into a vindictive one of taking from him by force. Thus the foundation is laid for a direct line of development to a later attitude, according to which she will not only deny her maternal instincts, but will have only one drive, i.e., to harm the male, to exploit him, and to suck him dry. She has become a vampire. Let us assume that there is a similar transformation from the wish to receive to the wish to take away. Let us further assume that the latter wish was repressed due to anxiety from a guilty conscience; then we have here the fundamental constellation for the formation of a certain type of woman who is unable to relate to the male because she fears that every male will suspect her of wanting something from him. This really means that she is afraid that he might guess her repressed desires. Or by completely projecting onto him her repressed wishes, she will imagine that every male merely intends to exploit her, that he wants from her only sexual satisfaction, after which he will discard her. Or let us assume that a reaction formation of excessive modesty will mask the repressed drive for power. We then have the type of woman who shies away from demanding or accepting anything from her husband. Such a woman, however, due to the return of the repressed, will react with depression to the nonfulfillment of her unexpressed, and often unformulated, wishes. She thus unwittingly jumps from the frying pan into the fire, as does her partner, because a depression will hit him much harder than direct aggression. Quite often the repression of aggression against the male drains all her vital energy. The woman then feels helpless to meet life. She will shift the entire responsibility for her helplessness onto the man, robbing him of the very breath of life. Here you have the type of woman who, under the guise of being helpless and childlike, dominates her man.

These are examples that demonstrate how the fundamental attitude of women toward men can be disturbed by childhood conflicts. In an attempt to simplify matters, I have stressed only one point, which, however, seems crucial to me—the disturbance in the development of motherhood.

I shall now proceed to trace certain traits of male psychology. I do not wish to follow individual lines of development, though it might be very instructive to observe analytically how, for instance, even men who consciously have a very positive relationship with women and hold them in high esteem as human beings, harbor deep within themselves a secret distrust of them; and how this distrust relates back to feelings toward their mothers, which they experienced in their formative years. I shall focus rather on certain typical attitudes of men toward women and how they have appeared during various eras of history and in different cultures, not only as regards sexual relationships with women, but also, and often more so, in nonsexual situations, such as in their general evaluation of women.

I shall select some random examples, starting with Adam and Eve. Jewish culture, as recorded in the Old Testament, is outspokenly patriarchal. This fact reflects itself in their religion, which has no maternal goddesses; in their morals and customs, which allow the husband the right to dissolve the marital bond simply by dismissing his wife. Only by being aware of this background can we recognize the male bias in two incidents of Adam's and Eve's history. First of all, woman's capacity to give birth is partly denied and partly devaluated: Eve was made of Adam's rib and a curse was put on her to bear children in sorrow. In the second place, by interpreting her tempting Adam to eat of the tree of knowledge as a sexual temptation, woman appears as the sexual temptress, who plunges man into misery. I believe that these two elements, one born out of resentment, the other out of anxiety, have damaged the relationship between the sexes from the earliest times to the present. Let us follow this up briefly. Man's fear of woman is deeply rooted in sex, as is shown by the simple fact that it is only the sexually attractive woman of whom he is afraid and who, although he strongly desires her, has to be kept in bondage. Old women, on the other hand, are held in high esteem, even by cultures in which the young woman is dreaded and therefore suppressed. In some primitive cultures the old woman may have the decisive voice in the affairs of the tribe; among Asian nations also she enjoys great power and prestige. On the other hand, in primitive tribes woman is surrounded by taboos during the entire period of her sexual maturity. Women of the Arunta tribe are able to magically influence the male genitals. If they sing to a blade of grass and then point it at a man or throw it at him, he becomes ill or loses his genitals altogether. Women lure him to his doom. In a certain East African tribe, husband and wife do not sleep together, because her breath might weaken him. If a woman of a South African tribe climbs over the leg of a sleeping man, he will be unable to run; hence the general rule of sexual abstinence two to five days prior to hunting, warfare, or fishing. Even greater is the fear of menstruation, pregnancy, and childbirth. Menstruating women are surrounded by extensive taboos—a man who touches a menstruating woman will die. There is one basic thought at the bottom of all this: Woman is a mysterious being who communicates with spirits and thus has magic powers that she can use to hurt the male. He must therefore protect himself against her powers by keeping her subjugated. Thus the Miri in Bengal do not permit their women to eat the flesh of the tiger, lest they become too strong. The Watawela of East Africa keep the art of making fire a secret from their women, lest women become their rulers. The Indians of California have ceremonies to keep their women in submission; a man is disguised as a devil to intimidate the women. The Arabs of Mecca exclude women from religious festivities to prevent familiarity between women and their overlords. We find similar customs during the Middle Ages —the Cult of the Virgin side by side with the burning of witches; the adoration of "pure" motherliness, completely divested of sexuality, next to the cruel destruction of the sexually seductive woman. Here again is the implication of underlying anxiety, for the witch is in communication with the devil. Nowadays, with our more humane forms of aggression, we burn women only figuratively, sometimes with undisguised hatred, sometimes with apparent friendliness. In any case "The Jew must burn."* In

* TRANSLATOR'S NOTE: This is a quote from *Nathan the Wise* by the eighteenth-century German author Gotthold Ephraim Lessing, a humanist and

friendly and secret autos-da-fé, many nice things are said about women, but it is just unfortunate that in her God-given natural state, she is not the equal of the male. Moebius pointed out that the female brain weighs less than the male one, but the point need not be made in so crude a way. On the contrary, it can be stressed that woman is not at all inferior, only different, but that unfortunately she has fewer or none of those human or cultural qualities that man holds in such high esteem. She is said to be deeply rooted in the personal and emotional spheres, which is wonderful; but unfortunately, this makes her incapable of exercising justice and objectivity, therefore disqualifying her for positions in law and government and in the spiritual community. She is said to be at home only in the realm of eros. Spiritual matters are alien to her innermost being, and she is at odds with cultural trends. She therefore is, as Asians frankly state, a second-rate being. Woman may be industrious and useful but is, alas, incapable of productive and independent work. She is, indeed, prevented from real accomplishment by the deplorable, bloody tragedies of menstruation and childbirth. And so every man silently thanks his God, just as the pious Jew does in his prayers, that he was not created a woman.

Man's attitude toward motherhood is a large and complicated chapter. One is generally inclined to see no problem in this area. Even the misogynist is obviously willing to respect woman as a mother and to venerate her motherliness under certain conditions, as mentioned above regarding the Cult of the Virgin. In order to obtain a clearer picture, we have to distinguish between two attitudes: men's attitudes toward motherliness, as represented in its purest form in th Cult of the Virgin, and their attitude toward motherhood as such, as we encounter it in the symbolism of the ancient mother goddesses. Males will always be in favor of motherliness, as expressed in certain spiritual qualities of women, i.e., the nurturing, selfless, self-sacrificing mother; for she is the ideal embodiment of the woman who could fulfill all his expectations and longings. In the ancient mother goddesses, man did not ven-

---

a spokesman for enlightenment and rationality. The expression became a colloquialism. It meant no matter how worthy and well-intentioned his acts, by virtue of being a Jew, a man was guilty.

erate motherliness in the spiritual sense, but rather motherhood in its most elemental meaning. Mother goddesses are earthy goddesses, fertile like the soil. They bring forth new life and they nurture it. It was this life-creating power of woman, an elemental force, that filled man with admiration. And this is exactly the point where problems arise. For it is contrary to human nature to sustain appreciation without resentment toward capabilities that one does not possess. Thus, a man's minute share in creating new life became, for him, an immense incitement to create something new on his part. He has created values of which he might well be proud. State, religion, art, and science are essentially his creations, and our entire culture bears the masculine imprint.

However, as happens elsewhere, so it does here; even the greatest satisfactions or achievements, if born out of sublimation, cannot fully make up for something for which we are not endowed by nature. Thus there has remained an obvious residue of general resentment of men against women. This resentment expresses itself, also in our times, in men's distrustful defensive maneuvers against the threat of women's invasion of their domains; hence their tendency to devalue pregnancy and childbirth and to over-emphasize male genitality. This attitude does not express itself in scientific theories alone, but is also of far-reaching consequence for the entire relationship between the sexes, and for sexual morality in general. Motherhood, especially illegitimate motherhood, is very insufficiently protected by law—with the one exception of a recent attempt at improvement in Russia. Conversely, there is ample opportunity for the fulfillment of the male's sexual needs. Emphasis on irresponsible sexual indulgence, and devaluation of women to an object of purely physical needs, are further consequences of this masculine attitude.

From Bachofen's investigations we know that this state of the cultural supremacy of the male has not existed since the beginning of time, but that women once occupied a central position. This was the era of the so-called matriarchy, when law and custom were centered around the mother. Matricide was then, as Sophocles showed in the *Eumenides*, the unforgivable crime, while patricide, by comparison, was a minor offense. Only in recorded historical times have men begun, with minor variations, to play the leading role in the political, economical, and judicial fields, as well as in the area of sexual morality. At present we seem to be going through a period of struggle in which women once more dare to fight for their equality. This is a phase, the duration of which we are not yet able to survey.

I do not want to be misunderstood as having implied that all disaster results from male supremacy and that relations between the sexes would improve if women were given the ascendency. However, we must ask ourselves why there should have to be any power struggle at all between the sexes. At any given time, the more powerful side will create an ideology suitable to help maintain its position and to make this position acceptable to the weaker one. In this ideology the differentness of the weaker one will be interpreted as inferiority, and it will be proven that these differences are unchangeable, basic, or God's will. It is the function of such an ideology to deny or conceal the existence of a struggle. Here is one of the answers to the question raised initially as to why we have so little awareness of the fact that there is a struggle between the sexes. It is in the interest of men to obscure this fact; and the emphasis they place on their ideologies has caused women, also, to adopt these theories. Our attempt at resolving these rationalizations and at examining these ideologies as to their fundamental driving forces, is merely a step on the road taken by Freud.

I believe that my exposition shows more clearly the origin of resentment than the origin of dread, and I therefore want to discuss briefly the latter problem. We have seen that the male's dread of the female is directed against her as a sexual being. How is this to be understood? The clearest aspect of this dread is revealed by the Arunta tribe. They believe that the woman has the power to magically influence the male genital. This is what we mean by castration anxiety in analysis. It is an anxiety of psychogenic origin that goes back to feelings of guilt and old childhood fears. Its anatomical-psychological nucleus lies in the fact that during intercourse the male has to entrust his genitals to the female body, that he presents her with his semen and interprets this as a surrender of vital strength to the woman, similar to his experiencing the subsiding of erection after intercourse as evidence of having been weakened by the woman. Although the following idea has not been thoroughly worked through yet, it is highly probable, according to analytical and ethnological data, that the relationship to the mother is more strongly and directly associated with the fear of death than the relationship to the father. We have learned to understand the longing for death as the longing for reunion with the mother. In African fairy tales it is a woman who brings death into the world. The great mother goddesses also brought death and destruction. It is as though we were possessed by the idea that the one who gives life is also capable of taking it away. There is a third aspect of the male's dread of the female that is more difficult to understand and to prove, but that can be demonstrated by observing certain recurrent phenomena in the animal world. We can see that the male is quite frequently equipped with certain specific stimulants for attracting the female, or with specific devices for seizing her during sexual union. Such arrangements would be incomprehensible if the female animal possessed equally urgent or abundant sexual needs as does the male. As a matter of fact, we see that the female rejects the male unconditionally, after fertilization has occurred. Although examples taken from the animal world may be applied to human beings only with the greatest of caution, it is permissible, in this context, to raise the following question: Is it possible that the male is sexually dependent on the female to a higher degree than the woman is on him, because in women part of the sexual energy is linked to generative processes? Could it be that men, therefore, have a vital interest in keeping women dependent on them? So much for the factors that seem to be at the root of the great power struggle between men and women, insofar as they are of a psychogenic nature and related to the male.

That many-faceted thing called love succeeds in building bridges from the loneliness on this shore to the loneliness on the other one. These bridges can be of great beauty, but they are rarely built for eternity and frequently they cannot tolerate too heavy a burden without collapsing. Here is the other answer to the question posed initially of why we see love between the sexes more distinctly than we see hate—because the union of the sexes offers us the greatest possibilities for happiness. We therefore are naturally inclined to overlook how powerful are the destructive forces that continually work to destroy our chances for happiness.

We might ask in conclusion, how can analytical insights contribute to diminish the distrust between the sexes? There is no uniform answer to this problem. The fear of the power of the affects and the difficulty in controlling them in a love relationship, the resulting conflict between surrender and self-preservation, between the I and the Thou, is an entirely comprehensible, unmitigatable, and as it were, normal phenomenon. The same thing applies in essence to our readiness for distrust, which stems from unresolved childhood conflicts. These childhood conflicts, however, can vary greatly in intensity, and will leave behind traces of variable depth. Analysis not only can help in individual cases to improve the relationship with the opposite sex, but it can also attempt to improve the psychological conditions of childhood and forestall excessive conflicts. This, of course, is our hope for the future. In the momentous struggle for power, analysis can fulfill an important function by uncovering the real motives of this struggle. This uncovering will not eliminate the motives, but it may help to create a better chance for fighting the struggle on its own ground instead of relegating it to peripheral issues.

PROBLEMS OF MARRIAGE*

oooooooooooooooooooooooooooooooooooooooooooooooooooo

*W*HY ARE GOOD MARRIAGES SO RARE—marriages that do not stifle the developmental potential of the partners, marriages in which undercurrents of tension do not reverberate in the home or in which they are so intense they have brought about a benevolent indifference? Could it be that the institution of marriage cannot be reconciled with certain facts of human existence? Is marriage perhaps only an illusion, about to disappear, or is modern man particularly incapable of giving it substance? Are we admitting to its failure or to our own, when we condemn it? Why is marriage so often the death of love? Must we succumb to this situation as if it were an unavoidable law, or are we subject to forces within us, variable in content and impact, and perhaps recognizable and even avoidable, yet playing havoc with us?

On the surface the problem appears to be very simple—and very hopeless. The routine of prolonged living with the same person makes for tiresome and boring relations in general, and especially in sex. Hence a gradual fading out and cooling off is said to be unavoidable. Van de Velde has given us an entire book filled with well-intentioned suggestions on how to correct the condition of sexual nonfulfillment. Yet he overlooked one thing, i.e., that he dealt with a symptom rather than the disease. Seeing marriage as losing its soul and its radiance because of the dull monotony of the years is only a surface view of the situation.

It is not really difficult to perceive the subterranean forces at work, but it is uncomfortable, as is every glimpse into the depths.

* "Zur Problematik der Ehe, *Psychoanalytische Bewegung*, IV (1932), pp. 212-23. Reprinted in translation with the permission of the Karen Horney Estate.

It is not necessary to have been schooled in Freud's ideas in order to recognize that the emptiness of a marriage is not due to simple fatigue, but is the result of hidden destructive forces, which were secretly at work and which have undermined its foundations; that it is simply the seed sprouting on the fertile soil of disappointments, distrust, hostility, and hatred. We do not like to recognize these forces, especially not in ourselves, because they are mysterious to us. Our mere recognition of them presupposes that we have to make uncomfortable demands upon ourselves. Yet it is this kind· of awareness that we must search for and deepen, if we seriously wish to be involved in the problems of marriage from the psychological point of view. The fundamental psychological question must be—how does the aversion to the marriage partner arise?

There are, first of all, several causes of a very general nature, almost too commonplace to be mentioned. They arise from our human limitations, which we know we have, whether we hold with the Bible that we are all sinners, or with Mark Twain that we are all partially insane, or whether in a more enlightened way we call this shortcoming a neurosis. All these assumptions admit of one exception only: ourselves. Whoever heard anybody who was weighing the decision to get married say: *I* shall develop such and such unpleasant traits in the long run? Imperfections—on the part of the spouse, to be sure—inevitably make their appearance during the long period of living closely together. They set in motion a minor avalanche, which automatically keeps growing, as it rolls down the mountain slope of time. If, perhaps, a husband clings to the illusion of his independence, he will react with secret bitterness to his feeling needed and tied down by his wife. She, in turn, senses his suppressed rebellion, reacts with hidden anxiety, lest she lose him, and out of this anxiety instinctively increases her demands on him. The husband reacts to this with heightened sensitivity and defensiveness—until finally the dam bursts, neither one having understood the underlying irritability. The explosion may happen on the occasion of an unimportant event. Compared to marriage, any transitory relationship, be it on the basis of prostitution, flirtation, friendship, or an affair— is simpler in nature, for here it is relatively easy to avoid rubbing against the partner's rough edges.

Furthermore, the usual human imperfections include our not liking to exert ourselves more than is absolutely necessary, internally as well as externally. The civil servant who has a lifetime job usually does not expend his very greatest efforts. His job is safe, anyway, and he does not have to compete and struggle for a career like the professional man or even the laborer. Let us look at the prerogatives of the marriage contract, which have been either sanctioned by law, or even without benefit of law, by prevailing standards. We can readily see that from a psychological point of view, the right to support, lifelong companionship, fidelity, and even sexual cooperation puts a tremendous burden on marriage and is a great danger lending it a fatal likeness to the case of the civil servant who cannot be fired. There is so little education for marriage that most of us don't even know that while we may be granted the gift of falling in love, we have to build up a good marriage step by step. For the time being there is but one known way to bridge the gap between the law and happiness. It involves a change of our personal attitude in the direction of an inner renunciation of claims on the partner. Let it be understood that I mean claims in the sense of demands and not wishes. In addition to these general difficulties there will be more personal ones, different in each individual case, varying in frequency of occurrence, in quality, and in intensity. There is a never-ending series of traps by which love has been interfered with and hate born. Little will be gained by enumerating and describing them. It is perhaps simpler and clearer to focus upon a few large groups and to delineate them.

A marriage may have a poor prognosis from the very start, if we do not choose the "right" partner. How are we to understand the fact that in choosing a person with whom we are to share our lives, we so often select an unsuitable partner? What exactly is going on here? Is it a lack of awareness of our own needs? Or lack of knowledge of the other person? Or is it temporary blindness under the impact of being in love? Certainly all these factors may play a part. However, it seems to me essential to keep in mind that, by and large, the choices in a voluntary marriage might not be altogether "wrong." Some quality in the partner really corresponded to some of our expectations; something in him really promised to fulfill a longing in us; perhaps it actually did so in marriage. If, however, the rest of the self stands aside and has little in common with the partner, this strangeness will inevitably prove disturbing to a lasting relationship. Thus, the essential error of such a choice lies in the fact that it was made to fulfill an isolated condition. One impulse alone, one sole desire emerged forcefully into the foreground and overshadowed everything else. In a man, for instance, it could be the irresistible urge to call a girl his own who is being wooed by many other men. This is an especially unfortunate condition for love, because the woman's appeal must fade away with the vanquishing of the rivals and can only be rekindled by the appearance of new rivals who, unconsciously, will be sought. Or a partner may appear desirable, because he or she might promise to fulfill all our secret strivings for recognition, be it on the economic, social, or spiritual level. Or in a different instance, still powerful infantile wishes might determine the choice. I think here of a young man, unusually gifted and successful, who harbored an especially deep longing for a mother, having lost his own at the age of four. He married an elderly, plump, motherly widow who had two children, and whose intelligence and personality were quite inferior to his. Or take the case of a woman who, at the age of seventeen, married a man thirty years her senior, who in his physical and psychological makeup, markedly resembled her dearly beloved father. This man kept her quite happy for a number of years, despite the complete absence of sexual relations, until she outgrew her childlike longings. She then became aware that she was actually alone, tied to a man who did not mean much to her, despite his many lovable qualities. In all such cases, and they are numerous indeed, too much in us remains empty and unfulfilled. Initial fulfillment is followed by later disappointment. Disappointment is not yet tantamount to dislike, but it does constitute a source of dislike, unless we have the extremely rare gift for acceptance and do not feel that a relationship on such a restricted basis will bar the way to other possibilities of finding happiness. Regardless of how civilized we are and how much we have controlled our instinctual life, it is in keeping with human nature that deep inside we will feel an ever-growing rage, directed against any man or power that threatens to block the fulfillment of vitally important strivings. This rage can and will creep in, without our being aware of it, yet it will be very active, even though we may close our minds to its consequences. The partner will sense that our attitude toward him becomes more critical, less patient, or more negligent.

I would like to add another group, in which the danger is not so much due to the increasing stringency of our requirements for love as to the conflict caused by contradictory expectations. We generally experience ourselves as more unified in our strivings than we actually are, because we instinctively feel—and not without reason—that contradictions within us constitute a threat to our personalities or to our lives. These contradictions are more apparent in people whose emotional equilibrium is disturbed, but it seems to be beside the point to draw a sharp demarcation line. It lies within the nature of things that such inner contradictions express themselves most easily and strongly in the realm of sex. For in other areas of life, such as in work and interpersonal relations, outer reality forces a more unified, and at the same time, more adaptive attitude upon us. Even those individuals who usually walk the straight and narrow are tempted most easily to make sex the playground of their contradictory dreams. And it is only natural that these varied expectations will be carried into marriage as well.

I am reminded of a case that represents the prototype for many similar ones. It is that of a man, himself soft, dependent, and somewhat effeminate, who married a woman who was much above him in vitality and caliber and who epitomized the maternal type. It was a real and true love match. However, this man's desires, as is so common in males, were contradictory. He was also attracted to a woman who was easy-going, flirtatious, and demanding, and who represented all that the first woman could not give him. And it was this dualism in his own wishes that wrecked this marriage.

Here we might also mention the cases of those individuals, who although closely tied to their own families, choose wives who are the direct opposites of their own background as far as race, appearance, interests, and social standing are concerned. At the same time, however, such people feel repelled by these differences, and without being aware of it, soon start looking for a more familiar type.

Or I can think of women who are ambitious for themselves and who always want to be on top, yet who do not dare to realize these ambitious dreams, and instead expect their husbands to fulfill these wishes for them. He should be accomplished, superior to all others, famous, and admired. Of course there are some women who will be satisfied with their husbands fulfilling all their expectations. However, it happens just as often that in the course of such a marriage, the wife will not tolerate fulfillment of her expectations by her partner, because her own craving for power does not tolerate her being overshadowed by her husband.

Finally, there are women who choose a feminine, delicate, and weak husband. They are motivated by their own masculine attitude, although they often are not aware of this fact. However, they also harbor a desire for a strong brutal male who will take them by force. Therefore, they will hold against the husband his inability to live up to both sets of expectations and will secretly despise him for his weakness.

There are various ways in which such conflicts may generate dislike for the marriage partner. We may hold against him his inability to give us what is essential to us, while taking for granted and devaluating into meaninglessness his very real gifts. All the while the unobtainable becomes a fascinating goal, brilliantly illuminated by the notion that it is the thing that we "really" craved from the very start. On the other hand we may even hold against him that he did fulfill our wishes, because the very fulfillment proved to be incompatible with our contradictory inner strivings.

During all these reflections so far, one fact has remained in the background, namely that marriage is also a sexual relationship between two individuals of the opposite sex. From this fact may derive the deepest sources of hatred, if the relationship of one sex to the other is already disturbed. Many a mishap in marriage gives the appearance of, and is felt as, a conflict centering about this particular partner only. Thus it is easy to become convinced that nothing of this kind could have happened to us, had we chosen a different mate. We are inclined to overlook the fact that the decisive factor may well be our own inner attitude toward the opposite sex and that it may express itself in a similar manner in our relationship with any other partner. In other words, of all the difficulties that appear in marriage often—or better, always—the lion's share is introduced by ourselves as a result of our own development. The struggle between the sexes furnishes not only the grand background for millenia of historical events, it also becomes the backdrop for the struggle within a particular marriage. The secret distrust between man and woman, which in one form or another we find so frequently, does not usually stem from bad experiences of our later years. Though we prefer to believe it derived from such happenings, this distrust originates in early childhood. Later experiences, as they occur during puberty and late adolescence, are generally conditioned by previously acquired attitudes, although we are not aware of these connections.

Let me add a few remarks for better understanding. It is one of those fundamental and probably indelible insights that we owe to Freud, that love and passion do not first appear at puberty, but that the young child is already capable of feeling, wanting, and demanding passionately. Since his spirit is not yet broken and inhibited, he is probably able to experience these feelings with quite a different intensity than is possible for us adults. If we accept these fundamental facts, and furthermore accept as self-evident that we, just like every animal, are subject to the great law of heterosexual attraction, then Freud's controversial postulate of the Œdipus complex, as a stage of development that every child has to go through, does not seem so peculiar or odd to us.

During these early love experiences the child will usually go through the unpleasantness of frustrations, disappointments, rejections, and feelings of helpless jealousy. Also, he will have had the experience of having been lied to and punished and threatened.

Some traces of these early love experiences will always remain and will affect the later relationship to the opposite sex. These traces vary endlessly in individual cases, yet in the diversity of attitudes of both sexes there emerges a recognizable pattern.

In the male we frequently find the following residuals of his early relationship to his mother. First of all there is the recoiling from the forbidding female. Since it is the mother who is usually entrusted with the care of the infant, it is the mother from whom we receive not only our earliest experience of warmth, care, and tenderness, but also our earliest prohibitions. It seems to be very difficult to fully free oneself from these early experiences. We often get the impression that traces of them remain alive in almost every man; especially when we see how happily relieved men are when they are among themselves, whether it be on the basis of sports, clubs, science, or even war. They look like relieved schoolboys who have escaped supervision! It is only natural that this attitude should repeat itself most clearly in their relationship to their wives, who more than other women, are destined to take the place of their mothers.

A second trait that betrays an unresolved dependency relation to the mother is the idea of the saintliness of woman, which has reached its most exalted expression in the cult of the Virgin. This idea may possibly have some beautiful aspects in everyday life, but the reverse side of the coin is quite dangerous. For in extreme cases it leads to the conviction that the decent, respectable woman is asexual and that one would humiliate her through having sexual desires for her. This conception furthermore implies that one cannot expect to have a full love experience with such a woman, even though one might love her very much, and that one would seek sexual satisfaction only with a debased type of woman, a harlot. In clear-cut cases this means that one may love and appreciate one's wife, but cannot desire her, and will therefore be more or less inhibited toward her. Some wives may be aware of this male attitude without objecting to it, particularly if they are frigid, yet it will almost inevitably lead to overt or covert dissatisfaction on both sides.

In this context I should like to mention a third trait that seems to me characteristic of the attitude of the male toward the female. It is man's dread of not being able to satisfy the woman. It is his fear of her demands in general and of her sexual demands in particular. This is a fear that is rooted to some extent in biological facts, insofar as the male must prove himself to the female again and again, while woman is able to have intercourse, to conceive, and to give birth even if she is frigid. From an ontological point of view, even this kind of fear has its origin in childhood, when the little boy felt himself to be a man, but was afraid his masculinity would be ridiculed and thereby his self-confidence hurt, when his childish wooing was made fun of and derided. Traces of this insecurity will remain more frequently than we are inclined to admit, frequently hidden behind an overemphasis on masculinity as a value in and of itself, yet these insecurities betray themselves through the ever-fluctuating self-confidence of the male in his relating to the female. Marriage can bring out a persisting oversensitivity regarding any frustration by the wife. If she is not available solely for him, if the best is not good enough for him, if he does not satisfy her sexually, all this must appear to the basically insecure husband as a grave insult to his masculine self-confidence. This reaction, in turn, will instinctively arouse his wish to humiliate his wife by undermining her self-confidence.

These few examples were selected to demonstrate some trends that are typical for the male. They may suffice to show that certain attitudes toward the opposite sex may have been acquired in childhood and will of necessity express themselves in later relationships, particularly in marriage, and are relatively independent of the personality of the partner. The less such attitudes have been overcome in the course of his development, the more uncomfortable the husband must feel in relation to his wife. The presence of such feelings will often be unconscious, and their sources always unconscious. The reaction to them can vary a great deal. It may lead to tensions and conflicts within the marriage, ranging from a hidden grudge to open hatred, or it may induce the husband to seek and find relief from tension in work, or in the company of men, or of other women whose demands he does not fear and in whose presence he does not feel burdened with all sorts of obligations. Again and again we see that it is the marital tie that proves to be the stronger one, for better or for worse. Yet the relationship with another woman frequently is the more relaxing, satisfying, and blissful one.

Of the difficulties the wife brings into the marriage, a gift of dubious value from her formative years, I shall mention only one: frigidity. Whether it is intrinsically important or not might be debatable, but it is an indication of a disturbance in the relationship with the male. Regardless of variations of the individual content, it is always an expression of rejection of the male, either of the specific individual or of the male sex in general. Statistics about the frequency of frigidity differ widely and seem to me basically unreliable, partly because the quality of a feeling cannot be expressed statistically, and partly because it is difficult to estimate how many women are deceiving themselves in one way or another about their capacity for sexual enjoyment. According to my own experience, I am inclined to assume that minor degrees of frigidity are more frequent than we might expect from the direct statements by women.

When I stated that frigidity is always an expression of rejection of the male, I did not mean the conspicuous appearance of hostility toward the male. Such women may be very feminine in their body build, way of dressing, and their behavior. They may give the impression that their whole life is "attuned to love alone."* What I mean is something far deeper—an inability to really love, to surrender to a man. These women will rather go their own way or drive the male away with their jealousy, demands, boredom, and nagging.

How does such an attitude arise? At first, one would be inclined to blame it all on the sins of our past and present methods of bringing up girls, with the pressures of sex prohibitions, the segregation from men that makes it impossible to see them in a normal light. Thus they appear either as heroes or monsters. However, evidence as well as reflection reveal that this concept is too superficial. It is a fact that greater strictness in raising girls does not run parallel with an increase in frigidity. Also, we find that where basic characteristics are concerned, human nature has never been essentially changed by prohibition and coercion.

There is perhaps only one factor that in the last analysis, is strong enough to frighten us away from the satisfaction of vital

---

* Quotation from Marlene Dietrich's famous song, "Love Alone."

needs: anxiety. If we want to understand its origin and development, as far as it is possible to grasp it genetically, we must take a closer look at the typical fate of the instinctual drives in the female child. Here we can find various factors that make the female role appear dangerous to the little girl and make her dislike it. The typical fears of early childhood with their transparent symbolism make it easy to guess at their hidden meaning. What else could be the meaning of the fear of burglars, snakes, wild animals, and thunderstorms, if not the feminine fear of overwhelming forces that can vanquish, penetrate, and destroy? There are additional fears in connection with the early instinctive premonition of motherhood. The little girl is half afraid of experiencing this mysterious and dreadful event in the future and at the same time is half afraid she may never have the opportunity to experience it.

The little girl escapes from these uneasy feelings in a typical way by flight into a desired or imagined masculine role. More or less distinct aspects of it can be easily observed in the four- to ten-year-old. Before and during puberty the noisy tomboyish behavior disappears to give way to a feminine attitude. However, some strong and disturbing residuals may continue to persist below the surface and be effective in several ways: as ambition, as drive for power, as resentment against the male who is seen as always having an advantage compared to herself, as a combative attitude toward the male, perhaps in the form of alternate kinds of sexual manipulation, and finally, in being inhibited or completely blocked in letting herself experience sexual fulfillment by a man.

One point will become clearer if we understand this roughly sketched developmental history of frigidity. If we look at marriage as a whole, we come to see that the background from which frigidity originates and the way it expresses itself in the total attitude toward the husband, are more serious than the symptom itself, which, as merely missed pleasures, is perhaps not so important.

Motherhood is one of the female functions that tend to be disturbed by such an unfavorable development. I would rather not discuss here the manifold ways in which such physical and emotional disturbances can be expressed, but limit myself to one question only. Is it likely that a basically good marriage will suffer through the arrival of a child? One can frequently hear this question posed in the apodictic form, of whether children cement or undermine a marriage. However, it is unproductive to ask the question in so general a form, because the answer will depend on the inner structure of the individual marriage. Therefore my question will have to be posed in a more specific form. Can a hitherto good relationship between marriage partners be damaged by the arrival of a child?

Although such a consequence seems to be biologically paradoxical, it may indeed occur under certain psychological conditions. It can, for instance, happen that a man who unconsciously is strongly attached to his mother, will come to experience his wife as a mother figure, once she actually has become a mother herself, so that it will become impossible for him to approach her sexually. Such a change in attitude can be defended through the rationalization that the wife lost her beauty through her pregnancy, childbirth, and nursing. It is by these kinds of rationalizations that we usually try to come to grips with those emotions or inhibitions which reach up into our lives from the incomprehensible depths of our being.

The corresponding case in a woman presupposes that by a certain distortion in her development, all of her feminine longings become focused on the child. Consequently, she loves in the grown man the child only, the child that he himself represents to her and the child he is supposed to give her. If such a woman really has a child, the husband will become unnecessary, even annoying, with his demands on her.

Thus, under certain psychological conditions, the child, too, can become a source of estrangement or dislike.

I would like to conclude at this point, at least for the time being, although I have not even touched on other important possibilities for conflict, such as the one arising out of latent homosexuality. A greater comprehensiveness would not add anything in principle to the viewpoints that result from the psychological insights discussed above.

My point of departure, therefore, is the following: As the

spark goes out of a marriage or a third person intrudes, the very things we usually hold responsible for the breaking down of a marriage, are already a consequence of a certain development. They are the result of a process that usually remains hidden from us, but that will gradually grow into a dislike of the partner. The sources of this dislike have to do much less than we think with the annoying qualities of the partner, and much more with the unresolved conflicts we bring into the marriage from our own development.

Hence problems in marriage are not to be solved by admonitions regarding duty and renunciation, nor by the recommendation of unlimited freedom for the instincts. The former no longer make sense to us nowadays, and the latter quite obviously does not serve well our striving for happiness, quite aside from the danger that our best values might get lost. Quite factually, the question should rather be posed as follows: What factors that lead to the dislike of the marriage partner can be avoided? Which ones can be alleviated? Which ones can be overcome? Excessively disruptive dissonances in development are avoidable, at least in intensity. One can rightfully say that the chances of a marriage are dependent on the degree of emotional stability acquired by both partners before marriage. Many of the difficulties seem unavoidable. It may be part of human nature to expect fulfillment to be presented to us as a gift, instead of having to work for it. An intrinsically good, i.e., anxiety-free, relationship between the sexes might remain an unreachable ideal. We also must learn to accept certain contradictory expectations within ourselves as partly pertaining to our nature, thus recognizing the impossibility of fulfilling them all within a marriage. Our attitudes toward renunciation will vary, depending on the moment in which the swing of history's pendulum will strike us. The generations preceding ours demanded too much renunciation of instincts. We, on the other hand, have the tendency to fear it excessively. The most desirable goal for marriage, as well as for any other relationship, seems to be to find an optimum between foregoing and granting, between restriction and freedom of drives. However, the essential renunciation that really threatens marriage is not the one imposed on us by the actual shortcomings of the partner. We could, after all, forgive him for not being able to give us more than the limitations of his nature permit him; but we would also have to give up our other claims, which, expressed or implied, poison the atmosphere all too easily. We would have to give up the claims to different ways of seeking and finding satisfaction of other drives within ourselves, not only sexual ones, which the partner let lie fallow and unfilled. In other words, we must seriously review the absolute standard of monogamy by reexamining with an open mind its origin, its values, and its dangers.

THE DREAD OF WOMAN

Observations on a Specific Difference in the Dread Felt by Men and by Women Respectively for the Opposite Sex*

○○

IN HIS BALLAD OF *The Diver*, Schiller tells how a squire leaps into a dangerous whirlpool in order to win a woman—at first symbolized by a goblet. Horror-struck, he describes the perils of the deep by which he is doomed to be engulfed:

Yet at length comes a lull o'er the mighty commotion,
As the whirlpool sucks into black smoothness the swell
Of the white-foaming breakers—and cleaves through the ocean
A path that seems winding in darkness to hell.
Round and round whirled the waves—deeper and deeper still driven,
Like a gorge through the mountainous main thunder-riven!

Happy they whom the rose-hues of daylight rejoice,
The air and the sky that to mortals are given!
May the horror below never more find a voice—
Nor man stretch too far the wide mercy of Heaven!
Never more—never more may he lift from the sight
The veil which is woven with Terror and Night!

Below at the foot of the precipice drear,
Spread the glowing, and purple, and pathless Obscure!

* "Die Angst vor der Frau Über einen spezifischen Unterschied in der männlichen und weiblichen Angst vor dem anderen Geschlecht," *Intern. Zeitschr. f. Psychoanal.* XVIII (1932), pp. 5-18; *Int. J. Psycho-Anal.* XIII (1932), pp. 348-60. Reprinted with the permission of *The International Journal of Psycho-Analysis.*

> *A silence of Horror that slept on the ear,*
> *That the eye more appalled might the Horror endure!*
> *Salamander—snake—dragon—vast reptiles that dwell*
> *In the deep, coil'd about the grim jaws of their hell.*
>
> (TRANSLATION BY BULWER LYTTON)

The same idea is expressed, though far more pleasantly, in the
Song of the Fisherboy in *Wilhelm Tell*:

> *The clear smiling lake woo'd to bathe in its deep,*
> *A boy on its green shore had laid him to sleep;*
> *Then heard he a melody*
> *Flowing and soft,*
> *And sweet as when angels are singing aloft.*
> *And as thrilling with pleasure he wakes from his rest,*
> *The waters are murmuring over his breast;*
> *And a voice from the deep cries,*
> *"With me thou must go, I charm the young shepherd,*
> *I lure him below."*
>
> (TRANSLATION BY THEODORE MARTIN)

Men have never tired of fashioning expressions for the violent
force by which man feels himself drawn to the woman, and side
by side with his longing, the dread that through her he might
die and be undone. I will mention particularly the moving expression of this dread in Heine's poem of the legendary Lorelei, who
sits high on the bank of the Rhine and ensnares the boatman
with her beauty.

Here once more it is water (representing, like the other "elements," the primal element "woman") that swallows up the man
who succumbs to a woman's enchantment. Ulysses had to bid
his seamen bind him to the mast in order to escape the allure-
ment and the danger of the sirens. The riddle of the Sphinx
can be solved by few, and most of those who attempt it forfeit
their lives. The royal palace in fairy tales is adorned with the
heads of the suitors who have had the hardihood to try to solve
the riddles of the king's beautiful daughter. The goddess Kali[1]

1. See Daly's account in his article, *"Hindumythologie und Kastrations-
komplex,"* Imago, Bd. XIII (1927).

dances on the corpses of slain men. Samson, whom no man could conquer, is robbed of his strength by Delilah. Judith beheads Holofernes after giving herself to him. Salome carries the head of John the Baptist on a charger. Witches are burnt because male priests fear the work of the devil in them. Wedekind's "Earth Spirit" destroys every man who succumbs to her charm, not because she is particularly evil, but simply because it is her nature to do so. The series of such instances is infinite; always, everywhere, the man strives to rid himself of his dread of women by objectifying it. "It is not," he says, "that I dread her; it is that she herself is malignant, capable of any crime, a beast of prey, a vampire, a witch, insatiable in her desires. She is the very personification of what is sinister." May not this be one of the principal roots of the whole masculine impulse to creative work —the never-ending conflict between the man's longing for the woman and his dread of her?[2]

To primitive sensibilities the woman becomes doubly sinister in the presence of the bloody manifestations of her womanhood. Contact with her during menstruation is fatal:[3] men lose their strength, the pastures wither away, the fisherman and the huntsman take nothing. Defloration involves the utmost danger to the man. As Freud shows in "The Taboo of Virginity,"[4] it is the husband in particular who dreads this act. In this work Freud, too, objectifies this anxiety, contenting himself with a reference to the castration-impulses that actually do occur in women. There are two reasons why this is not an adequate explanation of the phenomenon of the taboo itself. In the first place, women do not so universally react to defloration with castration-impulses recognizable as such; these impulses are probably confined to women with a strongly developed masculine attitude. And, secondly, even

2. Sachs explains the impulse to artistic creation as the search for companions in guilt. In this, I think, he is right, but he does not seem to me to go deeply enough into the question, since his explanation is one-sided and takes into account only part of the whole personality, namely, the superego. (Sachs, "Gemeinsame Tagträume," *Internationaler Psychoanalytischer Verlag*.)

3. Cf. Daly, "Der Menstruationscomplex," *Imago*, Bd. XIV (1928); and Winterstein, "Die Pubertätsriten der Mädchen und ihre Spuren im Märchen," *Imago*, Bd. XIV (1928).

4. Freud, "The Taboo of Virginity" (1918), *Collected Papers*, Vol. IV.

if defloration invariably aroused destructive impulses in the woman, we should still have to lay bare (as we should do in every individual analysis) the urgent impulses within the man himself which make him view the first—forcible—penetration of the vagina as so perilous an undertaking; so perilous, indeed, that it can be performed with impunity only by a man of might or by a stranger who chooses to risk his life or his manhood for a recompense.

Is it not really remarkable (we ask ourselves in amazement), when one considers the overwhelming mass of this transparent material, that so little recognition and attention are paid to the fact of men's secret dread of women? It is almost more remarkable that women themselves have so long been able to overlook it; I will discuss in detail elsewhere the reasons for their attitude in this connection (i.e., their own anxiety and the impairment of their self-respect). The man on his side has in the first place very obvious strategic reasons for keeping his dread quiet. But he also tries by every means to deny it even to himself. This is the purpose of the efforts to which we have alluded, to "objectify" it in artistic and scientific creative work. We may conjecture that even his glorification of women has its source not only in his cravings for love, but also in his desire to conceal his dread. A similar relief, however, is also sought and found in the disparagement of women that men often display ostentatiously in their attitudes. The attitude of love and adoration signifies: "There is no need for me to dread a being so wonderful, so beautiful, nay, so saintly." That of disparagement implies: "It would be too ridiculous to dread a creature who, if you take her all round, is such a poor thing."[5] This last way of allaying his anxiety has a special advantage for the man: It helps to support his masculine self-respect. The latter seems to feel itself far more threatened at its very core by the admission of a dread of women than by the admission of dread of a man (the father). The reason why the self-feeling of men is so peculiarly sensitive just in relation to

5. I well remember how surprised I was myself the first time I heard the above ideas asserted—by a man—in the shape of a universal proposition. The speaker was Groddeck, who obviously felt that he was stating something quite self-evident when he remarked in conversation, "Of course men are afraid of women." In his writings Groddeck has repeatedly emphasized this fear.

women can only be understood by reference to their early development, to which I will return later.

In analysis this dread of women is revealed quite clearly. Male homosexuality has for its basis, in common indeed with all the other perversions, the desire to escape from the female genital, or to deny its very existence. Freud has shown that this is a fundamental trait in fetishism,[6] in particular; he believes it to be based, however, not on anxiety, but on a feeling of abhorrence due to the absence of the penis in women. I think, however, that even from his account we are absolutely forced to the conclusion that there is anxiety at work as well. What we actually see is dread of the vagina, thinly disguised under the abhorrence. Only *anxiety* is a strong enough motive to hold back from his goal a man whose libido is assuredly urging him on to union with the woman. But Freud's account fails to explain this anxiety. A boy's castration anxiety in relation to his father is not an adequate reason for his dread of a being to whom this punishment has already happened. Besides the dread of the father, there must be a further dread, the object of which is the woman or the female genital. Now this dread of the vagina itself appears unmistakably not only in homosexuals and perverts, but also in the dreams of male analysands. All analysts are familiar with dreams of this sort and I need only give the merest outline of them: e.g., a motorcar is rushing along and suddenly falls into a pit and is dashed to pieces; a boat is sailing in a narrow channel and is suddenly sucked into a whirlpool; there is a cellar with uncanny, blood-stained plants and animals; one is climbing a chimney and is in danger of falling and being killed.

Dr. Baumeyer of Dresden[7] allows me to cite a series of experiments that arose out of a chance observation and illustrate this dread of the vagina. The physician was playing ball with the children at a treatment center, and after a time showed them that the ball had a slit in it. She pulled the edges of the slit apart and put her finger in, so that it was held fast by the ball. Of 28 boys whom she asked to do the same, only 6 did it without

---

6. Freud, "Fetishism," *Int. J. Psycho-Anal.*, Vol IX (1928).
7. The experiments were conducted by Frl. Dr. Hartung at a children's clinic in Dresden.

fear and 8 could not be induced to do it at all. Of 19 girls 9 put their fingers in without a trace of fear; the rest showed a slight uneasiness but none of them serious anxiety.

No doubt the dread of the vagina often conceals itself behind the dread of the father, which is also present; or in the language of the unconscious, behind the dread of the penis in the woman's vagina.[8]

There are two reasons for this. In the first place, as I have already said, masculine self-regard suffers less in this way, and secondly, the dread of the father is more tangible, less uncanny in quality. We might compare it to the difference between the fear of a real enemy and of a ghost. The prominence given to the anxiety relating to the castrating father is therefore tendentious, as Groddeck has shown, for example, in his analysis of the thumb-sucker in *Struwwelpeter;* it is a man who cuts off the thumb, but it is the mother who utters the threat, and the instrument with which it is carried out—the scissors—is a female symbol.

From all this I think it probable that the masculine dread or the woman (the mother) or of the female genital is more deep-seated, weighs more heavily, and is usually more energetically repressed than the dread of the man (father), and that the endeavor to find the penis in women represents first and foremost a convulsive attempt to deny the existence of the sinister female genital.

Is there any ontogenetic explanation of this anxiety? Or is it not rather (in human beings) an integral part of masculine existence and behavior? Is any light shed upon it by the state of lethargy—even the death—after mating, which occurs frequently in male animals?[9] Are love and death more closely bound up with one another for the male than for the female, in whom sexual union potentially produces a new life? Does the man feel, side by side with his desire to conquer, a secret longing for extinction

8. Boehm, "Beiträge zur Psychologie der Homosexualität," *Intern. Zeitschr. f. Psychoanal.,* XI (1925); Melanie Klein, "Early Stages of the Œdipus Conflict," *Int. J. Psycho-Anal.,* Vol. IX (1928); "The Importance of Symbol-Formation in the Development of the Ego," *Int. J. Psycho-Anal.,* Vol. XI (1930); "Infantile Anxiety-Situations reflected in a Work of Art and in the Creative Impulse," *Int. J. Psycho-Anal.,* Vol. X (1929), p. 436.

9. Bergmann, *Muttergeist und Erkenntnisgeist.*

in the act of reunion with the woman (mother)? Is it perhaps this longing that underlies the "death-instinct"? And is it his will to live that reacts to it with anxiety?

When we endeavor to understand this anxiety in psychological and ontogenetic terms, we find ourselves rather at a loss if we take our stand on Freud's notion that what distinguishes infantile from adult sexuality is precisely that the vagina remains "undiscovered" for the child. According to that view, we cannot properly speak of a genital primacy; we must rather term it a primacy of the phallus. Hence it would be better to describe the period of infantile genital organization as the "phallic phase."[10] The many recorded remarks of boys at that period of life leave no doubt of the correctness of the observations on which Freud's theory is based. But if we look more closely at the essential characteristics of this phase, we cannot help asking whether his description really sums up infantile genitality as such, in its specific manifestation, or applies only to a relatively later phase of it. Freud states that it is characteristic that the boy's interest is concentrated in a markedly narcissistic manner on his own penis: "The driving force which this male portion of his body will generate later at puberty expresses itself in childhood essentially as an impulsion to inquire into things—as sexual curiosity." A very important part is played by questions as to the existence and size of the phallus in other living beings.

But surely the essence of the phallic impulses proper, starting as they do from organ sensations, is a desire to *penetrate*. That these impulses do exist can hardly be doubted; they manifest themselves too plainly in children's games and in the analysis of little children. Again, it would be difficult to say what the boy's sexual wishes in relation to his mother really consisted in if not in these very impulses; or why the object of his masturbation anxiety should be the father as the castrator, were it not that masturbation was largely the autoerotic expression of heterosexual phallic impulses.

In the phallic phase the boy's psychic orientation is predominantly narcissistic; hence the period in which his genital impulses

10. Freud, "The Infantile Genital Organization of the Libido" (1923), *Collected Papers*, Vol. II.

are directed toward an object must be an earlier one. The possibility that they are not directed toward a female genital, of which he instinctively divines the existence, must certainly be considered. In dreams, both of earlier and later life, as well as in symptoms and particular modes of behavior, we find, it is true, representations of coitus that are oral, anal, or sadistic without specific localization. But we cannot take this as a proof of the primacy of corresponding impulses, for we are uncertain whether, or how far, these phenomena already express a displacement from the genital goal proper. At bottom, all that they amount to is to show that a given individual is influenced by specific oral, anal, or sadistic trends. Their evidential value is the less because these representations are always associated with certain affects directed against women, so that we cannot tell whether they may not be essentially the product or the expression of these affects. For instance, the tendency to debase women may express itself in anal representations of the female genital, while oral representations may express anxiety.

But besides all this, there are various reasons why it seems to me improbable that the existence of a specific female opening should remain "undiscovered." On the one hand, of course, a boy will automatically conclude that everyone else is made like himself; but on the other hand his phallic impulses surely bid him instinctively to search for the appropriate opening in the female body—an opening, moreover, that he himself lacks, for the one sex always seeks in the other that which is complementary to it or of a nature different from its own. If we seriously accept Freud's dictum that the sexual theories formed by children are modeled on their own sexual constitution, it must surely mean in the present connection that the boy, urged on by his impulses to penetrate, pictures in fantasy a complementary female organ. And this is just what we should infer from all the material I quoted at the outset in connection with the masculine dread of the female genital.

It is not at all probable that this anxiety dates only from puberty. At the beginning of that period the anxiety manifests itself quite clearly, if we look behind the often very exiguous façade of boyish pride that conceals it. At puberty a boy's task is obviously not merely to free himself from his incestuous attachment to his mother, but more generally, to master his dread of the whole female sex. His success is as a rule only gradual; first of all he turns his back on girls altogether, and only when his masculinity is fully awakened does it drive him over the threshold of anxiety. But we know that as a rule the conflicts of puberty do but revive, *mutatis mutandis,* conflicts belonging to the early ripening of infantile sexuality and that the course they take is often essentially a faithful copy of a series of earlier experiences. Moreover, the grotesque character of the anxiety, as we meet with it in the symbolism of dreams and literary productions, points unmistakably to the period of early infantile fantasy.

At puberty a normal boy has already acquired a conscious knowledge of the vagina, but what he fears in women is something uncanny, unfamiliar, and mysterious. If the grown man continues to regard woman as the great mystery, in whom is a secret he cannot divine, this feeling of his can only relate ultimately to one thing in her: the mystery of motherhood. Everything else is merely the residue of his dread of this.

What is the origin of this anxiety? What are its characteristics? And what are the factors that cloud the boy's early relations with his mother?

In an article on female sexuality [11] Freud has pointed out the most obvious of these factors: It is the mother who first forbids instinctual activities, because it is she who tends the child in its babyhood. Secondly, the child evidently experiences sadistic impulses against its mother's body,[12] presumably connected with the rage evoked by her prohibitions, and according to the talion principle, this anger has left behind a residue of anxiety. Finally—and this is perhaps the principal point—the specific fate of the genital impulses itself constitutes another such factor. The anatomical differences between the sexes lead to a totally different situation in girls and in boys, and really to understand both their anxiety and the diversity of their anxiety we must take into account first of all *the children's real situation* in the period of their early sex-

11. *Int. J. Psycho-Anal.,* Vol. XI (1930), p. 281.
12. Cf. the work of Melanie Klein, quoted above, to which I think insufficient attention has been paid.

uality. The girl's nature as biologically conditioned gives her the desire to receive, to take into herself;[13] she feels or knows that her genital is too small for her father's penis and this makes her react to her own genital wishes with direct anxiety; she dreads that if her wishes were fulfilled, she herself or her genital would be destroyed.[14]

The boy, on the other hand, feels or instinctively judges that his penis is much too small for his mother's genital and reacts with the dread of his own inadequacy, of being rejected and derided. Thus his anxiety is located in quite a different quarter from the girl's; his original dread of women is not castration anxiety at all, but a reaction to the menace to his self-respect.[15]

In order that there may be no misunderstanding, let me emphasize that I believe these processes take place purely instinctively on the basis of organ sensations and the tensions of organic needs; in other words, I hold that these reactions would occur even if the girl had never seen her father's penis or the boy his mother's genital, and neither had any sort of intellectual knowledge of the existence of these genitalia.

Because of this reaction on the part of the boy, he is affected in another way and more severely by his frustration at the hands of his mother than is the girl by her experience with her father. A blow is struck at the libidinal impulses in either case. But the girl has a certain consolation in her frustration—she preserves her physical integrity. But the boy is hit in a second sensitive spot —his sense of genital inadequacy, which has presumably accompanied his libidinal desires from the beginning. If we assume that the most general reason for violent anger is the foiling of impulses that at the moment are of vital importance, it follows that the boy's frustration by his mother must arouse a twofold fury in him: first through the thrusting back of his libido upon itself, and secondly, through the wounding of his masculine self-regard. At the same time old resentment springing from pregenital frustrations is probably also made to flare up again. The result is that his

13. This is not to be equated with passivity.
14. In another paper I will discuss the girl's situation more fully.
15. I would refer here also to the points I raised in a paper entitled "Das Misstrauen zwischen den Geschlechtern," *Die psychoanalytische Bewegung* (1930).

phallic impulses to penetrate merge with his anger at frustration, and the impulses take on a sadistic tinge.

Here let me emphasize a point that is often insufficiently brought out in psychoanalytical literature—namely, that we have no reason to assume that these phallic impulses are naturally sadistic and that therefore it is inadmissible, in the absence of specific evidence in each case, to equate "male" with "sadistic," and on similar lines "female" with "masochistic." If the admixture of destructive impulses is really considerable, the mother's genital must, according to the talion principle, become an object of direct anxiety. Thus, if it is first made distasteful to him by its association with wounded self-regard, it will by a secondary process (by way of frustration anger) become an object of castration anxiety. And probably this is very generally reinforced when the boy observes traces of menstruation.

Very often this latter anxiety in its turn leaves a lasting mark on the man's attitude to women, as we learn from the examples already given at random from very different periods and races. But I do not think that it occurs regularly in all men in any considerable degree, and certainly it is not a *distinctive* characteristic of the man's relation to the other sex. Anxiety of this sort strongly resembles, *mutatis mutandis*, anxiety we meet with in women. When in analysis we find it occurring in any noteworthy intensity, the subject is invariably a man whose whole attitude toward women has a markedly neurotic twist.

On the other hand I think that the anxiety connected with his self-respect leaves more or less distinct traces in every man and gives his general attitude toward women a particular stamp that either does not exist in women's attitude to men, or if it does, is acquired secondarily. In other words, it is no integral part of their feminine nature.

We can only grasp the general significance of this male attitude if we study more closely the development of the boy's infantile anxiety, his efforts to overcome it, and the ways in which it manifests itself.

According to my experience, the dread of being rejected and derided is a typical ingredient in the analysis of every man, no matter what his mentality or the structure of his neurosis. The analytic situation and the constant reserve of the woman analyst bring out this anxiety and sensitiveness more clearly than they appear in ordinary life, which gives men plenty of opportunity to escape from these feelings either by avoiding situations calculated to evoke them or by a process of overcompensation. The specific basis of this attitude is hard to detect, because in analysis it is generally concealed by a feminine orientation, for the most part unconscious.[16]

To judge by my own experience, this latter orientation is no less common, though (for reasons which I will give) less blatant, than the masculine attitude in women. I do not propose to discuss its various sources here; I will only say that I conjecture that the early wound to his self-regard is probably one of the factors liable to disgust the boy with his male role.

His typical reaction to that wound and to the dread of his mother that follows from it is obviously to withdraw his libido from her and to concentrate it on himself and his genital. From the economic point of view this process is doubly advantageous; it enables him to escape from the distressing or anxiety-fraught situation that has developed between himself and his mother, and it restores his masculine self-respect by reactively strengthening his phallic narcissism. The female genital no longer exists for him; the "undiscovered" vagina is a denied vagina. This stage of his development is fully identical with Freud's phallic phase.

Accordingly we must understand the inquiring attitude that dominates this phase and the specific nature of the boy's inquiries as expressing a retreat from the object followed by a narcissistically tinged anxiety.

His first reaction, then, is in the direction of a heightened phallic narcissism. The result is that to the wish to be a woman, which younger boys utter without embarrassment, he now reacts partly with renewed anxiety lest he should not be taken seriously and partly with castration anxiety. Once we realize that masculine castration anxiety is very largely the ego's response to the *wish to be a woman*, we cannot altogether share Freud's conviction that bisexuality manifests itself more clearly in the female than in the

16. Cf. Boehm, "The Femininity Complex in Men," *Int. J. Psycho-Anal.*, Vol. XI (1930).

male.[17] We must leave it an open question.

A feature of the phallic phase that Freud emphasizes shows up with special clearness the narcissistic scar left by the little boy's relation with his mother: "He behaves as if he had a dim idea that this member might be and should be larger." [18] We must amplify the observation by saying that this behavior begins, indeed, in the phallic phase, but does not cease with it; on the contrary, it is displayed naïvely throughout boyhood and persists later as a deeply hidden anxiety about the size of the subject's penis or his potency, or else as a less concealed pride about them.

Now one of the exigencies of the biological differences between the sexes is this: that the man is actually obliged to go on proving his manhood to the woman. There is no analogous necessity for her. Even if she is frigid, she can engage in sexual intercourse and conceive and bear a child. She performs her part by merely *being,* without any *doing*—a fact that has always filled men with admiration and resentment. The man on the other hand has to *do* something in order to fulfill himself. The ideal of "efficiency" is a typical masculine ideal.

This is probably the fundamental reason why, when we analyze women who dread their masculine tendencies, we always find that they unconsciously regard ambition and achievement as attributes of the male, in spite of the great enlargement of women's sphere of activity in real life.

In sexual life itself we see how the simple craving of love that drives men to women is very often overshadowed by their overwhelming inner compulsion to prove their manhood again and again to themselves and others. A man of this type in its more extreme form has therefore one interest only: to conquer. His aim is to have "possessed" many women, and the most beautiful and most sought-after women. We find a remarkable mixture of this narcissistic overcompensation and of surviving anxiety in those men who, while wanting to make conquests, are very indignant with a woman who takes their intentions too seriously, or who cherish a lifelong gratitude to her if she spares them any further

17. Freud, "Female Sexuality," *Inter. J. Psycho-Anal.,* Vol. XI (1930), p. 281.
18. Freud, "The Infantile Genital Organization of the Libido," *Collected Papers,* Vol. II.

proof of their manhood.

Another way of averting the soreness of the narcissistic scar is by adopting the attitude described by Freud as the propensity to debase the love object.[19] If a man does not desire any woman who is his equal or even his superior—may it not be that he is protecting his threatened self-regard in accordance with that most useful principle of sour grapes? From the prostitute or the woman of easy virtue one need fear no rejection, and no demands in the sexual, ethical, or intellectual sphere. One can feel oneself the superior.[20]

This brings us to a third way, the most important and the most ominous in its cultural consequences: that of diminishing the self-respect of the woman. I think that I have shown that men's disparagement of women is based upon a definite psychic trend toward disparaging them—a tendency rooted in the man's psychic reactions to certain given biological facts, as might be expected of a mental attitude so widespread and so obstinately maintained. The view that women are infantile and emotional creatures, and as such, incapable of responsibility and independence is the work of the masculine tendency to lower women's self-respect. When men justify such an attitude by pointing out that a very large number of women really do correspond to this description, we must consider whether this type of woman has not been cultivated by a systematic selection on the part of men. The important point is not that individual minds of greater or lesser caliber, from Aristotle to Moebius, have expended an astonishing amount of energy and intellectual capacity in proving the superiority of the masculine principle. What really counts is the fact that the ever-precarious self-respect of the "average man" causes him over and over again to choose a feminine type that is infantile, nonmaternal, and hysterical, and by so doing to expose each new generation to the influence of such women.

19. Freud, "Contributions to the Psychology of Love," *Collected Papers,* Vol. IV.

20. This does not detract from the importance of the other forces that drive men to prostitutes, which have been described by Freud in his "Contributions to the Psychology of Love," *Collected Papers,* Vol. IV; and by Boehm in his "Beiträge zur Psychologie der Homosexualität, *Intern. Zeitschr. f. Psychoanal.,* Bd. VI (1920) and Bd. VIII (1922).

THE DENIAL OF THE VAGINA

*A Contribution to the Problem of the Genital Anxieties Specific to Women**

○○○

THE FUNDAMENTAL CONCLUSIONS to which Freud's investigations of the specific character of feminine development have led him are as follows: first, that in little girls the early development of instinct takes the same course as in boys, both in respect of the erotogenic zones (in the two sexes only one genital organ, the penis, plays a part, the vagina remaining undiscovered) and also in respect of the first choice of object (for both the mother is the first love object). Secondly, that the great differences that nevertheless exist between the two sexes arise from the fact that this similarity of libidinal trend does not go with similar anatomical and biological foundations. From this premise it follows logically and inevitably that girls feel themselves inadequately equipped for this phallic orientation of their libido and cannot but envy boys their superior endowment in that respect. Over and above the conflicts with the mother, which the girl shares with the boy, she adds a crucial one of her own; she lays at her mother's door the blame for her lack of a penis. This conflict is crucial because it is just this reproach which is essential for her detachment from her mother and her turning to her father.

Hence Freud has chosen a happy phrase to designate the period of blossoming of childish sexuality, the period of infantile genital primacy in girls as well as boys, which he calls the *phallic phase*.

* "Die Verleugnung der Vagina. Ein Beitrag zur Frage der spezifisch weiblichen Genitalangst," *Intern. Zeitschr. f. Psychoanal*, XIX (1933), pp. 372-84; *Int. J. Psycho-Anal.*, 14 (1933), pp. 57-70. Reprinted with the permission of *The International Journal of Psycho-Analysis*.

I can imagine that a man of science who was not familiar with analysis would in reading this account pass over it as merely one of the many strange and peculiar notions that analysis expects the world to believe. Only those who accept the point of view of Freud's theories can gauge the importance of this particular thesis for the understanding of feminine psychology as a whole. Its full bearings emerge in the light of one of Freud's most momentous discoveries, one of those achievements which, we may suppose, will prove lasting. I refer to the realization of the crucial importance for the whole subsequent life of the individual of the impressions, experiences, and conflicts of early childhood. If we accept this proposition in its entirety, i.e., if we recognize the formative influence of early experience on the subject's capacity for dealing with his later experience and the way in which he does so, there ensue, at least potentially, the following consequences as regards the specific psychic life of women:

(1) With the onset of each fresh phase in the functioning of the female organs—menstruation, coitus, pregnancy, parturition, suckling, and the menopause—even a normal woman (as Helene Deutsch [1] has in fact assumed) would have to overcome impulses of a masculine trend before she could adopt an attitude of whole-hearted affirmation toward the processes taking place within her body.

(2) Again, even in normal women, irrespective of race and of social and individual conditions, it would happen altogether more readily than in men that the libido adhered, or came to be turned, to persons of her own sex. In a word, *homosexuality* would be incomparably and unmistakably more common among women than among men. Confronted with difficulties in relation to the opposite sex, a woman would plainly fall back more readily than a man into a homosexual attitude. For according to Freud, not only are the most important years of her childhood dominated by such an attachment to one of her own sex, but when she first turns to a man (the father), it is in the main only by way of the narrow bridge of resentment. "Since I cannot have a penis I want a child instead and 'for this purpose' I turn to my father. Since I have a grudge against my mother because of the anatomical inferiority

1. H. Deutsch, *Psychoanalyse der weiblichen Sexualfunktionen.*

for which I hold her responsible, I give her up and turn to my father." Just because we are convinced of the formative influence of the first years of life, we should feel it a contradiction if the relation of woman to man did not retain throughout life some tinge of this enforced choice of a substitute for that which was really desired.[2]

(3) The same character of something remote from instinct, secondary and substitutive, would, even in normal women, adhere to the *wish for motherhood,* or at least would easily manifest itself.

Freud by no means fails to realize the strength of the desire for children. In his view it represents on the one hand the principal legacy of the little girl's strongest instinctual object relation—i.e., to the mother—in the shape of a reversal of the original child-mother relationship. On the other hand, it is also the principal legacy of the early, elementary wish for the penis. The special point about Freud's viewpoint is rather that it sees the wish for motherhood not as an innate formation, but as something that can be reduced psychologically to its ontogenetic elements and draws its energy originally from homosexual or phallic instinctual desires.

(4) If we accept a second axiom of psychoanalysis, namely, that the individual's attitude in sexual matters is the prototype of his attitude toward the rest of life, it would follow, finally, that woman's whole reaction to life would be based on a strong subterranean resentment. For according to Freud, the little girl's penis envy corresponds to a sense of being at a radical disadvantage in respect to the most vital and elementary instinctual desires. Here we have the typical basis upon which a general resentment is liable to be built up. It is true that such an attitude would not follow inevitably; Freud says expressly that *where development proceeds favorably,* the girl finds her own way to the man and to motherhood. But here again, it would contradict all our analytical theory and experience if an attitude of resentment so early and so deeply rooted did not manifest itself extremely easily—by comparison much more easily than in men under similar conditions—or at any rate were not readily set going as an undercurrent detri-

2. In a later work I hope to discuss the question of early object relations regarded as the basis of the phallic attitude in little girls.

mental to the vital feeling-tone of women.

These are the very weighty conclusions with regard to the whole psychology of women, which follow from Freud's account of early feminine sexuality. When we consider them, we may well feel that it behooves us to apply again and again the tests of observation and theoretical reflection to the facts on which they are based and to their proper appraisal.

It seems to me that analytic experience alone does not sufficiently enable us to judge the soundness of some of the fundamental ideas that Freud has made the basis of his theory. I think that a final verdict about them must be postponed until we have at our disposal systematic observations of *normal* children, carried out on a large scale by persons trained in analysis. Among the views in question I include Freud's statement that "it is well-known that a clearly defined differentiation between the male and the female character is first established after puberty." The few observations that I have made myself do not confirm this statement. On the contrary I have always been struck by the marked way in which little girls between their second and fifth years exhibit specifically feminine traits. For instance, they often behave with a certain spontaneous feminine coquetry toward men, or display characteristic traits of maternal solicitude. From the beginning I have found it difficult to reconcile these impressions with Freud's view of the initial masculine trend of the little girl's sexuality.

We might suppose that Freud intended his thesis of the original similarity of the libidinal trend in the two sexes to be confined to the sphere of sex. But then we should come into conflict with the maxim that the individual's sexuality sets the pattern for the rest of his behavior. To clear up this point we should require a large number of exact observations of the differences between the behavior of normal boys and that of normal girls during their first five or six years.

Now it is true that in these first years, little girls who have not been intimidated very often express themselves in ways which admit of interpretation as early penis envy; they ask questions, they make comparisons to their own disadvantage, they say they want one too, they express admiration of the penis or comfort themselves with the idea that they will have one later on. Supposing for the moment that such manifestations occurred very frequently or even regularly, it would still be an open question as to what weight and place in our theoretical structure we should give them. Consistently with his total view, Freud utilizes these manifestations to show how much the little girl's instinctual life is already dominated by the wish to possess a penis herself.

Against this view I would urge the following three considerations:

(1) In boys of the same age, we meet with parallel expressions in the form of wishes to possess breasts or to have a child.

(2) In neither sex have these manifestations *any influence on the child's behavior as a whole.* A boy who wishes vehemently to have breasts like his mother's may at the same time behave in general with thorough-going boyish aggressiveness. A little girl who casts glances of admiration and envy at her brother's genital may simultaneously behave as a true little woman. Thus it seems to me still an open question as to whether such manifestations at this early age are to be deemed expressions of elementary instinctual demands or whether we should not perhaps place them in a different category.

(3) Another possible category suggests itself if we accept the assumption that there is in every human being a bisexual disposition. The importance of this for our understanding of the mind has, indeed, always been stressed by Freud himself. We may suppose that though at birth the definitive sex of each individual is already fixed physically, the result of the bisexual disposition, which is always present and merely inhibited in its development, is that *psychologically* the attitude of children to their own sexual role is at first uncertain and tentative. They have no consciousness of it and therefore naturally give naïve expression to bisexual wishes. We might go further and conjecture that this uncertainty only disappears in proportion as stronger feelings of love, directed to objects, arise.

To elucidate what I have just said, I may point to the marked difference existing between these diffuse bisexual manifestations of earliest childhood, with their playful, volatile character, and those of the so-called latency period. If, at *this* age, a girl wishes to be a boy—but here again the frequency with which these wishes occur and the social factors by which they are conditioned should be investigated—the manner in which this determines her whole behavior (preference for boyish games and ways, repudiation of feminine traits) reveals that such wishes emanate from quite another depth of the mind. This picture, so different from the earlier one, already represents, however, the outcome of mental conflicts [3] that she has been through and cannot therefore, without special theoretical assumptions, be claimed as a manifestation of masculinity wishes that had been laid down biologically.

Another of the premises on which Freud builds up his view relates to the erotogenic zones. He assumes that the girl's early genital sensations and activities function essentially in the clitoris. He regards it as very doubtful whether any early vaginal masturbation takes place and even holds that the vagina remains altogether "undiscovered."

To decide this very important question we should once more require extensive and exact observation of normal children. Josine Müller [4] and I myself, as long ago as 1925, expressed doubts on the subject. Moreover, most of the information we occasionally get from gynecologists and children's physicians interested in psychology suggests that, in the early years of childhood, vaginal masturbation is at least as common as clitoral. The various data that give rise to this impression are: the frequent observation of signs of vaginal irritation, such as reddening and discharge, the relatively frequent occurrence of the introduction of foreign bodies into the vagina, and finally, the fairly common complaints by mothers that their children put their fingers into the vagina. The well-known gynecologist Wilhelm Liepmann has stated [5] that his experience has led him to believe that in early childhood and even in the first years of infancy, vaginal masturbation is much more common than clitoral, and that only in the later years of childhood are the relations reversed in favor of clitoral masturbation.

3. Horney, "On the Genesis of the Castration Complex in Women," *Int. J. Psycho-Anal.*, Vol. V (1924).

4. Josine Müller, "The Problem of Libidinal Development of the Genital Phase in Girls," *Int. J. Psycho-Anal.*, Vol. XIII (1932).

5. In a private conversation.

These general impressions cannot take the place of systematic observations, nor therefore can they lead to a final conclusion. But they do show that the exceptions Freud himself admits seem to be of frequent occurrence.

Our most natural course would be to try to throw light upon this question from our analyses, but this is difficult. At very best, the material of the patient's conscious recollections or the memories that emerge in analysis cannot be treated as unequivocal evidence, because here as everywhere else, we must also take into account the work of repression. In other words, the patient may have good reason for not remembering vaginal sensations or masturbation, just as, conversely, we must feel sceptical about her ignorance of clitoral sensations.[6]

A further difficulty is that the women who come for analysis are just those from whom one cannot expect even an average naturalness about vaginal processes. For they are always women whose sexual development has departed somehow from the normal and whose *vaginal* sensibility is disturbed in a greater or lesser degree. At the same time it does seem as if even accidental differences in the material play their part. In approximately two-thirds of my cases I have found the following state of affairs:

(1) Marked vaginal orgasm produced by manual vaginal masturbation prior to any coitus. Frigidity in the form of vaginismus and defective secretion in coitus. (I have seen only two cases of this sort, which were quite unmistakable.) I think that, in general, preference is shown for the clitoris or the labia in manual genital masturbation.

(2) Spontaneous vaginal sensations, for the most part with noticeable secretion, aroused by unconsciously stimulating situations, such as that of listening to music, motoring, swinging, having the hair combed, and certain transference situations. No manual vaginal masturbation; frigidity in coitus.

(3) Spontaneous vaginal sensations produced by extragenital masturbation, e.g., by certain motions of the body, by tight lacing,

6. In a discussion following the reading of my paper on the phallic phase before the German Psychoanalytical Society in 1931, Boehm cited several cases in which only vaginal sensations and vaginal masturbation were recollected and the clitoris had apparently remained undiscovered.

or by particular sado-masochistic fantasies. No coitus, because of the overpowering anxiety aroused whenever the vagina is about to be touched, whether by a man in coitus, by a physician in a gynecological examination, or by the subject herself in manual masturbation, or in any douching prescribed medically.

For the time being, then, my impressions may be summed up as follows: In manual genital masturbation the clitoris is more commonly selected than the vagina, *but spontaneous genital sensations resulting from general sexual excitation are more frequently located in the vagina.*

From a theoretical standpoint I think that great importance should be attached to this relatively frequent occurrence of spontaneous vaginal excitations even in patients who were ignorant, or had only a very vague knowledge, of the existence of the vagina, and whose subsequent analysis did not bring to light memories or other evidence of any sort of vaginal seduction, nor any recollection of vaginal masturbation. For this phenomenon suggests the question *whether from the very beginning sexual excitations may not have expressed themselves perceptibly in vaginal sensations.*

In order to answer this question we should have to wait for very much more extensive material than any single analyst can obtain from his own observations. Meanwhile there are a number of considerations that seem to me to favor my view.

In the first place there are the fantasies of rape that occur before coitus has taken place at all, and indeed long before puberty, and are frequent enough to merit wider interest. I can see no possible way of accounting for the origin and content of these fantasies if we are to assume the nonexistence of vaginal sexuality. For these fantasies do not in fact stop short at quite indefinite ideas of an act of violence, through which one gets a child. On the contrary, fantasies, dreams, and anxiety of this type usually betray quite unmistakably an instinctive knowledge of the actual sexual processes. The guises they assume are so numerous that I need only indicate a few of them: criminals who break in through windows or doors; men with guns who threaten to shoot; animals that creep, fly, or run inside some place (e.g., snakes, mice, moths); animals or women stabbed with knives; or trains running into a station or tunnel.

I speak of an "instinctive" knowledge of the sexual processes because we meet typically with ideas of this sort—e.g., in the anxieties and dreams of early childhood—at a period when as yet there is no intellectual knowledge derived from observation or from explanations by others. It may be asked whether such instinctive knowledge of the processes of penetration into the female body necessarily presupposes an instinctive knowledge of the existence of the vagina as the organ of reception. I think that the answer is in the affirmative if we accept Freud's view that "the child's sexual theories are modelled on the child's own sexual constitution." For this can only mean that the path traversed by the sexual theories of children is marked out and determined by spontaneously experienced impulses and organ sensations. If we accept this origin for the sexual theories, which already embody an attempt at rational elaboration, we must all the more admit it in the case of that instinctive knowledge which finds symbolic expression in play, dreams, and various forms of anxiety, and which obviously has not reached the sphere of reasoning and the elaboration which takes place there. In other words, we must assume that both the dread of rape, characteristic of puberty, and the infantile anxieties of little girls are based on vaginal organ sensations (or the instinctual impulses issuing from these), which imply that something ought to penetrate into that part of the body.

I think we have here the answer to an objection which may be raised, namely, that many dreams indicate the idea that an opening was only created when the penis first brutally penetrated the body. For such fantasies would not arise at all but for the previous existence of instincts—and the organ sensations underlying them—having the passive aim of reception. Sometimes the connection in which dreams of this type occur indicates quite clearly the origin of this particular idea. For it occasionally happens that when a general anxiety about the injurious consequences of masturbation makes its appearance, the patient has dreams with the following typical content: she is doing a piece of needlework and all at once a hole appears, of which she feels ashamed; or she is crossing above a river or a chasm on a bridge that suddenly breaks off in the middle; or she is walking along a slippery incline and all at once begins to slide and is in danger of falling over a precipice.

From such dreams we may conjecture that when these patients were children and indulged in onanistic play, they were led by vaginal sensations to the discovery of the vagina itself, and that their anxiety took the very form of the dread that they had made a hole where no hole ought to be. I would here emphasize that I have never been wholly convinced by Freud's explanation why girls suppress direct genital masturbation more easily and frequently than boys. As we know, Freud supposes [7] that (clitoral) masturbation becomes odious to little girls because comparison with the penis strikes a blow at their narcissism. When we consider the strength of the drive behind the onanistic impulses, a narcissistic mortification does not seem altogether adequate in weight to produce suppression. On the other hand, the dread that she has done herself an irreparable injury in that region might well be powerful enough to prevent vaginal masturbation, and either to compel the girl to restrict the practice to the clitoris, or else permanently to set her against all manual genital masturbation. I believe that we have further evidence of this early dread of vaginal injury in the envious comparison with the man, which we frequently hear from patients of this type, who say that men are "so nicely closed up" underneath. Similarly, that deepest anxiety which springs out of masturbation for a woman, that dread that it has made her unable to have children, seems to relate to the inside of the body rather than to the clitoris.

This is another point in favor of the existence and the significance of early vaginal excitations. We know that observation of sexual acts has a tremendously exciting effect upon children. If we accept Freud's view we must assume that such excitation produces in little girls in the main the same phallic impulses to penetrate as are evoked in little boys. But then we must ask: Whence comes the anxiety met with almost universally in the analyses of female patients—the dread of the gigantic penis that might pierce her? The origin of the idea of an excessively large penis can surely not be sought anywhere but in childhood, when the father's penis must actually have appeared menacingly large and terrifying. Or again, whence comes that understanding of the female sexual role,

7. Freud, "Some Psychological Consequences of the Anatomical Distinction between the Sexes," *Int. J. Psycho-Anal.*, Vol. VIII (1927).

evinced in the symbolism of sexual anxiety, in which those early excitations once more vibrate? And how can we account at all for the unbounded jealous fury with the mother, which commonly manifests itself in the analyses of women when memories of the "primal scene" are affectively revived? How does this come about if at that time the subject could only share in the excitations of the father?

Let me bring together the sum total of the above data. We have: reports of powerful vaginal orgasm going with frigidity in subsequent coitus; spontaneous vaginal excitation without local stimulus, but frigidity in intercourse; reflections and questions arising out of the need to understand the whole content of early sexual games, dreams, and anxieties, and later fantasies of rape, as well as reactions to early sexual observations; and finally, certain contents and consequences of the anxiety produced in women by masturbation. If I take all the foregoing data together, I can see only one hypothesis that gives a satisfactory answer to all these questions, the hypothesis, namely, that *from the very beginning the vagina plays its own proper sexual part.*

Closely connected with this train of thought is the problem of frigidity, which to my mind lies *not* in the question how the quality of libidinal sensibility becomes transmitted to the vagina,[8] but rather, how it comes about that the vagina, in spite of the sensibility it already possesses, either fails altogether to react or reacts in a disproportionately small degree to the very strong libidinal exci-

8. In reply to Freud's assumption that the libido may adhere so closely to the clitoral zone that it becomes difficult or impossible for sensibility to be transferred to the vagina, may I venture to enlist Freud against Freud? For it was he who showed convincingly how ready we are to snatch at fresh possibilities of pleasure and how even processes that have no sexual quality—e.g., movements of the body, speech, or thought—may be eroticized and that the same is actually true of tormenting or distressing experiences such as pain or anxiety. Are we then to suppose that in coitus, which furnishes the very fullest opportunities for pleasure, the woman recoils from availing herself of them! Since to my thinking this is a problem that really does not arise, I cannot follow H. Deutsch and M. Klein in their conjectures about the transference of the libido from the oral to the genital zone. There can be no doubt that in many cases there is a close connection between the two. The only question is whether we are to regard the libido as being "transferred" or whether it is simply inevitable that when an oral attitude has been early established and persists, it should manifest itself in the genital sphere *also*.

tations furnished by all the emotional and local stimuli in coitus? Surely there could be only *one* factor stronger than the will for pleasure, and that factor is anxiety.

We are now immediately confronted by the problem of what is meant by this vaginal anxiety or rather by its infantile conditioning factors. Analysis reveals, first of all, castration impulses against the man, and associated with these, an anxiety whose source is twofold: on the one hand, the subject dreads her own hostile impulses, and on the other, the retribution she anticipates in accordance with the law of talion, namely, that the contents of her body will be destroyed, stolen, or sucked out. Now these impulses in themselves are, as we know, for the most part not of recent origin, but can be traced to infantile feelings of rage and impulses of revenge against the father, feelings called forth by the disappointments and frustrations the little girl has suffered.

Very similar in content to these forms of anxiety is that described by Melanie Klein, which can be traced back to early destructive impulses directed against the body of the mother. Once more it is a question of the dread of retribution, which may take various forms, but its essence is in general that everything which penetrates the body or is already there (food, faeces, children) may become dangerous.

Although at bottom these forms of anxiety are so far analogous to the genital anxiety of boys, they take on a specific character from that proneness to anxiety which is part of the biological make-up of girls. In this and earlier papers I have already indicated what are these sources of anxiety and here I need only complete and sum up what has been said before:

(1) They proceed first of all from the tremendous difference in size between the father and the little girl, between the genitals of father and child. We need not trouble to decide whether the disparity between penis and vagina is inferred from observation or whether it is instinctively apprehended. The quite comprehensible and indeed inevitable result is that any fantasy of gratifying the tension produced by vaginal sensations (i.e., the craving to take into oneself, to receive) gives rise to anxiety on the part of the ego. As I showed in my paper "The Dread of Woman," I believe that in this biologically determined form of feminine anxiety

we have something specifically different from the boy's original genital anxiety in relation to his mother. When he fantasies the fulfillment of genital impulses he is confronted with a fact very wounding to his self-esteem ("my penis is too small for my mother"); the little girl, on the other hand, is faced with destruction of part of her body. Hence, carried back to its ultimate biological foundations, the man's dread of the woman is genital-narcissistic, while the woman's dread of the man is physical.

(2) A second specific source of anxiety, the universality and significance of which is emphasized by Daly,[9] is the little girl's observation of menstruation in adult relatives. Beyond all (secondary!) interpretations of castration she sees demonstrated for the first time the vulnerability of the female body. Similarly, her anxiety is appreciably increased by observations of a miscarriage or parturition by her mother. Since, in the minds of children and (when repression has been at work) in the unconscious of adults, there is a close connection between coitus and parturition, this anxiety may take the form of a dread not only of parturition but also of coitus itself.

(3) Finally, we have a third specific source of anxiety in the little girl's reactions (again due to the anatomical structure of her body) to her early attempts at vaginal masturbation. I think that the consequences of these reactions may be more lasting in girls than in boys, and this for the following reasons: In the first place she cannot actually ascertain the effect of masturbation. A boy, when experiencing anxiety about his genital, can always convince himself anew that it does exist and is intact.[10] A little girl has no means of proving to herself that her anxiety has no foundation in reality. On the contrary, her early attempts at vaginal masturbation bring home to her once more the fact of her greater physical vulnerability,[11] for I have found in analysis that it is by no means

9. Daly, "Der Menstruationskomplex," *Imago*, Bd. XIV (1928).

10. These real circumstances must most certainly be taken into account, as well as the strength of unconscious sources of anxiety. For instance, a man's castration anxiety may be intensified as the result of phimosis.

11. It is perhaps not without interest to recall that the gynecologist Wilhelm Liepmann (whose standpoint is not that of analysis), in his book *Psychologie der Frau*, says that the "vulnerability" of women is one of the specific characteristics of their sex.

uncommon for little girls, when attempting masturbation or engaging in sexual play with other children, to incur pain or little injuries, obviously caused by infinitesimal ruptures of the hymen.[12]

Where the general development is favorable—i.e., where the object relations of childhood have not become a fruitful source of conflict—this anxiety is satisfactorily mastered and the way is then open for the subject to assent to her feminine role. That in unfavorable cases the effect of the anxiety is more persistent with girls than with boys is, I think, indicated by the fact that, with the former, it is relatively more frequent for direct genital masturbation to be given up altogether, or at least it is confined to the more easily accessible clitoris with its lesser cathexis of anxiety. Often everything connected with the vagina—the knowledge of its existence, vaginal sensations, and instinctual impulses—succumbs to a relentless repression; in short, the fiction is conceived and long maintained that the vagina does not exist, a fiction that at the same time determines the little girl's preference for the masculine sexual role.

All these considerations seem to me to be greatly in favor of the hypothesis that *behind the "failure to discover" the vagina is a denial of its existence.*

It remains to consider the question of what importance the existence of early vaginal sensations or the "discovery" of the vagina has for our whole conception of early feminine sexuality. Though Freud does not expressly state it, it is nonetheless clear that if the vagina remains originally "undiscovered," this is one of the strongest arguments in favor of the assumption of a biologically determined, primary penis envy in little girls or of their original phallic organization. For if no vaginal sensations or cravings existed, but the whole libido were concentrated on the clitoris, phallically conceived of, then and then only could we understand how little girls, for want of any specific source of

12. Such experiences often come to light in analysis, firstly, in the form of screen memories of injuries to the genital region, sustained in later life, possibly through a fall. To these recollections patients react with a terror and shame out of all proportion to the cause. Secondly, there may be an overwhelming dread lest such an injury should possibly occur.

pleasure of their own or of any specific feminine wishes, must be driven to concentrate their whole attention on the clitoris, to compare it with the boy's penis, and then, since they are in fact at a disadvantage in this comparison, to feel themselves definitely slighted.[13] If on the other hand, as I conjecture, a little girl experiences from the very beginning vaginal sensations and corresponding impulses, she must from the outset have a lively sense of this specific character of her own sexual role, and a primary penis envy of the strength postulated by Freud would be hard to account for.

In this paper I have shown that the hypothesis of a primary phallic sexuality carries with it momentous consequences for our whole conception of feminine sexuality. If we assume that there is a specifically feminine, primary, vaginal sexuality, the former hypothesis, if not altogether excluded, is at least so drastically restricted that those consequences become quite problematical.

13. Helene Deutsch arrives at this basis for penis envy by a process of logical argument. Cf. Deutsch, "The Significance of Masochism in the Mental Life of Women," *Int. J. Psycho-Anal.*, Vol. XI (1930).

PSYCHOGENIC FACTORS IN FUNCTIONAL

FEMALE DISORDERS*

∘∘∘

WITHIN THE LAST thirty or forty years there has been much discussion in the gynecologic literature on the influence of the psychic factors in female disorders. The spectrum of opinions is very wide. On the one hand there is a tendency to allow these factors to shrink to a minor significance —to emphasize, for instance, that of course there are emotional factors, but to consider them dependent on constitutional, glandular, and other bodily conditions.

On the other hand we see the tendency to ascribe to psychogenic factors a very great influence. The supporters of this point of view are inclined to see here the essential origin not only for more or less obvious functional disorders such as pseudocyesis, vaginismus, frigidity, menstrual disorders, hyperemesis, etc., but they also claim a psychological influence that seems to be beyond suspicion for diseases and disturbances, such as premature ad postmature delivery, certain forms of metritis, sterility, and some forms of leucorrhea.

The fact that physical changes can be brought about by psychic stimuli is not subject to doubt since Pavlov's experiments have put it on an empirical basis. We know that by stimulating the appetite the secretion of the stomach can be affected, that the heart rhythm and the bowel movements can be accelerated under the influence of fear, that certain vasomotor changes, as for instance blushing, can be an expression of a shame reaction.

* Read at a meeting of the Chicago Gynecological Society, November 18, 1932. Reprinted from the *American Journal of Obstetrics and Gynecology* 25:694 (1933), published by the C. V. Mosby Company, St. Louis, Missouri.

We have also a rather exact picture of the paths these stimuli follow from the central nervous system to the peripheral organs.

It seems to be quite a jump from these rather simple connections to raising the question of whether a dysmenorrhea can be brought about by psychic conflicts. Yet I think the fundamental difference is not so much in the process itself, but in the methodologic approach. You can arrange an experimental situation where you stimulate the appetite of a person and where you can measure the secretion of the stomach glands. You can measure exactly the changes in secretion that take place when you produce some sort of fright reaction in a person, but you cannot arrange an experimental situation where a dysmenorrhea is brought about. The emotional processes underlying a dysmenorrhea are much too complicated to be established in an experimental situation; but even if you could by experiment expose a person to certain very complicated emotional conditions, you could not expect any concrete results, because a dysmenorrhea is never the result of just one emotional conflict, but always presupposes a series of emotional preconditions whose foundation has been laid at different times.

For these reasons it is impossible to learn about these problems by way of experiment. A method that can reveal to us the connection between certain emotional forces and a symptom, as for instance dysmenorrhea, must obviously be a historical one. It must enable us to understand the specific emotional structure of a person and the correlation of the emotions with the symptom through a very detailed history of her life.

There is as far as I see only one psychological school that offers such an insight with any high degree of scientific exactness—namely, psychoanalysis. In psychoanalysis you get a picture of the nature, the content, and the dynamic strength of the psychic factors as they are effective in real life—a knowledge that is indispensable if one wants to discuss scientifically the question of whether or not functional disorders can be brought about by emotional factors.

I shall not go into the details of the method here, but shall only present in a very concise form some of the emotional factors that in my analytical work I found essential for the understanding of functional female disorders.

I start with the fact that struck my attention through its continuous repetition. My women patients came to be analyzed for
the most different psychical reasons: states of anxiety of all sorts,
compulsion neuroses, depressions, inhibitions in work and in
contact with people, character difficulties. In each neurosis their
psychosexual life was disturbed. Their relations with men or with
children or with both were in some way seriously hampered.
What struck me was this: Among these very different types of
neuroses there was not one case without some functional disturbance of the genital system—frigidity in all degrees, vaginismus,
all sorts of menstrual disorders, pruritus, pains and discharge that
had no organic basis and disappeared after uncovering certain
unconscious conflicts, various hypochondriacal fears, such as fears
of cancer or of not being normal, and some disturbances in pregnancy and childbirth that seemed to indicate a psychogenic origin.

Here three questions arise:

(1) This coincidence of a disturbed psychosexual life on the
one hand and functional female disorders on the other may be
very striking—but is this coincidence a regular one?

An analyst has the advantage of knowing a number of cases
very thoroughly, but after all, even a busy analyst sees only comparatively few cases. Therefore even if we find our results corroborated by other observations as well as ethnological facts, this
question about the frequency and the validity of our findings is
one to which the gynecologists should at some future date give
an answer.*

Of course, for them to do this investigation would require
time and psychological training; but if only part of the energy
that is put into laboratory work were put into psychological
training, it surely would help to clarify the problem.

(2) If we assume this coincidence exists regularly, could not
both the psychosexual disturbances and the functional ones arise
on the common basis of constitutional or glandular conditions?

* EDITOR'S NOTE: Dr. Horney is suggesting that gynecologists would be able
to evaluate their findings more accurately and to contribute significant statistics because of the large number of patients they see compared to psychoanalysts.

I do not wish to go into a detailed discussion of these very complicated problems now, but only to point out that according to my observations there is no regular coexistence of these functional factors and emotional disturbances. There are, for instance, frigid women with distinct masculine attitudes and strong feelings of aversion for the female role. The secondary sex characteristics—voice, hair, bones—of some of this group tend toward the masculine, but most of them have an absolutely female habitus. With both groups—the masculine-looking and the obviously feminine ones—you can find out from what conflicts the emotional changes started; but only in the first group could the conflicts have arisen on a constitutional basis. I have the impression that as long as we do not know more about constitutional factors and their particular influence on later attitudes it is pseudoexactness to assume too strict a connection. Furthermore, such an assumption can lead to very dangerous therapeutic consequences if one neglects the psychical factors. For instance, in the most modern German textbook of gynecology, by Halban and Seitz, one contributor, Matthes, describes the case of a girl seeking treatment for a dysmenorrhea that she had had for one and a half years. She told him that she had caught a cold at a dance. Later on he found out that she then had started a sexual relationship with a man. She told Matthes that she was strongly sexually aroused by the man but at the same time was enraged by him. As she represented what he calls an "intersexual type," Matthes advised her to give up the man, acting on the theory that she was the type of person who never can be happy in a sexual relationship. She tried to follow his advice and had two menstruations without pain. She then resumed her love affair and the pains recurred.

This seems to be a rather radical therapeutic conclusion on the basis of very slight knowledge and reminds me of the saying in the Bible, "If thine eye offend thee, pluck it out."

From the therapeutic point of view it seems better to look at the psychic level for conflicts that may have arisen from some constitutional factor, particularly as we often see these same conflicts without the presence of such a factor.

(3) It is the third question that I wish to discuss now. Its precise formulation would be, "Is there a specific correlation

between certain mental attitudes in psychosexual life and certain functional genital disturbances?" Unfortunately human nature is not so simple, and our knowledge is not far enough advanced to enable us to make very clear and rigid statements. In fact you will find certain fundamental psychosexual conflicts in all of these patients. These conflicts correspond to the fact that some degree of frigidity is present in all of the patients—at least a transitional frigidity; but in a regular correlation with certain functional symptoms, some specific emotions and factors play a predominant role.

With frigidity as the basic disturbance, one finds invariably the following characteristic mental attitudes:

In the first place frigid women have a very ambivalent attitude toward men, which invariably contains elements of suspicion, hostility, and fear. Very seldom are these elements completely overt.

For instance, one patient had the conscious conviction that all men were criminals and ought to be killed. This conviction was the natural consequence of her conception of the sexual act as something bloody and painful. She considered every woman who married as a heroine. Generally you find this antagonism in a disguised form; and one can get insight into a patient's real attitude toward men, not from her comments but from her behavior. Girls may tell you frankly how much they care for men, how they are inclined to idealize them, but at the same time you may see that they are likely to drop their "boy friends" very rudely without any apparent reason. To give a typical example: I had a patient X who had rather friendly sexual relations with men. These never lasted longer than about a year. Regularly after a short interval she felt increasingly irritated with the man until she could stand him no longer. She then sought and found some excuse to drop him. In fact her hostile impulses toward men became so strong that she was afraid she might do them harm and avoided them.

Sometimes you may find patients who tell you they feel devoted to their husbands, but a deeper investigation will show you all those small but very disturbing signs of hostility that come out in everyday life, such as a fundamental depreciative attitude toward the husband, belittling his merits, withdrawing from his interests or his friends, making too great financial claims, or waging a quiet but consistent fight for power.

You can in these cases not only get a more or less distinct impression that frigidity is a direct expression of undercurrent streams of hostility, but in certain advanced phases of the analysis you can also trace very accurately how the frigidity has been initiated when a new source of inner aversion against the man is revealed—and how it stops when these conflicts have been overcome.

Here is a marked difference in the psychology of men and of women. In the average case, sexuality in women is much more closely tied up with tenderness, with feelings, with affection, than in men. An average man will not be impotent even where he does not feel any particular tenderness for the woman. On the contrary, there is very often a split between sex life and love life so that in extremely pathologic cases such a man can only have sex relations with a woman whom he does not care for and can feel that he has no sexual desires for and is even impotent toward a woman of whom he is really fond.

With most women you will find a closer unity between sex feelings and their whole emotional life, probably for obvious biologic reasons. Therefore a secretly hostile attitude will express itself very easily in the inability to give or receive sexually.

This defensive attitude toward men need not be very deeply rooted. In some cases men who are able to awaken tender feelings in these women may be perfectly able to overcome the frigidity; but in another series of cases this attitude of hostile defense is very deep and the roots of it must be exposed if the woman is to be rid of it.

In this second series you will find that the feelings of antagonism toward men have been acquired in early childhood. To understand the far-reaching consequences of early experience in life it is not necessary to know much about analytical theory, but only to be clear on two points: that children are born with sexual feelings and that they can feel very passionately, probably much more so than we grownups with all our inhibitions.

You will find in the history of these women that there may

be deeply engraved disappointments in their early love life: a father or brother to whom they felt tenderly attached and who disappointed them; or a brother who was preferred to them; or a quite different situation, as in the following case. A patient had seduced a younger brother when she was eleven years old. Some years later this brother died of the grippe. She had intense guilt feelings. Still, after thirty years, when she came to be analyzed she felt convinced that she had caused her brother's death. She believed that as a consequence of her seduction her brother had started to masturbate and his death had been the consequence of his masturbation. This guilt feeling made her hate her own female role. She wanted to be a man, rather demonstratively envied men, let them down wherever she could, had fierce castration dreams and fantasies, and was absolutely frigid.

This case, by the way, throws some light on the psychogenesis of vaginismus. The patient had not been deflowered until four weeks after her marriage—and the defloration was done by a surgeon, even though there was nothing abnormal about her hymen and her husband was potent. The spasm was partly an expression of her strong aversion against the female role, partly a defense mechanism against her castration impulses toward the envied man.

This aversion to the female role often exerts a great influence, no matter how it may have started. In one case there was a younger brother who was preferred by both parents. The envy felt by the patient toward him poisoned her whole life and particularly her relations with men. She wanted to be a man herself and played this role in fantasies and dreams. During intercourse she sometimes quite consciously had the wish to change sex roles.

You will find in these frigid women another conflict situation that is often dynamically still more important—a conflict with the mother or with an older sister. Consciously the feeling toward the mother may be different. Sometimes these patients admit at the beginning of treatment—even to themselves—only the positive side of their relationship with their mothers. Possibly they have already felt struck by the observation that in spite of their craving for the mother's love, they have in fact always done just the contrary of what the mother would have liked them to do. In other cases there is overt hatred. But even if they realize the existence of a conflict, they know neither the essential reasons for it nor the influence it has on their psychosexual life. One of these essential features may be, for instance, that the mother keeps on representing for these women the agency which forbids sex life and sex pleasure. An ethnologist recently reported a primitive tribal custom that throws light on the ubiquity of these conflicts: When the father dies, the daughters remain in the house of the deceased, but the sons leave it, because they fear that the dead father's spirit might be hostile to them and do them harm. When the mother dies, the sons remain in the house, but the daughters leave it for fear that a spirit of the mother might kill them. This custom expresses the same antagonism and fear of retaliation that is found in the analysis of frigid women.

Here one who does not know the process of analysis may ask: If these conflicts are not conscious to the patients, how can you believe so definitely that they exist and that they play this particular role? There is an answer to this question, which however may be difficult for someone lacking in analytic experience to understand. The patient's old irrational attitudes are revived and reactivated toward the analyst. For instance, the patient X had consciously an affectionate attitude toward me, though it was always intermingled with some fear. But at the time when her old infantile hatred against her mother came nearer to the surface, she trembled with fear in the waiting room and emotionally saw in me something like a ruthless evil spirit. It became evident that in these situations she had transferred an old fear of her mother to me. One particular incident gave us insight into the important part this fear of the forbidding mother played in her frigidity. At a period in the analysis when her sexual inhibitions had already diminished I was away for a fortnight. She told me afterward that one evening she had been together with some friends and had drunk some alcohol—but not more than she could ordinarily tolerate—and that she had no memory of what followed. But her boy friend told her that she had been very excited, that she had asked to have intercourse and had a full orgasm (she had been completely frigid until then) and that she had exclaimed several times in a sort of triumphant voice, "I have Horney holidays." I, as the forbidding mother in her fantasy, was absent and therefore she could be a loving woman without fear.

Another patient with a vaginismus and later frigidity had transferred to me the old fear she had felt toward her mother and particularly toward her sister who was eight years older than she. The patient made several attempts to have relationships with men but always failed because of her complexes. Regularly in such situations she would feel infuriated about me and sometimes even expressed the rather paranoid idea that I had kept the man away from her. Though she realized intellectually that I was the one who wanted to help her to find an adjustment, the old fear of her sister then had the upper hand. And at the time when she had had her first sexual experience with a man she promptly had an anxiety dream in which her sister chased her.

There are in every case of frigidity other psychical factors involved, some of which I shall now mention. But I shall not go into the connections they have with frigidity and shall only point out the importance they may have for certain other functional disorders.

There is above all the influence that masturbation fears may exert on mental attitudes as well as on bodily processes. It is well known that, given such fears concerning masturbation, nearly every disease can be regarded as a result of them. The particular form these fears often take with women is the fear that the genital organs are physically damaged by masturbation. This fear is often connected with a very fantastic idea that they once were like a boy and have been castrated. Such a fear may express itself in different forms:

(1) In a vague but deep fear of not being "normal."

(2) In hypochondriacal fears and symptoms, such as pains and discharges without an organic basis, which drive them to seek gynecologic advice. They then will get suggestive treatment or some sort of reassurance and will feel better—but naturally the fear returns and they come back with the same complaints. Sometimes this fear leads them to insist upon an operation. They have the feeling that something is physically wrong with them, which

can be corrected only by such radical means as an operation.

(3) The fears may furthermore take this form: Because I have damaged myself, I will never be able to have a child. In very young girls the fear in this connection may be sometimes quite conscious. But even these young patients usually will tell you first that they consider having children disgusting and never wish to have any. Only much later you learn that this feeling of disgust represents for them a kind of "sour grapes" reaction against their very intense earlier wishes to have many children and that the above-mentioned fear has led them to deny this wish.

There may be many conflicting unconscious tendencies connected with the wish for a child. The natural maternal instinct may be counteracted by certain unconscious motives. I cannot go into details now and shall only mention one possibility: For those women who in some part of their mind have an intense wish to be a man, pregnancy and motherhood, which represent the equivalent female accomplishment, have an enhanced significance.

I have unfortunately never seen a case of pseudocyesis, but probably it too results from unconscious reinforcement of the wish for a child. Certainly a temporary amenorrhea will indicate a wish to have a child at any price. Every gynecologist knows women who are unusually nervous and depressed, but are perfectly happy and poised as long as they are pregnant. For them, too, pregnancy represents a particular form of satisfaction.

What is reinforced in the cases I have in mind is not so much the idea of having a child, nursing and caressing it, but the idea of pregnancy itself; of bearing the child in their body. The state of pregnancy has for them an exquisite narcissistic value. Two such cases had a postmature delivery. It is too soon to draw any conclusions, but with all critical cautiousness one could at least think here of the possibility that the unconscious wish of keeping the child within might be an explanation for some cases of postmature delivery that are otherwise inexplicable.

Another factor that sometimes plays a role is an intense fear of dying at delivery. This fear itself may or may not be conscious. The real origin of the fear is never conscious. One essential element in it, according to my experience, is an old antagonism against the pregnant mother. One patient I have in mind, who had an extreme fear of dying in childbirth, remembered that she had as a child for many years anxiously watched her mother to see if she was pregnant again. She never could see a pregnant woman on the street without feeling the impulse to kick her womb and naturally had the retaliation fear that something equally awful would happen to her.

On the other hand the maternal instinct may be counteracted by unconscious hostile impulses against the child. Here very interesting problems are the possible influence of such impulses on hyperemesis, premature delivery, and depressions after childbirth.

To go back once more to the masturbation fears, I have already mentioned that they might result from the patient's idea of being physically damaged and that this fear might lead to hypochondriacal symptoms. There is another way in which these fears may be expressed: in the attitude toward menstruation. The idea of being damaged makes these women resent their own genitals as a sort of wound, and menstruation is therefore emotionally conceived of as a corroboration of this assumption. For these women there is a close association between bleeding and a wound. It is understandable from this that for these women menstruation can never be a natural process, and that they will have a deep feeling of disgust about it.

This leads me to the problem of menorrhagia and dysmenorrhea. Of course, I am only speaking of those cases in which there is neither any local nor other organic cause. The basis for an understanding of any functional menstrual disorder is this: The psychical equivalent of the bodily processes in the genital organs at that time is increased libidinal tension. A woman who is very poised in her psychosexual development will meet this without any particular difficulties. But there are many women who barely succeed in maintaining some sort of balance and for whom this increased libidinal tension is the straw that breaks the camel's back.

Under the pressure of this tension, all sorts of infantile fantasies will be revived; particularly those having some connection with the process of bleeding. These fantasies have, generally speaking, the content that the sex act is something cruel, bloody, and painful. I found without any exception that fantasies of this kind played a determining role in all patients with menorrhagia and dysmenorrhea. The dysmenorrhea usually starts, if not in puberty, at the time when the patient comes in contact with adult sex problems.

I shall try to give some examples: One patient of mine who always suffered from a profuse menorrhagia when thinking of intercourse, had a vision of blood. In analysis we found that certain childhood memories contained determinants for this vision, which appeared under certain circumstances.

She was the oldest of eight children and her most frightening memories concerned the time when a new child was born. She had heard her mother scream and had seen bowls of blood carried out of her mother's room. The early association between childbirth, sex, and blood was so close for her that one night when her mother had a lung hemorrhage, she immediately connected the hemorrhaging with the occurrence of marital relations between her parents. Her menstruation revived for her these old infantile impressions and fantasies of a very bloody sex life.

The patient I have just mentioned had a severe dysmenorrhea. She herself was perfectly aware that her real sex life had to do with all sorts of sadistic fantasies. Whenever she heard or read of cruelties, she felt sexually aroused. She described the pains she had at the time of menstruation as being as if her insides were torn out. This specific form was determined by infantile fantasies. She remembered having had as a small girl the idea that in intercourse the man tore out something from the body of the woman. In the dysmenorrhea she emotionally acted out these old fantasies.

I suppose that a great many of my statements concerning the psychogenic factors may sound utterly fantastic, though perhaps all this is not really fantastic but only foreign to our usual medical thinking. If one wishes to have more than a mere emotional judgment, there is only one scientifically valid way—a testing of the facts. The idea that uncovering brings to light specific psychical roots and that symptoms disappear during this process is no proof that it was the uncovering process that brought about this cure. Any skillful suggestion may have the same result.

Scientific testing* ought to be the same here as in other fields of science: to apply the psychoanalytical technique of free association, and see if the findings are similar. Every judgment that has not met this requirement lacks scientific value.

Yet it seems to me that there is still another way for the gynecologist to get at least a feeling of evidence for the specific correlation of certain emotional factors and certain functional disturbances. If only some time and attention were given to the patients, at least some of them would reveal their conflicts very easily. I think this way of proceeding might even have some direct therapeutic value. A correct analysis can only be done by a physician who has had adequate psychoanalytic training. It is a procedure not less incisive than an operation. Yet there is not only major but also minor surgery. A minor psychotherapy would consist in dealing with the more recent conflicts and uncovering their connection with the symptoms. The work already being done in this area could easily be greatly extended.

There is only one limitation to such a possibility, which one has to realize: One must have a thorough psychologic knowledge if one wishes to avoid mistakes; particularly those that may stir up emotions with which one is not able to cope.

* EDITOR'S NOTE: A reformulation of Horney's statements may further clarify her meaning. The requirements for scientific validity are that a number of trained psychoanalysts, using the technique of free association in the investigation of a series of patients with functional female disorders and psychosexual disturbances, would uncover similar psychodynamic configurations; that these patients would respond to psychoanalytic therapy with an amelioration of their symptoms and a resolution of the specific psychic conflicts and defenses uncovered; and that more analysts would reconfirm these findings with increasing numbers of such patients.

MATERNAL CONFLICTS*

‹‹‹

DURING THE LAST 30 or 40 years there have been contrasting evaluations of the educational capacities innate in mothers. About 30 years ago the maternal instinct was considered an infallible guide in the upbringing of children. When this proved inadequate it was followed by an equally overstressed belief in theoretical knowledge about education. Unfortunately, equipment with the tools of scientific educational theories proved to be no more perfect guarantee against failure than the maternal instinct had been. And now we are in the midst of a return to stressing the emotional side of the mother-child relationship. This time, however, not with a vague conception of instincts to be relied upon, but with one definite problem: What are the emotional factors that can disturb a desirable attitude and from what sources do they originate?

Without attempting to discuss the great variety of conflicts that one sees when analyzing mothers, I will endeavor to present here only one particular type, in which the relation of the mother to her own parents is reflected in her attitude toward her children. I have in mind the example of a woman who came to me at the age of thirty-five. She was a teacher, endowed with intellect and capacity, a striking personality and, on the whole, appeared to be very well balanced. One of her two problems concerned a moderate depression she suffered upon learning that her husband had deceived her with another woman. She herself was a woman of high moral standards, reinforced by her education and vocation, but she had cultivated a tolerant attitude toward others, and

* Presented at the 1933 meeting of the American Orthopsychiatric Association. Reprinted from *The American Journal of Orthopsychiatry*, Vol. III, No. 4 (October 1933). Copyright, The American Orthopsychiatric Association, Inc. Reproduced by permission.

therefore her naturally existing hostile reactions toward her husband were not consciously acceptable to her. Still, this loss of faith in her husband affected her attitude toward life and held her in its toils. Her other problem concerned her thirteen-year-old son, who was afflicted with a severe obsessional neurosis and suffered states of anxiety, which his own analysis showed were related to his unusual attachment for his mother. Both of these problems were satisfactorily cleared up. Then it was five years before she returned, this time with a difficulty that had remained concealed during the first period. She had remarked that some of her male pupils displayed more than tender feelings for her—in fact, there was evidence that certain boys had fallen passionately in love with her and she asked herself if she had had anything to do with stimulating such passion and love. She felt that she was at fault in her attitude toward these pupils. She accused herself of responding emotionally to this passion and love, and indulged in severe self-reproach. She was firmly convinced that I must condemn her for her part and when I did not she was incredulous. I tried to reassure her, saying that there was nothing extraordinary in the situation and that if one is able to work so intensely in a field as to do really fine creative work, it is most natural that the deeper instincts should be functioning. That explanation did not relieve her, and so we had to seek for the deeper emotional sources of these relations.

What finally came out was the following. First, the sexual nature of her own feelings became apparent. One of the boys followed her to the city where she was analyzed, and she actually fell in love with this young boy, who was twenty years of age. It was rather striking to see this poised and restrained woman fighting with herself and with me, fighting against the urge to have a love relationship with a comparatively immature boy, and combatting all the conventional barriers that she thought were the only hindrance to the love relation.

It then developed that this love did not really apply to the boy himself. This boy and others before him represented for her, in an obvious way, the image of the father. All these boys had certain physical and mental trends that reminded her of her father, and in dreams these boys and the father often appeared as one and the same person.

She became aware, consciously, that behind rather bitter opposition toward her father in her adolescent years, a deep, passionate love for him was concealed. In the case of a father fixation the subject usually shows a pronounced preference for older men, because they seem to suggest the father. In this case, the infantile age relationships were reversed. Her attempts to solve the problem had taken this form in fantasy: "I am not the small child who cannot get the love of my unattainable father, but if I am big, then he will be small, then I shall be the mother, and my father will be my son." She remembered that at the death of her father her wish had been to lie down beside him and put him on her breast as a mother would do with her child.

Further analysis made it apparent that these boy pupils represented only a second phase of the transference of her love for her father. Her son was the first recipient of this transferred love, and then it was turned toward these boys who were of the same age as her son, in order to divert her mind from concentrating on an incestuous love object. Her love for her pupils was an escape, a second form of her love for her own son, who represented the primary incarnation of her father. As soon as she became aware of her passion for this other boy, the enormous tension that she felt toward her son was diminished. Hitherto she had insisted upon receiving a letter from him every day, or otherwise she was very much worried. When her passion for the other boy took hold of her, the emotional overcharge toward her son diminished immediately, which is proof of how this boy, and others before him, actually were substituted for her own son. Her husband, too, had been younger and a much weaker personality than she was, and her relation to him also had quite distinctly a mother-son character. Her bond to her husband had lost its emotional significance for her as soon as the son was born. In fact it was this emotional overcharge toward her son that had created in him a severe obsessional neurosis at the beginning of his puberty.

One of our basic analytic conceptions is that sexuality does not start at puberty but at birth, and consequently our early love feelings always have a sexual character. As we see it in the whole animal kingdom, sexuality means attraction between the different sexes. We see this expressed in childhood in that the daughter feels instinctively a greater attraction toward her father and the son toward his mother. The factors of competition and jealousy with regard to the parent of the same sex is responsible for conflicts arising from this source. In the above case we have seen the working of the conflict in a tragic way, as it progresses through three generations.

I have seen such transference of a love from the father to the son in five cases. This revival of the feelings for the father usually remains unconscious. The sexual nature of the feeling for the son was conscious in only two cases; what is usually conscious is only the high emotional charge of this mother-son relationship. To understand the features of such a relation, one has to realize that by its very nature it will be a disturbed one. Not only the incestuous sexual elements are transferred from the infantile relation to the father, but also the hostile elements that necessarily were once connected with them. A certain residue of hostile feelings is unavoidable, as a result of equally unavoidable affects caused by jealousy, frustration, and guilt feelings. If the feelings toward the father are in their entity transferred to the son, the son will receive not only the love but the old hostility. As a rule, both will be repressed. The one form in which the conflict between love and hate may consciously come out is an over-solicitous attitude. These mothers see their children constantly beset by dangers. They have an exaggerated fear that the little ones may contract illnesses or infections, or meet with accidents. They are fanatical about their care. The woman of whom we have spoken protected herself by absolutely immersing herself in the care of her son, whom she saw surrounded by innumerable perils. When he was a small boy everything near him had to be sterilized. And even later, if he met with the slightest mishap she would remain home from school and devote herself to his care.

In other cases, such mothers do not dare to touch their sons, for fear of injuring them themselves. Two women whom I have in mind kept a nurse exclusively for the small son's care, although this expense did not fit in with their budgets, and the nurse's presence was, from the emotional side as well, a great inconvenience to the household. Yet the mothers preferred to suffer the presence of the nurses, because their function of protecting the sons from alleged dangers was too important.

There is still another reason for the over-solicitous attitude of such mothers. Their love having the character of a forbidden incestuous love, they constantly feel the threat of the son's being taken away from them. One woman dreamed, for instance, that she was standing in a church with her son in her arms, and she had to sacrifice him to some gruesome mother-goddess.

Another complication in the case of a father-fixation often is due to the jealousy existing between mother and daughter. A certain amount of competition between mother and maturing daughter is a natural thing. But when the mother's own Œdipus situation has caused an excessively strong sense of rivalry, it may take grotesque forms and start early in the infancy of the daughter. Such a rivalry may show in a general intimidation of the child, efforts to ridicule and belittle her, prevent her from looking attractive or meeting boys, and so on, always with the secret aim of thwarting the daughter in her female development. Though it may be difficult to detect the jealousy behind the various forms in which it is expressed, the whole psychological mechanism is of a simple basic structure and therefore needs no detailed description.

Let us consider the more complicated solution that arises when a woman has felt a particularly strong tie, not to her father, but to her own mother. Certain features have stood out consistently in cases of this sort that I have analyzed. The following is typical: A girl may have reasons to acquire a dislike for her own female world very early, perhaps because her mother has intimidated her, or she has experienced a thoroughly disillusioning disappointment from the side of the father or brother; she may have had early sexual experiences that frightened her; or she may have found that her brother was greatly preferred to herself.

As a result of all this she emotionally turns away from her innate sexual role and develops masculine tendencies and fantasies. The masculine fantasies, if once established, lead to a competitive attitude toward men that adds itself to the original resentment toward men. It is obvious that women with such attitudes are not very well fitted for marriage. They are frigid and dissatisfied and their masculine tendencies will show, for instance, in the wish to be domineering. When these women marry and have children, they are likely to show an exaggerated attachment to them, which is often described as a pent-up libido fastened upon the child. This description, though correct, does not give any insight into the particular processes going on. Realizing the origin of such development, we can understand the single features as the result of attempts to solve certain early conflicts.

The masculine tendencies are shown by the woman's domineering attitude and her desire to control the children absolutely. Or she may be afraid of this, and therefore be too lax with them. One of the two extremes may show. She may pry into the children's affairs relentlessly or she may be afraid of the sadistic tendencies involved, and remain passive, not daring to interfere. The resentment against the female role comes out in teaching the children that men are brutes and women are suffering creatures, that the female role is distasteful and pitiable, that menstruation is a disease ("curse") and sexual intercourse a sacrifice to the lusts of the husband. These mothers will be intolerant of any sexual manifestations, particularly on the side of the daughters, but very frequently on the part of the sons, too.

Very often these masculine mothers will develop an over-attachment to the daughter, similar to that which other mothers feel toward the son. Very often the daughter reciprocates with a too strong attachment to the mother. The daughter becomes alienated from her own female role and as a consequence of all these factors, she finds it difficult in later life to achieve normal relationships with men.

In still another important manner the children may actually and directly revive the images and functions of the parents. The parents are not only the objects of love and hatred during infantile and adolescent years, but also of infantile fears. Much of the formation of our conscience, particularly the unconscious part of it that we call superego, is due to the incorporation of the frightening images of the parents in our personalities.

This old infantile fear once attached to the father or mother may also be transferred to the children and may lead to an immense but vague feeling of insecurity with regard to them. This seems to be particularly true in this country, for complicated reasons. Parents show this fear in two main forms. They are in terror of being disapproved of by their children, afraid that their own conduct, their drinking, smoking, sexual relations, will be criticized by the children. Or they worry incessantly about whether they are giving the children the proper education and training. The reason is a secret sense of guilt with regard to the children, and leads either to overindulgence, in order to avoid their disapproval, or to open hostility—that is, the instinctive use of attack as a means of defense.

The subject is not exhausted. There are many indirect outgrowths of conflicts with the mother's own parents. My aim has been to make clear the manner in which children may quite directly represent old images, and thus stimulate compulsively the same emotional reactions that once were present.

The question may be raised, "Of what practical use are these various insights in our efforts at child guidance and the improvement of the conditions for raising children?" In a single case the analysis of the maternal conflict would be the best way to help any child, but this cannot be done on a broad scale. However, I think that the very detailed knowledge gained from the analyses of these relatively few cases may point out the direction in which the genetic factors really lie, for the guidance of future work. And furthermore, the knowledge of the disguised forms in which pathogenic factors appear may be helpful in detecting them more easily in practical work at present.

THE OVERVALUATION OF LOVE

A Study of a Common Present-Day
Feminine Type*

○○○

WOMAN'S EFFORTS TO ACHIEVE independence and an enlargement of her field of interests and activities are
continually met with a skepticism which insists that
such efforts should be made only in the face of economic necessity, and that they run counter to her inherent character and her
natural tendencies. Accordingly, all efforts of this sort are said
to be without any vital significance for woman, whose every
thought, in point of fact, should center exclusively upon the
male or upon motherhood, in much the manner expressed in
Marlene Dietrich's famous song, "I know only love, and nothing
else."

Various sociological considerations immediately suggest themselves in this connection; they are, however, of too familiar and
obvious a character to require discussion. This attitude toward
woman, whatever its basis and however it may be assessed, represents the patriarchal ideal of womanhood, of woman as one whose
only longing is to love a man and be loved by him, to admire him
and serve him, and even to pattern herself after him. Those who
maintain this point of view mistakenly infer from external behavior the existence of an innate instinctual disposition thereto;
whereas, in reality, the latter cannot be recognized as such, for the
reason that biological factors never manifest themselves in pure
and undisguised form, but always as modified by tradition and

* The Psychoanalytic Quarterly, Vol. III (1934), pp. 605-38. Reprinted
with the permission of The Psychoanalytic Quarterly.

environment. As Briffault has recently pointed out in some detail in *The Mothers*, the modifying influence of "inherited tradition," not only upon ideals and beliefs but also upon emotional attitudes and so-called instincts, cannot possibly be overestimated.[1] Inherited tradition means for women, however, a compressing of her participation (which originally was probably very considerable) in general tasks into the narrower sphere of eroticism and motherhood. The adherence to inherited tradition fulfills certain day-to-day functions for both society and the individual; of their social aspect we shall not speak here. Considered from the standpoint of the psychology of the individual, it need only be mentioned that this mental construction is for the male at times a matter of great inconvenience, yet on the other hand constitutes for him a source from which his self-esteem can always derive support. For woman, conversely, with her lowered self-esteem of centuries' duration, it constitutes a haven of peace in which she is spared the exertions and anxieties associated with the cultivation of other abilities and of self-assertion in the face of criticism and rivalry. It is comprehensible, therefore—speaking solely from the sociological standpoint—that women who nowadays obey the impulse to the independent development of their abilities are able to do so only at the cost of a struggle against both external opposition and such resistances within themselves as are created by an intensification of the traditional ideal of the exclusively sexual function of woman.

It would not be going too far to assert that at the present time this conflict confronts every woman who ventures upon a career of her own and who is at the same time unwilling to pay for her daring with the renunciation of her femininity. The conflict in question is therefore one that is conditioned by the altered position of woman and confined to those women who enter upon or follow a vocation, who pursue special interests, or who aspire in general to an independent development of their personality.

1. Briffault, R., *The Mothers* (London, 1927, Vol. II), p. 253: "The sexual division of labour upon which social development had been founded in primitive societies was abolished in the great economic revolution brought about by agriculture. Woman, instead of being the chief producer, became economically unproductive, destitute, and dependent. . . . One economic value alone was left to woman, her sex."

Sociological insight makes one fully cognizant of the existence of conflicts of this kind, of their inevitability, and in broad outline, of many of the forms in which they are manifested and of their more remote effects. It enables one—to give but a single instance—to understand how there result attitudes that vary from the extreme of complete repudiation of femininity on the one hand to the opposite extreme of total rejection of intellectual or vocational activities on the other.

The boundaries of this field of inquiry are marked off by such questions as the following: Why is it that in a given case the conflict takes the particular form it does, or why is its solution reached in just the manner it is? Why do some women fall ill in consequence of this conflict, or suffer a considerable impairment in the development of their potentialities? What predisposing factors on the part of the individual are necessary to such a result? And what types of outcome are possible? At the point where the problem of the fate of the individual emerges, one enters the domain of individual psychology, in fact of psychoanalysis.

The observations to be presented do not proceed from a sociological interest, but arise out of certain definite difficulties encountered in the analysis of a number of women which compelled a consideration of the specific factors responsible for these difficulties. The present report is based upon seven analyses of my own, and upon a number of additional cases familiar to me through analytic conferences. The majority of these patients had no prominent symptoms, in the main; two had a tendency to not at all typical depression and occasional hypochondriacal anxiety; two had infrequent attacks that had been diagnosed as epileptic. But in every case the symptoms, so far as they were present at all, were overshadowed by certain difficulties connected in each instance with the patient's relations to men and to work. As so often happens, their difficulties as such were more or less clearly sensed by the patients as arising out of their own personalities.

But it was by no means a simple matter to grasp the actual problem involved. The first impression did not yield much more than the fact that for these women their relation to men was of great importance to them, but that they had never succeeded in establishing a satisfactory relationship of any duration. Either attempts to form a relationship had failed outright, or there had been a series of merely evanescent relationships, broken off either by the man in question or the patient—relationships that moreover often showed a certain lack of selectivity. Or if a relationship of greater duration and deeper significance were entered into, it invariably foundered in the end on the rocks of some attitude or behavior on the part of the woman.

There was at the same time in all these cases an inhibition in the sphere of work and accomplishment and a more or less well-marked impoverishment of interests. To some extent these difficulties were conscious and immediately evident, but in part the patients were unaware of them as such until the analysis brought them to light.

It was only after somewhat prolonged analytic work that I recognized in certain gross examples that the central problem here consisted not in any love-inhibition, but in an entirely too exclusive concentration upon men. These women were as though possessed by a single thought, "I must have a man"—obsessed with an idea overvalued to the point of absorbing every other thought, so that by comparison all the rest of life seemed stale, flat, and unprofitable. The capabilities and interests that most of them possessed either had no meaning at all for them or had lost what meaning they had once had. In other words, conflicts affecting their relations to men were present and could be to a considerable extent relieved, but the actual problem lay not in too little but in too much emphasis on their love life.

In some instances inhibitions respecting work first appeared in the course of analysis and increased, while simultaneously the relation to men improved through the analysis of the anxieties associated with sexuality. This change was variously evaluated by the patient and her associates. On the one hand it was regarded in the light of progress—as in the case of the father who expressed pleasure in the fact that his daughter had become so feminine as a result of her analysis that she now wanted to get married and had lost all interest in study. On the other hand, in the course of consultations I repeatedly encountered complaints that this or that patient had attained to a better relationship with men through the analysis, but had lost her previous efficiency, ability, and pleasure in work and was now exclusively occupied with the desire for male companionship. This was food for thought. Evidently such a picture might also represent an artifact of analysis, a miscarriage of treatment. Still, this was the outcome only in the case of certain women, and not in others. What were the predisposing factors that determined the one outcome or the other? Was there something in the total problem of these women which had been overlooked?

Finally, another trait characterized all these patients in more or less striking degree—*a fear of not being normal*. This anxiety appeared in the sphere of erotism, in relation to work, or in a more abstract and diffuse form as a general feeling of being different and inferior, which they attributed to an inherent and hence unalterable predisposition.

There are two reasons why this problem only gradually became clarified. On the one hand, the picture represents to a great extent our traditional conception of the truly feminine woman, who has no other aim in life than to lavish devotion upon a man. The second difficulty lies in the analyst himself, who, convinced of the importance of the love life, is consequently disposed to regard the removal of disturbances in this domain as his prime task. He will therefore be glad to follow patients who emphasize of their own accord the importance of this sphere into the problems of this kind which they present. If a patient were to tell him that the great ambition of his life was to take a trip to the South Sea Islands and that he expected the analysis to resolve the inner conflicts standing in the way of the fulfillment of this wish, the analyst would naturally put the question, "Tell me, why is this trip of such vital importance to you?" The comparison is of course inadequate, because sexuality is really of greater importance than a journey to the South Seas; but it serves to show that our discernment, quite right and proper in itself, of the importance of heterosexual experience can on occasion blind us to a neurotic overvaluation of and overemphasis upon this sphere.

Seen from this standpoint, these patients present a discrepancy of a double sort. Their feeling for a man is in reality so complicated—I should like to say descriptively, so loose—that their estimate of a heterosexual relationship as the only valuable thing in life is undoubtedly a compulsive overvaluation. On the other hand, their gifts, abilities, and interests, and their ambition and the corresponding possibilities of achievement and satisfaction, are very much greater than they assume. We are dealing, therefore, with a displacement of emphasis from attainment or the struggle for achievement, to sex; indeed, so far as one may speak of objective facts in the field of values, what we have here is an objective falsification of values. For although in the last analysis sex is a tremendously important, perhaps the most important, source of satisfaction, it is certainly not the only one, nor the most trustworthy.

The transference situation relative to a woman analyst was dominated throughout by two attitudes: by rivalry, and by recourse to activity in relations with men.[2] Every improvement, every advance, seemed to them not progress of their own but exclusively the success of the analyst. The subject of a didactic analysis projected upon me the idea that I did not really want to cure her, or that I advised her to settle in another city because I was afraid of her rivalry. Another patient reacted to every (correct) interpretation by pointing out that her capacity for work had not improved. Still another was in the habit of remarking, whenever I had the feeling that progress was being made, that she was sorry to take up so much of my time. Desperate complaints of discouragement barely veiled the obstinate wish to discourage the analyst. These patients emphasized that unmistakable improvement was attributable in reality to factors outside the analysis, while any change for the worse was laid at the door of the analyst. They very frequently experienced difficulty in associating freely because it meant a giving in on their part and a triumph for the analyst, and because it would assist the analyst to succeed. In a word, they wanted to prove that the analyst could not do anything. A patient expressed this jokingly in the following fan-

2. Toward a male analyst the attitude may be the same. Or the transference may present, temporarily or permanently, the picture described by Freud as "the logic of soup and noodles." In the first case the analyst represents predominantly the mother or sister (but by no means always, and hence each situation must be considered on its merits). In the second case the chronic urge to win a man, characteristic of this group of patients, is related to the analyst himself.

tasy: She would settle in the house opposite mine and put on my house a conspicuous placard pointing to her sign and bearing the legend, "Over there lives the only good woman analyst."

The other transference attitude consists in this, that, as in life too, the relation to men is pushed into the foreground, and this with conspicuous frequency in the form of acting out. Often one man after another plays a part, ranging from mere approaches to sexual relations; while accounts of what he has done or not done, whether he loves or disappoints them, and of how they have reacted to him, take up at times the greater part of the hour and are tirelessly spun out to the smallest detail. The fact that this represents an acting out and that this acting out subserved the resistance was not always immediately evident. At times it was veiled because of the patient's endeavor to demonstrate that a satisfactory relation with a man, perhaps one of vital significance, was getting under way—an endeavor that accorded with a similarly directed wish on the part of the analyst. In retrospect I can say, however, that with a more exact knowledge of the specific problem of these patients and of their specific transference reaction, it is possible as a rule to see through this game and thus considerably to limit their acting out.

In this activity three kinds of tendencies come to the fore. They may be described as follows:

(1) "I am afraid of being dependent upon you as a woman, a mother image. Therefore I must avoid tying myself to you by any feeling of love. For love is dependence. And so, fleeing from this, I must try to attach my feelings elsewhere, to a man." Thus a dream that ushered in the analysis of a woman who was very definitely of the type in question showed the patient trying to come to the analysis but running away with a man whom she saw in the waiting room. This reserve is often rationalized by the idea that since the analyst will not reciprocate her love, it is useless to let one's feelings become involved.

(2) "I would rather make you dependent upon me (in love with me). Therefore I woo you, and try to arouse your jealousy by the attention I pay to men." Here a deeply rooted, largely preconscious conviction is expressed that jealousy is a sovereign means of evoking love.

(3) "You begrudge me relations with men; in fact, you try to prevent me in every possible way from having them, and do not even wish me to be attractive. But I will show you, out of spite, that I can, just the same." The willingness of the analyst to help is granted only intellectually at the most, sometimes not even that; and when at long last the ice is broken, the frank astonishment displayed at someone's actually wanting to help a person to attain happiness in this sphere is striking. On the other hand, even where there exists an intellectual superstructure of confidence, the patient's real mistrust and real anxiety, as well as anger at the analyst, came to light when the attempt to form a bond with the analyst miscarries. This anger is sometimes almost paranoid in character, the content being that the analyst is responsible for this or that, that he even actively intervened to bring it about.

Insight along lines such as these tempts us to assume that the key to this behavior with men lies in a strong and at the same time dreaded homosexuality that causes a pathological flight to the man—homosexuality, indeed, in the sense of "true masculine behavior," of which the effort to make men and women dependent upon one is merely the conscious expression. This would also render intelligible the characteristic looseness and unselectivity in these subjects' relationships with men. The ambivalence toward women that invariably characterizes homosexuality would explain the necessity for flight from homosexuality and specifically the flight to men, as well as the distrust, anxiety, and rage manifested toward the analyst insofar as the latter plays the mother role.

The clinical findings would not at first contradict such an interpretation. In dreams we meet the definite expression of the wish to be a man, and in life masculine patterns of behavior are exhibited in various disguises. Very characteristic is the fact that in well-defined cases these wishes are rejected vigorously, for the reason that these women regard being a man and being homosexual as identical. The rudiments of a homosexually colored relationship are almost always present at some period of life. That such relationships do not develop beyond the rudimentary stage is also in accord with the foregoing interpretation, as is the fact that in most cases feminine friendships play a strikingly minor role. All these phenomena might well be regarded in the light of measures of defense against a pronounced homosexuality.

One is rather taken aback to find, however, that in all these cases an interpretation based upon unconscious homosexual tendencies and flight therefrom remains completely ineffectual therapeutically. Some other interpretation, and a more correct one, must therefore be possible. An example from the transference situation supplies the answer.[3]

A patient at the beginning of her treatment repeatedly sent me flowers, at first anonymously and then openly. My first interpretation, that she was behaving like a man wooing a woman, did not alter her behavior, although she admitted it laughingly. My second interpretation, that the presents were intended as a compensation for the aggression she abundantly exhibited, was equally without effect. On the other hand, the picture changed as if by magic when the patient brought associations that stated unequivocally that by means of presents one can make a person dependent upon one. A fantasy that followed brought to light the deeper destructive content behind this wish. She would like, she said, to be my maid and do everything for me to perfection. Thus I would become dependent upon her, trust her completely, and then one day—she would put poison in my coffee. She concluded her fantasy with a phrase that is absolutely typical of this group of individuals: "Love is a means of murder." This example reveals particularly clearly the attitude characteristic of this whole group. Insofar as sexual impulses toward women are consciously perceived, they are often as a matter of fact experienced *sub specie* criminality. The instinctive attitude in the transference, insofar as the analyst represents a mother or sister image, is likewise unequivocally destructive, so that the aim is to dominate and to destroy; in other words, the latter is destructive and not sexual. The term "homosexual" is therefore misleading, for by homosexuality is usually meant an attitude in which sexual aims, even though mixed with destructive elements, are directed toward a

3. It struck me repeatedly that whenever I demonstrated to these patients the wish to be a man completely freed from every object relation, they reacted with invariable promptitude and naïveté as though I had "reproached" them with homosexuality.

partner of the same sex. In the present case, however, the destructive impulses are only loosely combined with the libidinal ones. The sexual elements that are commingled meet the same fate as in puberty: a satisfactory relationship to a man is for internal reasons impossible, and a quantity of free-floating libido exists, therefore, which can be directed upon women. There are reasons, as I shall show later, why other outlets for the libido, such as work or autoerotism, are not available. There is in addition, as a positive factor in the impulse toward other women, a turning—unsuccessful in all these cases—toward their own masculinity, as well as an equally unsuccessful attempt to render the destructive impulses harmless by means of libidinal ties. This combination of factors explains, in part, the anxiety in regard to homosexuality—why it is that in these cases sexual or tender or even friendly feelings are not to any great extent directed toward women.

However, a glance at the women in whom such a development has taken place reveals immediately the inadequacy of this explanation. For, although hostile trends directed against women are plainly and abundantly present in these groups (as seen in the transference and in their lives), the same trends are to be found in unconsciously homosexual women (*per* the definition just given) in no less a degree. Anxiety with regard to these trends cannot, therefore, be the decisive factor. It seems to me, rather, that in women whose development has been in the homosexual direction the decisive factor lies in a very early and far-reaching resignation—for no matter what reasons—with regard to men; so that erotic rivalry with other women recedes relatively into the background in these subjects, and in them there results not only, as occasionally also among the group in question, a *coupling* of sexual and destructive impulses, but as well a *love that overcompensates* these destructive trends.

In the type of woman we have in mind, this overcompensation either does not occur or does not assume much importance; and we find at the same time not only that rivalry with women persists but that this rivalry is in fact sharply aggravated because the aim of the struggle (colored as the latter is by a tremendous hatred), the winning of a man, has not been given up. Thus there exists anxiety with regard to this hatred and a fear of retaliation, but no motive to compel its cessation; indeed, there is rather an interest in having it kept up. This enormous hatred of women, born of rivalry, is enacted in the transference situation in other spheres than the erotic, but is expressed perfectly clearly in the erotic sphere in the form of projection. For if the fundamental feeling is that the [woman] analyst stands in the way of the patient's relations to men, the reference here is by no means solely to the forbidding mother but in particular to the jealous mother or sister who will not tolerate a feminine type of development or success in the feminine sphere.

It is only on this basis that one can fully understand the meaning of playing off the man against the woman analyst in the resistance. The intention is to show the jealous mother or sister, out of spite, that the patient can have or get a man. But this is possible only at the price of a bad conscience or anxiety. From this fact proceed also the open or concealed reactions of rage upon any frustration. A struggle is enacted beneath the surface, somewhat as follows: When the analyst insists upon analyzing instead of allowing the acting out of the relations to the man, this is unconsciously interpreted as a prohibition, as opposition, on the part of the analyst. If on occasion the analyst points out that without the analysis these attempts to establish a relationship with a man cannot possibly lead anywhere, this signifies emotionally to the patient a repetition of attempts by the mother or sister to suppress the patient's feminine self-esteem—as if the analyst had said: You are too little, or of too little account, or not sufficiently attractive; you cannot attract or hold a man. And comprehensibly enough, her reaction is to demonstrate that she can. In the case of younger patients this jealousy is expressed directly in their emphasis upon their own youth and the greater age of the analyst, in some such form as that the analyst is too old to be able to understand that it is natural for a girl to want a man above everything else, and that this should be of greater importance to her than the analysis. Not infrequently the family situation, in the sense of the Oedipus complex, is reenacted in almost unchanged form, as for example when a patient feels a relation to a man to be disloyal to the analyst.

What takes place here in the transference is, as always, a particularly clear and uncensored edition of what takes place in the rest of the patient's living. The patient almost always seeks to win a man who is desired by or in some way bound to other women—often quite irrespective of his other qualities. Or in cases of severe anxiety there exists an absolute taboo in regard to precisely a man of this description. This, as in one case, may even go so far that all men are taboo—for in the last analysis every man is taken away from some possible woman. In another patient, where the rivalry was primarily with an older sister, an anxiety dream occurred after her first intercourse, in which dream the sister chased her threateningly around the room. The forms that pathologically increased rivalry may assume are so well known that I need not go into further particulars here. That a large share of erotic inhibition and frustration is caused by the anxiety associated with rivalry of a destructive type is an equally familiar fact.

But the primary question is: What so tremendously increases this attitude of rivalry and imparts to it such an enormously destructive character?

In the previous histories of these women there is one factor that is striking in the regularity of its occurrence and the marked affect with which it is characterized: All these women in child-hood had come off second best in competition for a man (father or brother). Conspicuously often—in seven cases out of thirteen—there was, above all, an older *sister* who was able by various means to command a place in the sun, that is, in the favor of the father, or in one case that of an older brother, in another of a younger. Except in one case, where a much older sister was the father's very obvious favorite and evidently did not have to make any special exertions to prevent the younger from having his attention, the analysis brought to light a tremendous anger against these sisters. The anger is centered on two points. It may refer to the feminine coquetry by which the sister has succeeded in winning the father, brother, or, later, other men. And in these cases it is so great that for a long period, by way of protest, it prevents the patient's own development in this direction, in the sense of a complete repudiation of feminine wiles; thus she refrains from wearing attractive clothes, dancing, and participation in general in anything in the sphere of the erotic. The second type of anger concerns the sisters' hostility to the patient; its full extent is divined only by degrees. Reduced to a common formula, it may be expressed as follows: The older sisters have intimidated the younger ones, in part by direct threats that they were capable of putting into effect because of their greater physical strength and more advanced mental development, in part by ridiculing all the efforts of the younger sisters to be erotically attractive, and in part—as was certainly true in three cases and possibly in four —by making the younger ones dependent upon them by means of sexual games. The last method, as may easily be conceived, left the deepest impress of anger, since it rendered the younger children defenseless—partly because of the sexual dependence involved, partly because of feelings of guilt. It was in these cases, too, that the most definite tendency to homosexuality in the overt sense was to be found. In one of these cases the mother was a particularly attractive woman, surrounded by a crowd of male acquaintances, and kept the father in a state of absolute dependence upon her. In another instance not only was the sister preferred, but the father had a love affair with a relative living in the house and in all probability with other women. In yet another case the still young and unusually beautiful mother was the absolute center of attention on the part of the father as well as of the sons and the various men who frequented the house. In this last case there was the complicating factor superadded that the little girl from her fifth to her ninth year had had a sexually intimate relationship with a brother some years her senior, although the latter was the mother's favorite and had continued to be more closely tied to her than to his sister. On account of his mother, moreover, he suddenly broke off the relationship with his sister, at least as regards its sexual character, at the time of puberty. In still another case the father had made sexual advances to the patient from her fourth year, which became more outspoken in their character at the approach of puberty. At the same time he not only continued to be extremely dependent upon the mother, who received devotion on all sides, but was likewise very susceptible to the charms of other women, so that the girl got the impression of being merely her father's plaything, to be cast aside at his convenience or when grownup women appeared on the scene.

Thus all these girls experienced throughout their childhood an intensified rivalry for the attention of a man, which either was hopeless from the beginning or resulted ultimately in defeat. This defeat in relation to the father is, of course, the typical fate of the little girl in the family situation. But in these cases it produces specific and typical consequences because of the intensification of the rivalry brought about by the presence of a mother or a sister who absolutely dominates the situation erotically or by the awakening of specific illusions on the part of the father or brother. There is also operative an additional factor, to the significance of which I shall return in another connection. In the majority of these cases, sexual development has received an impulse more precipitate and intensified than in the average case, by reason of exaggerated early experience of sexual excitation called forth by other persons and occurrences. This premature experience of a genital excitation much greater and more intense than the physical pleasure derivable from other sources (oral, anal, and muscle erotism) not only results in bringing the genital sphere into much greater prominence but also lays the foundation for instinctively appreciating earlier and more fully the importance of the struggle for the possession of a man.

In the fact that such a struggle brings in its train a permanent and destructive attitude of rivalry with women, the same psychology is evident as holds true of every competitive situation—the vanquished feels lasting anger toward the victor, suffers injury to his self-esteem, will consequently be in a less favorable psychological position in subsequent competitive situations, and will ultimately feel either consciously or unconsciously that his only chance of success lies in the death of his opponent. Exactly the same consequences can be traced in the cases under discussion: a feeling of being downtrodden, a permanent feeling of insecurity with regard to feminine self-esteem, and a profound anger with their more fortunate rivals. There takes place in all cases, as a result of these, a partial or complete avoidance or inhibition in regard to rivalry with women, or on the other hand, a compulsive rivalry of exaggerated proportions—and the greater the feeling of being worsted, the more intent will the victim be upon the death of the rival, as though to say: Only when you are dead can I be free.

This hatred of the victorious rival may eventuate in either of two ways. If it remains in large measure preconscious, the blame for the erotic failure is placed upon other women. If it is more deeply repressed, the reason for lack of success is sought in the patient's own personality; the self-tormenting complaints that arise combine with the sense of guilt that originates in the repressed hatred. In the transference one can often clearly observe not only how one attitude alternates with the other but how the suppression of the one automatically strengthens the other. If anger toward the mother or sister is suppressed, the patient's feelings of guilt increase; if the patient's self-reproaches diminish, anger against the others wells up. Someone must be responsible for my misfortune: if it is not I, it must be others; if not others, then it is I. Of these two attitudes the feeling that it is one's own fault is much more strongly repressed.

This gnawing doubt as to whether one is not oneself to blame for the fact of not effecting a satisfactory relationship with men does not appear in the analysis in this form at first, as a rule, but rather is expressed in a general conviction that things are not what they should be; the patients feel, and have always felt, anxiety as to whether they are "normal." Sometimes this is rationalized as a fear that they are not constitutionally or organically sound. Occasionally a mechanism of defense against such doubts is conspicuous in the form of an extreme emphasis upon their normality. If there is this emphasis upon the defensive aspect, the analysis is often regarded as something to be ashamed of, since this is evidence that everything is not as it should be; and accordingly they try to keep the analysis a secret. The mental attitude may vary from one extreme to the other in the same patient, from hopelessness that even the analysis cannot change what is so fundamentally amiss, to the opposite certainty that everything is all right and hence they do not need analysis.

The most frequent form that these doubts assume in consciousness is the conviction that the patient is ugly and therefore cannot possibly be attractive to men. This conviction is quite independent of whatever the actual facts may be; it may be found, for example, even in girls who are unusually pretty. The feeling is referred to some real or imaginary defect—straight hair, large hands or feet, too stout a figure, too large or small a stature, their age, or a poor complexion. These self-criticisms are invariably associated with a deep feeling of shame. One patient, for example, was for some time disturbed about her feet; she hurried to museums in order to compare her feet with those of statues, feeling that she would have to commit suicide if she were to discover that her feet were unsightly. Another patient could not understand, in the light of her own feelings, why her husband was not mortally ashamed of his crooked toes. Another fasted for weeks because her brother had remarked that her arms were too fat. In some instances the feeling was referred to dress, the idea being that one could not be attractive without pretty clothes.

In the attempt to get the best of these tormenting ideas, dress plays a very important part, and yet without any permanent success, since doubts invade this sphere as well and make it a perpetual affliction. It becomes unendurable not to have articles of dress match perfectly, and the same if a dress makes the wearer look stout, or if it seems too long or too short, too plain or too elegant, too conspicuous, too youthful, or not modern enough. Granting that the matter of clothes is of importance to a woman, there can be no question but that quite inappropriate affects here come into play—affects of shame, insecurity, and even anger. One patient, for example, was in the habit of tearing up a dress if she thought that it made her appear stout; in others the anger was directed at the dressmaker.

Another attempt at defense is the wish to be a man. "As a woman I am nothing," said one of these patients; "I should be much better off to be a man," and accompanied this remark with markedly masculine gestures. The third and most important means of defense consists in the patient's proving nevertheless that she can attract a man. Here again we encounter the same gamut of emotions. To be without a man, never to have had anything to do with one, to have remained a virgin, to be unmarried—all these things are a disgrace and cause people to look down upon one. Having a man—whether he be admirer, friend, lover, or husband—is the proof that one is "normal." Hence the frantic pursuit of a man. *Au fond,* he need fulfill only the single requirement of being a man. If he has other qualities that enhance the woman's narcissistic satisfaction, so much the better. Otherwise a striking degree of unselectivity on her part may be exhibited, which is in conspicuous contrast to her level in other respects.

But this attempt too, like that in regard to dress, remains unsuccessful—unsuccessful, at any rate, so far as proving anything is concerned. For even when these women succeed in getting one man after another to fall in love with them, they are able to conjure up reasons for depreciating their success—reasons such as the following: There was no other woman about for the man to fall in love with; or, he does not amount to much; or, "I forced him into the situation anyway"; or, "He loves me because I am intelligent, or because I can be useful to him in this or that way."

In the first place, analysis reveals an anxiety in regard to the sexual organs, the content of this anxiety being that the subject has harmed herself by masturbation, has done herself some injury in this way. Frequently these fears are expressed in the specific idea that the hymen has been destroyed or that as a result of masturbation the subject cannot have children.[4] Under the pressure of this anxiety, masturbation is completely suppressed as a rule, and all recollection of it repressed; at any rate, the allegation of never having masturbated is typical. In the relatively infrequent cases in which masturbation was indulged in at a later period of life it was followed by severe feelings of guilt.

The essential basis of this extreme defense against masturbation is to be found in the extraordinary sadistic fantasies that accompany it, fantasies of the infliction of injury in various ways upon some woman who is imprisoned or humiliated or degraded or tortured or, in particular, whose genitalia are mutilated. This last named fantasy is the most strongly repressed, but seems to be the essential element, dynamically. So far as my experience

4. One repeatedly gains the impression that this latter anxiety is the "deepest" anxiety in connection with masturbation, but one hesitates to express quantitative judgments of this kind without accurate data in support of them. In any event, the desire for children is an extraordinarily powerful one in all these women, and is originally strongly repressed in the majority of cases.

goes, this fantasy is never expressed directly, even when the onanistic fantasies revel in cruelty of other kinds. It can be reconstructed, however, from such data as the following: In the case of the patient who tore her clothing when she felt that it made her appear stout, it was evident in the first place that this behavior was an onanistic equivalent, secondly that she afterward felt as though she had committed a murder of which she had anxiously to efface the traces, further that stoutness meant pregnancy to her and reminded her of her mother's pregnancy (when she was five years old), then the thought that the analyst's pregnancies must have caused internal tears, and finally a spontaneous feeling, while she was tearing her dress, as though she were tearing her mother's sexual organs.

Another patient who had completely overcome the masturbatory habit had a feeling in connection with the pain of her menses as though her insides were being torn out. She experienced sexual excitement when she heard of an abortion; she recalled having had the idea as a child that the husband drew something out of his wife with a knitting needle. Reports of rape and murder were exciting to her. Various dreams contained the idea of a girl's sexual organs being injured or operated upon by a woman, so that they bled. Once this happened to a girl in a reformatory at the hands of one of the teachers—the opposite of what she would have liked to do to the analyst or to her greatly hated mother.

In other patients one may infer the presence of these destructive impulses from a similarly expressed fear of reprisal, that is, exaggerated anxiety lest every female sexual function be painful and bloody, in particular defloration and birth.

In brief, one quite evidently finds still operative in the unconscious, in unchanged form and undiminished strength, the destructive impulses directed against the mother or sister in early childhood; Melanie Klein has laid much emphasis on the significance of these impulses. By way of accounting for this, it is easy to believe that it is augmented and embittered rivalry, which has not permitted them to become quiescent. The original impulses against the mother have the meaning: You must not have intercourse with my father; you must not have children by him; if you do, you will be so damaged that you cannot do so again

and will be rendered harmless forever; or—as further elaborated
—you will appear hideous and repulsive to all men. But this,
according to the inexorable law of talion that prevails in the
unconscious, brings in its train fears of exactly the same kind.
Thus if I wish this injury to befall you and inflict it upon you
in my masturbation fantasies, I have to fear that the same thing
will happen to me; not only this, but I have to fear that the same
thing will happen to me when I am in the same situation as that
in which I have wished pain and injury upon my mother. As a
matter of fact, in a certain number of these cases, a dysmenorrhœa
develops at the very time when they begin to play with the idea
of a sex relationship. Sometimes, moreover, the dysmenorrhœa
developing at this time is regarded quite consciously and explicitly as a punishment for the sexual wishes in question. In other
cases the patient's fears are of a less specific character, manifesting
themselves primarily in their effect, which is to interdict sexual
intercourse for the individual.

These retributive anxieties have reference in part to the
future, as just indicated; but in part also to the past, as follows:
Because I have lived out these destructive impulses in masturbation, the same thing has happened to me; I am damaged in the
same way as she, or—as further elaborated—I am as hideous as
she. This connection was entirely conscious and outspoken in
one patient in whom actual sexual approaches on the part of the
father had engendered an unusually intense rivalry: prior to the
analysis she had hardly dared to look at herself in the mirror
because she thought she was ugly, although in fact she was decidedly pretty. When here conflicts with her mother had been
worked through and lived through in the analysis, in a moment
of released affects she saw herself in the mirror with the features
of her mother.

Destructive impulses toward men are also present in every
case. In dreams these are expressed as castration impulses, in life
in the various familiar forms of desiring to injure or in the form
of defense against these impulses. These impulses directed against
men, however, are evidently only slightly connected with the
idea of not being normal, their uncovering in the analysis proceeds usually with little resistance, and alters the picture not at

all. On the other hand, anxiety disappears with the uncovering and working through of the destructive drives directed against women (mother, sister, analyst), and conversely persists unaltered as long as an excess of anxiety prevents the taking in hand of the severe feelings of guilt connected with these drives. The defenses here instituted—the appearance of which I have referred to as a resistance against analysis—is a defense against the sense of guilt, with some such meaning as: I have not injured myself in any way, I am made this way. This serves at the same time as a complaint against fate that one is made in this way and not differently; or against hereditary predisposition that is what it is once and for all; or as in two cases, against a sister who had done something to the patient's genital; or against oppression in childhood for which amends had never been made. Here it is clearly apparent that the function these complaints serve, and the reason for their retention, is that of a defense against the individual's sense of guilt.

Originally I supposed that the adherence to the idea of not being normal was determined by the illusion of masculinity, the concomitant sense of shame by the idea of having forfeited the penis, or the possibility of its growing, through masturbation; I regarded the pursuit of a man as determined in part by a secondary overemphasis of femininity and in part by a wish to be supplemented by a man if one cannot be a man oneself. But from the dynamics of the course of events, such as I have described above, I have come to the conviction that the fantasies of masculinity do not represent the *dynamically effective agency*, but are merely an *expression of secondary tendencies* that have their root in the rivalry with women described above, being at the same time an accusation against unjust fate or against the mother, rationalized in this way or that, for not having been born a man, or an expression of the need to create in dreams or fantasies a means of escape from the torment of feminine conflicts.

There are, of course, cases in which adherence to the illusion of being a man does play a dynamic part, but these cases seem to be of quite a different structure, since in them a conspicuous degree of identification with a specific man—generally the father or the brother—has taken place, on the basis of which development in a homosexual direction or the formation of a narcissistic attitude and orientation occurs.

The overvaluation of relationships with men has its sources, so far as we have up to this point discussed them, not in any unusual strength of sexual impulse, but in factors lying outside the male-female relationship, namely, restoration of wounded self-esteem and defiance of the victorious (female) rival. And so it becomes needful to inquire whether, and to what extent, the desire for sexual gratification plays an essential part in the pursuit of the male. That consciously it is striven for is certain, but is this also true from an instinctual standpoint?

It is quite essential to keep in mind in this connection the important fact that this gratification is not sought with average zeal but is definitely and unequivocally overvalued. This attitude was at times made quite prominent on a conscious level also, but at first I was inclined to underestimate it because of the strength of sexual inhibitions on the one hand and on the other of the force of the urge toward the male deriving from other sources; hence I regarded the attitude in question as being in large measure a rationalization serving to conceal the unconscious motives and to represent the desire for men as something "quite normal and natural." Now this emphasis doubtless does serve these ends as well, as a matter of fact; but we here find confirmation also of the old dictum that the patient is always—in some sense—right. Given the natural desire for sexual gratification and with due regard for all extrasexual elements, there nevertheless still remains an excess of sexual desire, and specifically for heterosexual intercourse. This impression is based upon the consideration that if in these women it was *in essence* merely a matter of protest against women on the one hand and of self-assertion ("narcissistic compensation") on the other, it would not be easy to explain the fact that in reality, often without being aware of it and often, indeed, in contradiction of their conscious attitude, they eagerly seek sexual intercourse with the partner in question. One often finds them entertaining the idea that they cannot be healthy or efficient in their work without it. This is rationalized from a half-understood analytic point of view, or with some theory of hormones, or simply by means of the masculine ideology of the harmfulness of abstinence. How important sexual intercourse is to them is shown in efforts that, however variously determined in other respects, have the one common denominator of assuring themselves sexual intercourse, that is, of not being in the position of being suddenly cut off from the possibility of intercourse. These efforts seek realization in three ways, intrinsically as different as possible, yet interchangeable with each other owing to their common underlying motivation: prostitution fantasies, the desire to marry, and the wish to be a man. Prostitution fantasies and marriage signify on this basis that there will always be a man available. The wish to be a man, or resentment against the male, derives in this connection from the idea that a man can always have sexual intercourse when he wants it.

I believe that the following three factors contribute to this overvaluation of sexuality:

(1) From the economic standpoint there is much in the typical psychological configuration of these women to force them into the sphere of sexuality, because the path to other kinds of possibilities of satisfaction has been made extremely difficult. Homosexual impulses are rejected because they are coupled with destructive impulses and because of the attitude of rivalry toward other women. Masturbation is unsatisfactory, if it has not been, as is true in most cases, completely suppressed. But in large measure all other forms of autoerotic gratification in the broader sense, both of a direct and a sublimated sort, everything that one does or enjoys "only by oneself," such as the enjoyment of eating, of earning money, of art or nature, are inhibited, and this in chief measure because these women, like all people who feel themselves at a decided disadvantage in life, harbor a tremendously strong wish to have everything for themselves alone, not to allow anybody else to enjoy the slightest thing, to take everything away from everybody else—a wish that is repressed because of the reactive anxiety it gives rise to and because of its incompatibility with the individual's standards of behavior in other respects. In addition to this there is the inhibition present in all spheres of activity, which when coupled with ambition, results in great inward dissatisfaction.

(2) This first factor might explain an actual intensification of

sexual need; but a further factor might constitute a root of this increased valuation—one based upon the individual's original defeat in the sphere of feminine rivalry, and resulting in a deep-seated fear lest other women should constantly be a disturbing element in heterosexual activities, as indeed is manifested clearly enough in the transference situation. This is in fact something like the "aphanisis" described by Ernest Jones, except that here it is not a question of anxiety regarding the loss of one's own capacity for sexual experience, but rather the fear of being balked of it for all time by an external agency. This anxiety is warded off by the attempts to gain security mentioned above, and con-tributes to the overestimation of sexuality insofar as any purpose that becomes an object of controversy is always overrated.

(3) The third source seems to me the least well-established since I could not detect its presence in all cases and therefore cannot vouch for its relevance in every instance. Some of these women, as has already been mentioned, recall experiencing in early childhood sexual excitation similar to orgasm. In still others one may infer with some justification the occurrence of such an experience, this on the grounds of subsequent phenomena such as the fear of orgasm coupled though this is with knowledge of it as betrayed in dreams. The excitation experienced in early life was terrifying either because of the specific conditions under which it was experienced or simply on account of its overwhelm-ing strength relative to the subject's immaturity, so that it was repressed. The experience left certain traces in its wake, however —of a pleasure far in excess of that from any other source, and of something strangely vitalizing to the whole organism. I am inclined to think that these traces cause these particular women— to a greater extent than in the average instance—to conceive of sexual gratification as a kind of elixir of life that only men are able to provide and without which one must dry up and waste away, while the lack of it makes achievement in any other direction impossible. This point, however, must be further corroborated.

Despite this multiple determination of the intensive pursuit of men, and despite the strenuous efforts indulged in for the attainment of this goal, all these attempts are doomed to failure.

The reasons for this failure are to be found in part in what has already been said. They have their root in the same soil as engendered defeat in the competition for the male, yet which at the same time gives rise to the very special efforts made to win him.

The embittered attitude of rivalry with women forces them, of course, constantly to demonstrate afresh their erotic superiority, but at the same time their destructive impulses toward women cause any rivalry over a man to be inevitably bound up with deep anxiety. In accordance with the strength of this anxiety, and perhaps even more in accordance with the subjective realization of defeat and the consequent lowering of self-esteem, the conflict between an increased urge to engage in rivalry with other women and the increased anxiety engendered thereby, results outwardly either in an avoidance of such rivalry or in increased efforts in that direction. The manifest picture may therefore run the gamut from women who are extremely inhibited in making any advances in establishing relationships with men, though craving for them to the exclusion of any other wish, to women of a veritable Don Juan type. The justification for including all these women within a single category, despite their outward dissimilarities, lies not only in the similarity of their fundamental conflicts, but also in the similarity of their emotional orientation, in spite of the extreme difference in their outward careers—this, more accurately, with special reference to their attitude regarding the sphere of the erotic. The factor already mentioned, that "success" with men is not emotionally esteemed as such, contributes to an important extent to this similarity. Furthermore, no relationship with a man that is satisfactory either mentally or physically is achieved in any instance.

The insult to their femininity drives these women, both directly and *via* the fear of not being normal, to prove their feminine potency to themselves; but since this goal is never reached on account of the self-depreciation that instantly occurs, such a technique leads of necessity to a rapid change from one relationship to another. Their interest in a man, such as may even amount to an illusion of being tremendously in love with him, vanishes as a rule as soon as he is "conquered"—that is, as soon as he has become emotionally dependent on them.

This tendency to make a person dependent through love, as I have already described as being characteristic of the transference, has still another determinant. It is determined by an anxiety which says that dependence is a danger to be avoided at all costs, that therefore, since love or any emotional bond is that which creates the greatest degree of dependence, these latter constitute the very evil to be avoided. The fear of dependence is, in other words, a profound fear of the disappointments and humiliations that they expect to result from falling in love, humiliations that they have themselves experienced in childhood and would like subsequently to pass on to others. The original experience that has thus left behind it such a strong feeling of vulnerability was presumably caused by a man, but the resultant behavior is directed almost equally toward men and women. The patient, for example, who wanted to make me dependent upon her by means of presents expressed regret on one occasion that she had not gone to a male analyst, for one can more easily make a man fall in love with one and then the game is won.

Protection of oneself against emotional dependence thus corresponds to the desire to be invulnerable, much as Siegfried in the German saga bathed in the dragon's blood for that purpose.

In still other instances, the mechanism of defense manifests itself in a tendency toward despotism as well as in vigilance to make sure that the partner will remain more dependent upon her than she upon him, and this is accompanied, of course, by correspondingly violent overt or repressed reactions of rage whenever the partner gives any sign of independence.

The doubly determined inconstancy toward men serves further to gratify a deep-seated desire for revenge, a desire which likewise has developed on the basis of her original defeat; the desire is to get the better of a man, to cast him aside, to reject him just as she herself once felt cast aside and rejected. From what has already been said, it is evident that the chances of a suitable object choice are very slight, indeed are nonexistent; for reasons having to do in part with their relations to other women and in part with their own self-esteem, these women snatch blindly at a man. These chances, moreover, in two-thirds of the cases dealt with here, were still further reduced by a fixation on the father, who was the person about whom the struggle in childhood primarily centered. These cases at first gave the impression that as a matter of fact they were seeking the father or a father image, and that later on they dropped men very quickly because the latter did not correspond to this ideal or also because they became the recipient of the repetitive revenge originally intended for the father; or in other words, that the fixation on the father constituted the nucleus of these women's neurotic difficulties. Although as a matter of fact this fixation intensifies the difficulties in many of these women, it is nevertheless certain that it is not a specific factor in the genesis of this type. At any rate, it does not constitute the dynamic kernel of the specific problem with which we are here concerned, for in about one-third of these cases nothing was found in this respect that transcended the ordinary in intensity or in any particular characteristic. I mention the matter here only for technical reasons. For one learns by experience that when one follows through these early fixations without having first worked through the entire problem involved, one readily reaches an impasse.

For the patient there is but one way out of a situation so totally unsatisfactory, namely, by means of achievement, of esteem, of ambition. These women without exception seek this way out, in that they all develop tremendous ambition. They are motivated by powerful impulses emanating from wounded feminine self-esteem and from an exaggerated sense of rivalry. One can build up one's self-esteem by achievement and success, if not in the erotic sphere, then in any other field of endeavor, the choice of which is determined by the individual's particular abilities, and thus triumph over all rivals.

However, they are foredoomed to failure along this path as well as in the erotic sphere. We must now consider the reasons for the inevitability of this failure. We can do this briefly because the difficulties in the sphere of accomplishment are essentially the same as we have seen them to be in the erotic sphere, and all that needs to be considered here is the form in which these manifest themselves. It is in the matter of rivalry, of course, that the parallelism is most clearly discernible between these individuals' behavior in the erotic sphere and in that of accomplishment. In those who have an almost pathologically increased need to drive every other woman from the field, there exists a conscious ambition and desire for recognition in every sort of competitive activity, but the underlying insecurity is of course obvious. It manifested itself in the three cases that exhibited this particular pattern in their absolute failure to pursue a given goal perseveringly in spite of tremendous ambition. Even kindly criticism discourages them, and the same holds true of praise. Criticism touches off their secret fear of inability to compete successfully, and praise the fear of any rivalry whatever, but especially, of course, successful rivalry. A second element that recurred in these cases with monotonous regularity was their Don Juanism. In the same way as they are in constant need of new males, they are also incapable of tying themselves down to any particular work. They are fond of pointing out that tying themselves down to a particular type of work deprives them of the possibility of pursuing other interests. That this fear is a rationalization is betrayed by the fact that they do not in actuality pursue any interest with any real degree of energy.

In those who avoid any rivalry in the erotic sphere under an obsession of their inability to please, ambition as such is also almost always repressed. In the presence of those who give merely the appearance of being able to do things better than they, they feel completely relegated to the background, feel unwanted, and react with tremendous outbursts of rage to such situations—just as in the transference situation—and readily react with a depression.

When it comes to marriage, their own repressed ambition is often transferred to the husband, so that with the whole momentum of their own ambition they demand that he be successful. But this transference of ambition has only partial success, for on account of their own unintermitting attitude with regard to rivalry, they are at the same time unconsciously lying in wait for failure on his part. Which attitude toward the husband predominates depends upon the strength of their own need for sex-maximation. Thus from the very outset he may be regarded as himself a rival, in relation to whom they fall into an abyss of feelings of incompetence, accompanied by the deepest feelings of resentment toward him—in the same way that they avoid erotic rivalry.

There occurs in all these cases a further difficulty of prime importance, which arises from the striking discrepancy between their increased ambition and their weakened self-confidence. All these women would be capable of productive work, in accordance with their individual endowments, as writers, as scientists, as painters, as physicians, as organizers. It is perfectly self-evident that in every productive activity a certain amount of self-confidence is a prerequisite, and a noticeable lack of it has a paralyzing effect. This holds true, of course, equally here. Hand in hand with their excessive ambition, there is from the very outset a lack of courage resulting from their broken morale. At the same time the majority of these patients are unaware of the tremendous tension under which they labor, due to their ambition.

This discrepancy has a further practical result. For they expect, without being aware of it, to achieve distinction from the very outset—to master the piano, for example, without practice, or to paint brilliantly without technique, to achieve scientific success without hard labor, or to diagnose correctly heart murmurs and pulmonary sounds without training. Their inevitable failure they do not ascribe to their unreal and excessive expectations, but regard it as due to their general lack of ability. They then are inclined to drop whatever work they are doing at the time; they thus fail to attain that knowledge and skill, through patient labor, which is indispensable to success: and thereby they bring about a further and permanent increase in the discrepancy between increased ambition and weakened self-confidence.

This feeling of an inability to achieve anything, which is just as tormenting here as in the erotic sphere from which it originates, is as a rule maintained with equal tenacity. The patient is determined to prove to herself and to others, and above all to the analyst, that she is incompetent to do anything, that she is just awkward or stupid. She discards any proofs to the contrary and takes every praise as a deceitful flattery.

What is it that maintains these tendencies? On the one hand, the conviction of one's own incapacity affords an excellent protection against achieving anything worthwhile, and thus insures one against the dangers of successful competition. Adherence to the incapacity to do things subserves this defense far less than it does the positive striving that dominates the entire picture, namely, that of obtaining a man, or rather of extorting from fate a man in spite of all the powers that be—and of doing so by giving proof of one's own weakness, dependence, and helplessness. This "scheme" is always entirely unconscious, but is pursued all the more obstinately for that reason; and that which is seemingly meaningless betrays itself as a planned and purposeful striving toward a definite end, when regarded from the standpoint of this unconscious expectation.

This appears on the surface in various ways, such as certain vague but nevertheless persistent conceptions implying that there exists an alternative between man and work, that the path to work and independence interferes with or cuts off the path to men. To impress upon these patients that such conceptions have no basis in reality leaves them completely unmoved. The same holds true of the interpretation of the supposed alternative between masculine and feminine, penis and child. Their obstinacy becomes intelligible if regarded as the expression, even if not understood, of the scheme described above. One patient, in whom this idea of the alternative referred to above played a considerable part in her extreme resistance to all work, exhibited the underlying wish during transference in the following fantasy: Through the payment of the analytic fee she would gradually lose all her money and become impoverished. The analysis, however, would not be able to help her overcome her inhibitions in regard to work. She would be deprived in consequence of all means of support and would be unable to earn her livelihood. In that case her analysts would have to take care of her—in particular, her first (male) analyst. The same patient tried to get the analyst to prohibit her working by insistently putting forward not only her incapacity for doing so but likewise the harmful results attending it. When urged to work on the ground of suitability and competence, she reacted—in quite logical fashion, indeed—with anger that sprang from the frustration of her secret scheme, while its conscious content was that the analyst looked upon her as fit only for work and wished to frustrate her feminine development.

In other cases the fundamental expectation is expressed in envy of the woman who is supported by a man or furthered in her work by a man. Fantasies having a similar meaning occur in abundance, fantasies of receiving from a man support or gifts, children or sexual gratification, spiritual aid or moral support. Corresponding oral-sadistic fantasies make their appearance in dreams. In two cases it was the father himself whom the patients compelled to support them, by demonstrating their inability to do so themselves.

Their whole attitude remains unchanged, as regards its dynamics, until one has fitted it into the framework of their secret expectation, which is to the following effect: If I cannot obtain the love of my father—that is, a man—in a natural way, I will extort it by the device of being helpless. This is, as it were, a magic appeal to their pity. The function of this masochistic attitude is therefore a neurotically distorted means of attaining a heterosexual goal, which these patients believe they cannot reach in any other way.[5]

To put it simply, one might say that the solution of the problem of their feeling of inhibition in regard to work lies in these cases in their inability to bring to the work in question a sufficient amount of interest. In fact, the term "inhibition in regard to work" does not cover the matter adequately, for in most cases there comes about eventually a complete mental aridity. The aims remain fixed in the erotic sphere, the conflicts existing in that sphere are transferred to the field of work, and finally the inhibition in regard to work is itself utilized by the desire to extort love, at least in this roundabout way, in the form of commiseration and tender care.

Since work must of necessity remain not only unproductive and unsatisfactory but becomes actually painful, these patients are thrust back with redoubled force—in a *secondary* manner—into the erotic sphere. This secondary process may be set in motion by a personal sexual experience such as marriage, but also by any other similar occurrences in the environment. This may also serve to explain the possibility already mentioned, that the

5. The train of thought is here the same, in the main, as has been expressed by Reich in "Der masochistische Charakter," *Intern. Zeitschr.* (1932), insofar as he also was able to demonstrate masochistic behavior as subserving the attainment of pleasure in the end.

analysis also may become an exciting factor, namely when the analyst, misjudging the true state of affairs, puts all the emphasis upon the sexual sphere from the outset.

The difficulties naturally become more pronounced with increasing age. A young person is easily consoled in the face of erotic failures and hopes for a better "fate." Economic independence is, at least in the middle classes, not as yet a pressing problem. And the narrowing down of the spheres of interest does not as yet make itself very severely felt. With increasing years, say in about the thirties, continued failure in love comes to be regarded as a fatality, while gradually at the same time the possibilities of a satisfactory relationship become more hopeless, chiefly for internal reasons: increasing insecurity, retardation of general development, and therefore failure to develop the charms characteristic of mature years. Furthermore, the lack of economic independence gradually becomes more of a burden. And finally, the emptiness that comes to pervade the sphere of work and achievement is felt in increasing degree as increased emphasis is, with increasing age, placed by the subject or by the environment upon achievement. Life seems increasingly to lack meaning, and gradually bitterness develops because these persons necessarily lose themselves more and more in their twofold self-deception. They think that they can be happy only through love, whereas, constituted as they are, they can never be, while on the other hand they have an ever-diminishing faith in the worth of their abilities.

Every reader will in all probability have noticed that the type of woman depicted here occurs frequently today in less exaggerated form, at any rate in our middle-class intellectual circles. At the outset I expressed the opinion that this is largely determined by social reasons, reasons that lie in the social narrowing of women's sphere of work. In the cases described here, however, the particular neurotic entanglement nevertheless arises clearly from an unfortunate individual development.

This description might give the impression that the two sets of forces, social and individual, are separated from each other. This is certainly not the case. I believe that I can show in each instance that the type of woman described can only result in this form on the basis of individual factors, and I assume that the *frequency* of the type is explained by the fact that, given the social factors, relatively slight difficulties in personal development suffice to drive women in the direction of this type of womanhood.

THE PROBLEM OF FEMININE

MASOCHISM*

○○○

*I*NTEREST IN THE PROBLEM of feminine masochism extends far beyond the merely medical and psychological spheres, for to students of the Western culture at least, it touches on the very roots for evaluating woman in her cultural definition. The facts appear to be that in our cultural areas, masochistic phenomena are more frequent in women than in men. Two ways of approaching an explanation of this observation have appeared. By one, there is an attempt to discover if masochistic trends are inherent in, or akin to, the very essence of female nature. By the other, one undertakes to evaluate the weight of social conditionings in the genesis of any sex-limited peculiarities in the distribution of masochistic trends.

In psychoanalytic literature—taking the views of Rado and Deutsch as representative in this connection—the problem has been tackled only from the viewpoint of regarding feminine masochism as one psychic consequence of anatomical sex differences. Psychoanalysis thus has lent its scientific tools to support the theory of a given kinship between masochism and female biology. The possibility of social conditioning has as yet not been considered from the psychoanalytical side.

The task of this paper is to contribute to the efforts of determining the weight of biological and cultural factors in this problem; to review carefully the validity of the psychoanalytical data given in this direction; and to raise the question of whether psy-

* Expanded from a paper presented at the mid-year meeting of the American Psychoanalytic Association in Washington, December 26, 1933. *The Psychoanalytic Review*, Vol. XXII, No. 3 (1935), pp. 241-57. Reprinted with the permission of *The Psychoanalytic Review*.

choanalytical knowledge can be utilized for an investigation of a possible connection with social conditionings.

One may summarize the psychoanalytic views thus far presented somewhat as follows:

The specific satisfactions sought and found in female sex life and motherhood are of a masochistic nature. The content of the early sexual wishes and fantasies concerning the father is the desire to be mutilated, that is, castrated by him. Menstruation has the hidden connotation of a masochistic experience. What the woman secretly desires in intercourse is rape and violence, or in the mental sphere, humiliation. The process of childbirth gives her an unconscious masochistic satisfaction, as is also the case with the maternal relation to the child. Furthermore, as far as men indulge in masochistic fantasies or performances, these represent an expression of their desire to play the female role.

Deutsch[1] assumes a genetic factor of a biological nature, which inevitably leads up to a masochistic conception of the female role. Rado[2] points out a genetic factor that forces the sexual development into a masochistic channel. There is a difference of opinion as to whether or not these specifically female forms of masochism arise from deviations in the female development, or represent the "normal" female attitude.

It is assumed at least implicitly that masochistic character trends of all kinds also are much more frequent in women than in men. This conclusion is inevitable when one holds the basic psychoanalytic theory that general behavior in life is modeled on the sexual behavior pattern, which in women is deemed masochistic. It then follows that if most or all women are masochistic in their attitude toward sex and reproduction, they would indubitably reveal masochistic trends in their nonsexual attitude toward life more frequently than would men.

This consideration shows that these authors are dealing in fact with a problem of normal female psychology, and not only with one of psychopathology. Rado affirms that he is concerned

1. Deutsch, H., "Der feminine Masochismus und seine Beziehung zur Frigidität," *Intern. Zeitschr. f. Psychoanal.*, II (1930).

2. Rado, S., "Fear of Castration in Woman," *Psychoanalytic Quarterly*, III-IV (1933).

only with pathologic phenomena, but from his deduction as to the origin of feminine masochism, one cannot but conclude that the sex life of the vast majority of women is pathologic. The difference between his views and those presented by Deutsch, who affirms that to be feminine is to be masochistic, is thus seen to be theoretical rather than factual.

There is no need to question the fact that women may seek and find masochistic satisfaction in masturbation, menstruation, intercourse, and childbirth. Beyond doubt this occurs. What remains for discussion is the genesis and frequency of occurrence. Both Deutsch and Rado, in dealing with the problem, completely ignore discussion of frequency, because they maintain that the psychologic genetic factors are so forceful and ubiquitous that a consideration of frequency becomes superfluous.

On the matter of genesis, both authors assume that the decisive turning point in female development is the awareness of the little girl that she has no penis, the assumption being that the shock of this realization exerts a lasting influence. There are two sources of data for this assumption: the findings in the analyses of neurotic women concerning fantasies and wishes to possess, or to have possessed a penis; and the observation of little girls expressing the wish to have a penis when they discover its existence in others.

The foregoing observations are sufficient to build a working hypothesis to the effect that wishes for masculinity of some origin or other, play a role in female sex life, and this hypothesis may be used in seeking explanations for certain neurotic phenomena in women. It must be realized, however, that this is an hypothesis, not a fact; and that it is not even indisputably useful as an hypothesis. When it is claimed, moreover, that the desire for masculinity is not only a dynamic factor of primary order in neurotic females, but in every human female, independent of individual or cultural conditions, one cannot but remark that there are no data to substantiate this claim. Unfortunately little or nothing is known of psychically healthy women, or of women under different cultural conditions, due to limitations of historical and ethnological knowledge.

Therefore, as there are no data about frequency, conditioning, and weight of the observed reactions of the little girl to the discovery of the penis, the assumption that this is a turning point in female development is stimulating, but can scarcely be used in a chain of proof. Why, indeed, should the girl turn masochistic when she realizes the lack of a penis? Deutsch and Rado account for this further assumption in very different ways. Deutsch believes that "the hitherto active-sadistic libido attached to the clitoris rebounds from the barricade of the subject's inner realization of her lack of the penis . . . and most frequently of all is deflected in a regressive direction to masochism." This swinging in the direction of masochism is "part of the woman's anatomical destiny."

Let us ask again: What are the data? As far as I can see, only the fact that there may exist in small children early sadistic fantasies. This is partly elicited by direct psychoanalytic observation of neurotic children (M. Klein), and partly by reconstruction out of analysis of neurotic adults. There is no evidence for the ubiquity of these early sadistic fantasies, and I wonder, for instance, whether little American Indian girls, or little Trobriand girls have them. However, even taking for granted that this occurrence was in fact ubiquitous, there still remain three further assumptions necessary for completion of the picture:

(1) That these sadistic fantasies are generated by the active-sadistic libido cathexis of the clitoris.

(2) That the girl renounces her clitoris-masturbation in consequence of the narcissistic injury of having no penis.

(3) That the hitherto active-sadistic libido turns automatically inward and becomes masochistic.

All three assumptions seem highly speculative. It is known that people can become frightened of their hostile aggressions and subsequently prefer the suffering role, but how a libido-cathexis of an organ can be sadistic and then turn inward, seems mysterious.

Deutsch wanted "to examine the genesis of femininity," by which she means "the feminine, passive-masochistic disposition of the mental life of women." She affirms that masochism is the most elemental power in female mental life. No doubt that is the case in many neurotic women, but the hypothesis offered that it is psycho-biologically necessary in all women is unconvincing.

Rado proceeds in a more careful way. First, he does not start with the endeavor to point out the "genesis of femininity," but wants to account only for certain clinically observable pictures in neurotic women and he gives valuable data about various defenses against masochistic drives in women. Furthermore, he does not take the wish for penis-possession as a given fact, but recognizes that there may be a problem here. It will be remembered that I formerly raised the same question, as did Jones and Lampl-de Groot subsequently. The various solutions suggested are by no means congruent. Jones, Rado, and I agree insofar as we see in the masculinity wish, or masculinity fiction, a defense. Jones suggests that it is a defense against the danger of aphanisis; Rado, one against masochistic drives; and I, one against incestuous wishes for the father.[3] Lampl-de Groot suggests that the desire for masculinity is due to early sexual wishes for the mother. It would surpass the scope of this paper to discuss the ramifications of this problem here; briefly, in my opinion the problem is not yet solved.

Rado offers the following formula for the masochistic development in woman following the discovery of the penis: He agrees with Freud that this discovery is inevitably a narcissistic shock for the girl, but he thinks the effect varies with different emotional conditions. If it occurs in the period of early sex efflorescence, it represents, according to Rado, in addition to the narcissistic blow, a peculiarly painful experience because it arouses in the girl the belief that the male can derive much more pleasure from masturbation than the female. This experience, he thinks, is so painful that it destroys forever the pleasure the girl hitherto found in masturbation. Before we see how Rado deduces the genesis of female masochism from this alleged reaction, it is necessary to discuss the underlying premise that the awareness of the possibility of a major pleasure definitely destroys the enjoyment of an attainable pleasure that is considered inferior to it.

3. I am no longer committed to this view for reasons that will be elucidated in an article of later date. In fact I am inclined to agree with Rado's opinion, though I arrive at my conclusions for different reasons.

How does this assumption coincide with the data of everyday life? It would imply, for instance, that a man who thought Greta Garbo more attractive than other women, but had no chance of meeting her, would as a result of the "discovery" of her superior charms lose all pleasure in having relations with other women available to him. It would imply that one who is fond of mountains would find his pleasure in them utterly spoiled by imagining that a sea resort might offer a greater pleasure. Of course reactions of this kind are occasionally observed, but only in persons of a certain type, namely, in persons excessively or pathologically greedy. The principle applied by Rado is certainly not the pleasure-principle, but might better be called the greediness-principle, and as such, though valuable for the explanation of certain neurotic reactions, can scarcely be assumed to work in "normal" children or adults, and is in fact contradictory to the pleasure-principle. The latter implies that one is bound to seek satisfaction in every given situation, even when it does not provide the maximal pleasure possibilities, and even though the possibilities are meager. The normal occurrence of this reaction is accounted for by two factors: the high adaptability and flexibility of our pleasure-seeking strivings pointed out by Freud as characteristic of the healthy person in contrast to the neurotic one; and an automatic reality-testing process, which results in an automatic conscious or unconscious registering of what is attainable and what is not. Even assuming that this latter process functions more slowly in children than in adults, a little girl who is fond of her rag doll, though she may for a while ardently desire the well-dressed doll in the toyshop, will go on playing cheerfully with her own doll after realizing the impossibility of getting the more beautiful one.

Let us, however, accept for a moment Rado's assumption that the girl hitherto satisfied in her sexual outlets finds her pleasure in masturbation destroyed by the discovery of the penis. What then might one expect this to contribute toward her development of masochistic drives? Rado argues as follows. The extreme mental pain caused by the penis discovery excites the girl sexually and this provides her with a substitute gratification. Having been robbed thus of her natural means of satisfaction, she has thenceforth only the one way of craving satisfaction through suffering. Her sexual strivings become and remain masochistic. She may then later, conceiving the aim of her strivings as dangerous, build up various defenses, but the sex strivings themselves are definitely and permanently shifted into masochistic channels.

One question intrudes itself. Granting that the girl would really suffer severely from the vision of an unattainable major source of pleasure, why should this pain excite her sexually? As this assumed reaction is the cornerstone upon which the author builds a subsequent lifelong masochistic attitude, one would like to hear evidence of its factual occurrence.

As the evidence has not yet been presented, one looks around for analogous reactions that might lend plausibility to the assumption. A correspondent example would have to fulfill the same preconditions given in the case of the little girl: a sudden interruption of customary sexual outlets by the occurrence of some painful event. Consider, for example, the case of a man who has led a hitherto satisfactory sex life, and is then jailed and placed under such close supervision that all sexual outlets are barred. Will such a man become masochistic? That is, will he become sexually incited by witnessing beatings, by imagining beatings, or receiving actual beatings and maltreatment? Will he indulge in fantasies of persecution and inflicted suffering? No doubt such masochistic reactions may occur. But no doubt also this represents only one of several possible reactions, and such masochistic reactions will occur only in a man who *previously* had masochistic tendencies. Other examples lead to the same conclusion. A woman deserted by her husband, and without any immediate sexual outlet or the anticipation of one, may react masochistically; but the more poised she is, the better able she will be to renounce sexuality temporarily and find some satisfaction in friends, children, work, or pleasure. Again, a woman in such a situation will react masochistically only if she already had an established pattern of masochistic trends.

If I may venture a guess as to what implicit premise induced the author to regard such a challenging statement as self-evident, I should say it is an overvaluation of the urgency of sexual needs —as if he supplied the sexual urge with the same impatient greediness that he attributed to the general pleasure-seeking strivings; more concretely, as if when one's sexual outlet is barred, one immediately has to seize upon the next opportunity available for sexual excitement and satisfaction.

In other words, reactions like the one assumed by Rado certainly exist, though by no means self-evident or inevitable; they presuppose when they occur, masochistic drives previously existing; *they are an expression of masochistic tendencies, but not their root.*

Following Rado's train of reasoning, is it not curious indeed, that the little boy does not turn masochistic? Nearly every little boy obtains a view of the much larger penis of some adult. He perceives that the adult—the father—can obtain a much greater pleasure than he does. The idea of the greater obtainable pleasure should spoil his own enjoyment in masturbation. He should give up masturbation. He should suffer a severe mental pain, which excites him sexually, and he should adopt this pain as a substitute gratification and from then on be masochistic. This seems to happen very infrequently.

I proceed to a last critical point. Assuming the girl did react to the discovery of the penis with a severe mental pain; assuming the idea of a possibly greater pleasure destroying her attainable pleasure; assuming she did become sexually excited by the mental pain and found a substitute sexual satisfaction in it; assuming all these debatable considerations for the purpose of argument: Why then should she *lastingly* be driven to seek satisfaction in suffering? There seems to be a discrepancy between cause and effect here. A stone that has fallen to the ground will remain there unless it is removed by some external power. A living organism, when hit by some traumatic event adapts itself to the new situation. While Rado assumes subsequent defense reactions built up as a protection against the dangerous masochistic drives, he does not question the enduring character of the strivings themselves, which once established, are believed to retain their motivating force unchanged. It is one of the great scientific merits of Freud to have vigorously stressed the tenacity of childhood impressions; yet psychoanalytic experience shows also that an emotional reaction which has once occurred in childhood is maintained throughout life only if it continues to be supported by various dynamically important drives. If Rado does not assume that a single traumatic shock can exert a lasting influence without being supported by any needs within the personality, then he must assume that though the shock is passing, the allegedly painful fact of lacking a penis remains, with the consequence that masturbation is abandoned, and the sexual libido is permanently redirected along masochistic channels. But clinical experience indicates that absence of masturbation is by no means invariable in masochistic children.[4] This chain of alleged causation therefore also fails.

Although Rado does not assume, as does Deutsch, that this traumatic event is a regular, inevitable occurrence in female development, he states correctly that it is bound to happen with "striking frequency," and in fact a girl could, according to his assumptions, only exceptionally escape the fate of a masochistic deflection. In coming to this implied conclusion that women must be almost universally masochistic, he has made the same error that physicians tend to make if they endeavor to account for pathologic phenomena on a broader basis—namely, unwarranted generalization from limited data. It is in principle the same error that psychiatrists and gynecologists have made before him: Krafft-Ebing, observing that masochistic men often play the role of the suffering female, speaks of masochistic phenomena as representing a sort of rank overgrowth of female qualities; Freud, starting from the same observation, assumes a close connection between masochism and femininity; the Russian gynecologist Nemilow, being impressed by women's suffering in defloration, menstruation, and childbirth, speaks of the "bloody tragedy of woman"; the German gynecologist Liepman, being impressed by the frequency of illnesses, accidents, and pains in the life of women, assumes that vulnerability, irritability, and sensitivity are the fundamental triad of female qualities.

Only one justification could be adduced for such generalizations, namely, Freud's hypothesis that there is no fundamental

4. In a communication from David M. Levy he cites instances in which girls with fantasies of being beaten also masturbated while indulging in these fantasies. He states that he knows of no direct relationship between masochistic phenomena and the absence of genital manipulation.

difference between pathologic and "normal" phenomena; that pathologic phenomena merely show more distinctly as through a magnifying glass the processes going on in all human beings. There can be little doubt that this principle has broadened the horizon, but one should be aware of its limitations. These have had to be considered, for instance, in dealing with the Œdipus complex. First, its existence and implications were seen distinctly in neuroses. This knowledge sharpened the observation of psychoanalysts, so that slighter indications of it were frequently observed. The conclusion was then drawn that this was an ubiquitous phenomenon, which in neurotic persons was only more accentuated. This conclusion is disputable, because ethnological studies have shown that the peculiar configuration denoted by the term Œdipus complex is probably nonexistent under widely different cultural conditions.[5] One must, therefore, narrow down the assumption to the statement that this peculiar emotional pattern in the relations between parents and children arises only under certain cultural conditions.

The same principle can in fact be found to apply to the question of feminine masochism. Deutsch and Rado have been impressed by the frequency with which they found a masochistic conception of the female role in neurotic women. I suppose every analyst will have made the same observations, or will be assisted by their findings in making them more accurately. Masochistic phenomena in women can be detected as a result of directed and sharpened observation, where they might otherwise have passed unnoticed, as in social rencontres with women (entirely outside the field of psychoanalytic practice), in feminine character portrayals in literature, or in examination of women of somewhat foreign mores, such as the Russian peasant woman who does not feel she is loved by her husband unless he beats her. In the face of this evidence, the psychoanalyst concludes that he is here confronted with an ubiquitous phenomenon, functioning on a psychobiological basis with the regularity of a law of nature.

The onesidedness or positive errors in the results obtained by a partial examination of the picture are due to a neglect of cul-

5. Boehm, F., "Zur Geschichte des Ödipuskomplexes," *Int. Zeitschr. f. Psychoanal.*, I (1930).

tural or social factors—an exclusion from the picture of women living under civilizations with different customs. The Russian peasant woman of the Tsaristic and patriarchal regime was invariably cited in discussions aimed at proving how deeply masochism is ingrained in female nature. Yet this peasant woman has emerged into the self-assertive Soviet woman of today who would doubtless be astonished if beatings were administered as a token of affection. The change has occurred in the patterns of culture rather than in the particular women.

More generally speaking, whenever the question of frequency enters into the picture, sociological implications are involved, and the refusal to be concerned with them from the psychoanalytic angle does not shut out their existence. Omission of these considerations may lead to a false valuation of anatomical differences and their personal elaboration as causative factors for phenomena actually partially or wholly the result of social conditioning. Only a synthesis of both series of conditions can lead to a complete understanding.

For sociological and ethnological approaches, data concerning the following questions would be pertinent:

i—What is the frequency of occurrence of masochistic attitudes towards female functions under various social and cultural conditions?

ii—What is the frequency of general masochistic attitudes or manifestations in women, as compared with men, under various social and cultural conditions?

If both these inquiries gave color to the view that under all social conditions there is a masochistic conception of the female role, and if equally there is a decided preponderance of general masochistic phenomena among women as compared with men, then, and only then, would one be justified in seeking further psychologic reasons for this phenomenon. If, however, such an ubiquitous feminine masochism did not appear, one would wish of the sociological-ethnological research the answer to the further questions:

(1) What are the special social conditions under which masochism connected with female functions is frequent?

(2) What are the special social conditions under which gen-

eral masochistic attitudes are more frequent in women than in men?

The task of psychoanalysis in such an investigation would be to supply the anthropologist with psychological data. With the exception of perversions and masturbatory fantasies, masochistic tendencies and gratifications are unconscious. The anthropologist cannot explore these. What he needs are criteria by which he can identify and observe the manifestations that in high probability indicate the existence of masochistic drives.

To give these data is comparatively simple as in question (1), concerning masochistic manifestations in female functions. On the basis of psychoanalytic experience it is reasonably safe to assume masochistic tendencies:

(1) When there is a great frequency of functional menstrual disorders, such as dysmenorrhea and menorrhagia.

(2) When there is great frequency of psychogenic disturbance in pregnancy and childbirth, such as fear of childbirth, fuss about it, pains, or elaborate means to avoid pain.

(3) When there is a frequency of such attitudes toward sexual relations as to imply that it is debasing for, or an exploitation of, women.

These indications are not to be taken as absolute, but rather with the following two restricting considerations:

(a) It seems to have become habitual in psychoanalytic thinking to assume that pain, suffering, or fear of suffering are prompted by masochistic drives, or result in masochistic gratification. It is therefore necessary to point out that such assumptions require evidence. Alexander, for instance, assumes that people climbing mountains with heavy knapsacks are masochistic, particularly if there is a car or railway by which they might get to the top of a mountain more easily. This may be true, but more frequently the reasons for carrying heavy knapsacks are very realistic ones.

(b) Suffering, or even self-inflicted pain, in more primitive tribes, may be an expression of magical thinking meant to ward off danger, and may have nothing to do with individual masochism. Therefore, one can only interpret such data in connection with a basic knowledge of the entire structure of the tribal history concerned.

The task of psychoanalysis in regard to question (2), data concerning indications for general masochistic attitudes is much more difficult, because understanding of the whole phenomenon is still limited. In fact, it has not advanced much beyond Freud's statement that it has something to do with sexuality and with morality. There are, however, these open questions: Is it a primarily sexual phenomenon that extends also into the moral sphere, or a moral phenomenon extending also into the sexual sphere? Are the moral and the erogenic masochism two separate processes, or only two sets of manifestations arising from a common underlying process? Or is masochism perhaps a collective term for very complex phenomena?

One feels justified in using the same term for widely discrepant manifestations because all of them have some trends in common: tendencies to arrange in fantasies, dreams, or in the real world, situations that imply suffering; or to feel suffering in situations that would not have this concomitant for the average person. The suffering may concern the physical or the mental sphere. There is some gratification or relief of tension connected with it, and that is why it is striven for. The gratification or relief of tension may be conscious or unconscious, sexual or nonsexual. The nonsexual functions may be very different: reassurances against fears, atonements for committed sins, permission to commit new ones, strategy in reference to goals otherwise unattainable, indirect forms of hostility.

The realization of this wide range of masochistic phenomena is more bewildering and challenging than encouraging, and these general statements certainly cannot be of much help to the anthropologist. More concrete data are at his disposal, however, if all scientific worries about conditions and functions are swept aside, and only those surface attitudes that have been observable in patients with distinct and widespread masochistic tendencies within the psychoanalytic situation are made the basis of his investigations. For this purpose, therefore, it may suffice to enumerate these attitudes without tracing them back in detail to their individual conditions. Needless to say, they are not all present in every patient belonging to this category; yet the whole syndrome is so typical (as every analyst will recognize), that if some of these trends are apparent at the beginning of a treatment, one can safely predict the entire picture, though of course the details vary. The details concern sequence of appearance, distribution of weight among the single trends, and particularly form and intensity of defenses built up for protection against these tendencies.

Let us consider what observable data there are in patients with widespread masochistic trends. As I see it, the main lines of the surface structure in such personalities are somewhat as follows:

There are several ways in which one can find reassurance against deep fears. Renunciation is one way; inhibition, another; denying the fear and becoming optimistic, a third one; and so on. Being loved is the particular means of reassurance used by a masochistic person. As he has a rather free-floating anxiety, he needs constant signs of attention and affection, and as he never believes in these signs except momentarily, he has an excessive need for attention and affection. He is therefore, generally speaking, very emotional in his relations with people; easily attached because he expects them to give him the necessary reassurance; easily disappointed because he never gets, and never can get, what he expects. The expectation or illusion of the "great love" often plays an important role. Sexuality being one of the most common ways of getting affection, he also tends to overvalue it and clings to the illusion that it holds the solution of all life's problems. How far this is conscious, or how easily he has actual sexual relations, depends on his inhibitions on this score. Where he has had sexual relations, or attempts at such, his history shows a frequency of "unhappy loves"; he has been deserted, disappointed, humiliated, badly treated. In nonsexual relations, the same tendency appears in all gradations from being or feeling incompetent, self-sacrificing, and submissive, to playing the martyr role and feeling or actually being humiliated, abused, and exploited. While he otherwise feels it as a given fact that he *is* incompetent or that life *is* brutal, one can see in the psychoanalytic situation that it is not facts, but an obstinate tendency, which makes him insist upon seeing or arranging it this way. This tendency, moreover, is revealed in the psychoanalytic situation as an unconscious arrangement motivating him to provoke attacks, to feel ruined, damaged, ill-treated, humiliated, without any real cause.

Because other people's affection and sympathy are of vital importance to him, he easily becomes extremely dependent, and this hyperdependency also shows clearly in relations with the analyst.

The next observable reason he never believes in any form of affection he may actually receive (instead of clinging to it as representing the coveted reassurance) lies in his greatly diminished self-esteem; he feels inferior, absolutely unlovable and unworthy of love. On the other hand, just this lack of self-confidence makes him feel that appealing to pity by having and displaying inferiority feelings, weakness, and suffering is the only means by which he can win the affection he needs. One sees that the deterioration of his self-esteem lies rooted in his paralysis of what may be termed "adequate aggressiveness." By this I mean the capacities for work, including the following attributes: taking initiative; making efforts; carrying things through to completion; attaining success; insisting upon one's rights; defending oneself when attacked; forming and expressing autonomous views; recognizing one's goals and being able to plan one's life according to them.[6] In masochistic persons one usually finds widespread inhibitions on this score, which in their entirety account for the feeling of insecurity, or even helplessness, in the life struggle, and explain the subsequent dependency on other people, and a predisposition to look to them for support or help.

Psychoanalysis reveals the tendency to recoil from competition of any kind as the next observable reason for their incapacity to be self-assertive. Their inhibitions thus result from efforts to check themselves in order to avoid the risk of competition.

The hostile feelings inevitably generated on the basis of such self-defeating tendencies, also cannot be expressed freely because they are conceived as jeopardizing the reassurance attendant on being loved, which is the mainspring of protection against anxieties. Weakness and suffering, therefore, already serving many

6. In the field of psychoanalytic literature Schultz-Hencke, "Schicksal und Neurose," has particularly emphasized the pathogenic importance of these inhibitions.

functions, now also act as a vehicle for the indirect expression of hostility.

The use of this syndrome of observable attitudes for anthropologic investigation is subject to one source of possible major error; namely, masochistic attitudes are not always apparent as such because they are frequently concealed by defenses, often appearing clearly only after the latter have been removed. As an analysis of these defenses clearly is beyond the sphere of such an investigation, the defenses must be taken at face value, with the result that these instances of masochistic attitudes must escape observation.

Reviewing then, the observable masochistic attitudes, regardless of their deeper motivation, I suggest that the anthropologist seek data concerning questions like these: under what social or cultural conditions do we find more frequently in women than in men

(1) the manifesting of inhibitions in the direct expression of demands and aggressions;

(2) a regarding of oneself as weak, helpless, or inferior and implicitly or explicitly demanding considerations and advantages on this basis;

(3) a becoming emotionally dependent on the other sex;

(4) a showing of tendencies to be self-sacrificing, to be submissive, to feel used or to be exploited, to put responsibilities on the other sex;

(5) a using of weakness and helplessness as a means of wooing and subduing the other sex.[7]

Besides these formulations, which are direct generalizations of the psychoanalytic experience with masochistic women, I may also present certain generalizations as to the causative factors that predispose to the appearance of masochism in women. I should ex-

---

7. It may strike the psychoanalytic reader that in the enumeration of factors, I have not restricted myself to those that are influential in childhood only. One has to consider, however, that (1) the child is bound to feel the influence of those factors indirectly through the medium of the family, and particularly through the influence they have exerted on the women in her surroundings; and (2) though masochistic attitudes (like other neurotic attitudes) generate primarily in childhood, the conditions of later life determine for the average case (that is, cases in which childhood conditions have not been so severe that they alone definitely shape the characteristics).

pect these phenomena to appear in any culture-complex that included one or more of the following factors:

(1) Blocking of outlets for expansiveness and sexuality.

(2) Restriction in the number of children, inasmuch as having and rearing children supplies the woman with various gratifying outlets (tenderness, achievement, self-esteem), and this becomes all the more important when having and rearing children is the measuring rod of social evaluation.

(3) Estimation of women as beings who are, on the whole, inferior to men (insofar as it leads to a deterioration of female self-confidence).

(4) Economic dependence of women on men or on family, inasmuch as it fosters an emotional adaptation in the way of emotional dependence.

(5) Restriction of women to spheres of life that are built chiefly upon emotional bonds, such as family life, religion, or charity work.

(6) Surplus of marriageable women, paricularly when marriage offers the principal opportunity for sexual gratification, children, security, and social recognition.[8] This condition is relevant inasmuch as it favors [as do also (3) and (4)] emotional dependence on men, and generally speaking, a development that is not autonomous but fashioned and molded by existing male ideologies. It is pertinent also insofar as it creates among women a particularly strong competition from which recoil is an important factor in precipitating masochistic phenomena.

All the factors enumerated overlap; for example, strong sexual competition among women will be more potent if other outlets for competitive strivings (as for professional eminence) are concurrently blocked. It would seem that no one factor is ever solely responsible for the deviating development, but rather a con-

8. It must be borne in mind, however, that social regulations, such as marriage arrangement by families, would greatly reduce the effectiveness of this factor. This consideration also throws a light on Freud's assumption that women generally are more jealous than men. The statement probably is correct so far as the present German and Austrian cultures are concerned. To deduce this, however, from more purely individual anatomical-physiological sources (penis envy) is not convincing. While it may be so in individual cases, the generalization—independent of consideration of the social conditions—is subject to the same fundamental objection as previously mentioned.

catenation of factors.

In particular one must consider the fact that when some or all of the suggested elements are present in the culture-complex, there may appear certain fixed ideologies concerning the "nature" of woman; such as doctrines that woman is innately weak, emotional, enjoys dependence, is limited in capacities for independent work and autonomous thinking. One is tempted to include in this category the psychoanalytic belief that woman is masochistic by nature. It is fairly obvious that these ideologies function not only to reconcile women to their subordinate role by presenting it as an unalterable one, but also to plant the belief that it represents a fulfillment they crave, or an ideal for which it is commendable and desirable to strive. The influence that these ideologies exert on women is materially strengthened by the fact that women presenting the specified traits are more frequently chosen by men. This implies that women's erotic possibilities depend on their conformity to the image of that which constitutes their "true nature." It therefore seems no exaggeration to say that in such social organizations, masochistic attitudes (or rather, milder expressions of masochism) are favored in women while they are discouraged in men. Qualities like emotional dependence on the other sex (clinging vine), absorption in "love," inhibition of expansive, autonomous development, etc., are regarded as quite desirable in women but are treated with opprobrium and ridicule when found in men.

One sees that these cultural factors exert a powerful influence on women; so much so, in fact, that in our culture it is hard to see how any woman can escape becoming masochistic to some degree, from the effects of the culture alone, without any appeal to contributory factors in the anatomical-physiological characteristics of woman, and their psychic effects.

Certain writers, however—among them H. Deutsch—have generalized from psychoanalytical experience with neurotic women, and have held that the culture complexes to which I have referred are themselves the very effect of these anatomical-physiological characteristics. It is useless to argue this overgeneralization until the type of anthropological investigation suggested has been made. Let us look, however, at the factors in the somatic organization of women, which actually contribute to their acceptance of a masochistic role. The anatomical-physiological factors in women that may prepare the soil for the growth of masochistic phenomena, seem to me to be the following:

(a) Greater average physical strength in men than in women. According to ethnologists this is an acquired sex difference. Nevertheless it exists nowadays. Though weakness is not identical with masochism, the realization of an inferior physical strength may fertilize an emotional conception of a masochistic female role.

(b) The possibility of rape similarly may give rise in women to the fantasy of being attacked, subdued, and injured.

(c) Menstruation, defloration, and childbirth, insofar as they are bloody or even painful processes, may readily serve as outlets for masochistic strivings.

(d) The biologic differences in intercourse also serve for masochistic formulation. Sadism and masochism have fundamentally nothing whatsoever to do with intercourse, but the female role in intercourse (being penetrated) *lends* itself more readily to a personal misinterpretation (when needed) of masochistic performance; and the male role, to one of sadistic activity.

These biological functions have in themselves no masochistic connotation for women, and do not lead to masochistic reactions; but if masochistic needs of other origin[9] are present, they may easily be involved in masochistic fantasies, which in turn causes them to furnish masochistic gratifications. Beyond admitting the possibility of a certain preparedness in women for a masochistic conception of their role, every additional assertion as to the relation of their constitution to masochism is hypothetical; and such facts as the disappearance of all masochistic tendencies after a successful psychoanalysis, and the observations of nonmasochistic women (which, after all, exist), warn us not to overrate even this element of preparedness.

In summary: The problem of feminine masochism cannot be related to factors inherent in the anatomical-physiological-psychic characteristics of woman alone, but must be considered as importantly conditioned by the culture-complex or social organization

9. What I have in mind as the sources of masochistic attitudes, I shall present in a later communication.

in which the particular masochistic woman has developed. The precise weight of these two groups of factors cannot be assessed until we have the results of anthropological investigations using valid psychoanalytical criteria in several culture areas significantly different from ours. It is clear, however, that the importance of anatomical-psychological-psychic factors has been greatly overestimated by some writers on this subject.

PERSONALITY CHANGES IN

FEMALE ADOLESCENTS*

○○

*I*N ANALYZING ADULT WOMEN with neurotic troubles or character disturbances, one frequently finds these two conditions:
(1) Although in all cases the determining conflicts have arisen
in early childhood, the first personality changes have taken place
in adolescence. At this time they often have not been alarming
to the environment and have not given the impression of being
pathological manifestations endangering future development or
requiring treatment, but have been regarded as transient troubles natural for this period of life, or even as desirable and
promising signs. (2) The onset of these changes coincides approximately with the beginning of menstruation. This connection has
not been apparent either because the patients have not been
aware of the coincidence, or even if they have observed a temporal coincidence, they have not attributed any significance to it,
because they have not noticed or have "forgotten" the psychic
implications menstruation has had for them. Personality changes,
in contrast to neurotic symptoms, develop gradually and this also
helps to disguise and obscure the real connection. Usually it is
only after the patients have gained insight into the emotional
effect that menstruation has had on them that they spontaneously
see the connection. Tentatively I am inclined to distinguish these
four types of changes:

(1) girl becomes absorbed in sublimated activities; develops
aversion against erotic sphere;

(2) girl becomes absorbed in erotic sphere (boy-crazy); loses

* Presented at the 1934 meeting of the American Orthopsychiatric Asso-
ciation. Reprinted from *The American Journal of Orthopsychiatry*, Vol. V,
No. 1 (January 1935), pp. 19-26. Copyright, The American Orthopsychiatric
Association, Inc. Reproduced by permission.

interest in and capacity for work;

(3) girl becomes emotionally "detached," acquires a "don't care" attitude; cannot put energy into anything;

(4) girl develops homosexual tendencies.

This classification is incomplete and certainly does not cover the entire range of existing possibilities (for instance, the development of the prostitute and criminal) but refers only to those changes that I had the opportunity of observing, directly or by inference, among the patients who incidentally came in for treatment. Besides, the division is arbitrary, as divisions of behavior types necessarily are, involving the fiction that clearcut types always appear, while in reality all sorts of transitions and mixtures are frequently present.

The first group consists of girls who have shown a natural curiosity regarding questions of anatomical and functional differences in the two sexes and the riddles of propagation and who have felt attracted to boys and have liked to play with them. Around the time of puberty they suddenly become absorbed in mental problems, in religious, ethical, artistic, or scientific pursuits, while at the same time they lose interest in the erotic sphere. Usually the girl who undergoes this change does not come for treatment at this time because the family is pleased at her seriousness and her lack of flirtatious tendencies. Difficulties are not apparent. They will appear only later in life, particularly after marriage. It is easy to overlook the pathological nature of this change for these two reasons: (1) To develop intense interest in some mental activity is expected during these years. (2) The girl herself is for the most part not conscious that she really has an aversion against sexuality. She only feels that she loses interest in boys and more or less dislikes dances, dates, and flirtations and gradually withdraws from them.

The second group presents the reverse picture. Very gifted, promising girls at this time lose interest in everything except boys, cannot concentrate, and drop all mental activities a short time after undertaking them. They become completely absorbed in the erotic sphere. This transformation, just as the reverse one, is regarded as "natural" and defended as such with the similar rationalization that it is "normal" for a girl at this age to turn her attention to boys, dances, and flirtations. Surely that is so, but what about the following trends? The girl compulsively falls in love with one boy after the other, without really caring for any of them, and after she is sure of having conquered them she either drops them or provokes them to drop her. She feels utterly unattractive in spite of evidence to the contrary and usually she shrinks from having actual sexual relations, rationalizing this attitude on the basis of social demands, although the real reason is that she is frigid, as is shown when she eventually hazards this step. She becomes depressed or apprehensive as soon as there is no man around to admire her. On the other hand her attitude toward work is not, as the defense would imply, the "natural" outcome of the fact that her other interests have been forced into the background because of her preoccupation with boys, but the girl is in reality very ambitious and suffers intensely from a feeling of inability to accomplish anything.

The third type becomes inhibited in the spheres of both work and love. Again this is not necessarily apparent on the surface. Superficially observed, she may give the impression of being well-adjusted. She has no difficulty in making social contacts, has girl and boy friends, is sophisticated, talks frankly about everything sexual, pretends to have no inhibitions at all, and sometimes also enters into one or the other kind of sexual relations without becoming emotionally involved in any of them. She is detached, remote, an observer of herself and of others, a spectator of life. She may deceive herself about the existing aloofness, but at times, at least, she is keenly aware that there is no deep, positive emotional tie to anyone or anything. Nothing matters much. There is a marked inconsistency between her vitality and gifts, and her lack of expansiveness. Usually she feels her life to be hollow and boring.

The fourth group is the easiest to characterize and best known. Here the girl turns away from boys altogether and develops crushes and intense friendships with girls, the sexual character of which may or may not be conscious. If she becomes aware of the sexual character of these tendencies such a girl may suffer from intense feelings of guilt as though she were a criminal. Her attitude toward work may vary. Ambitious and at times very capable, she often has difficulty in asserting herself or has "nervous breakdowns" in between times of efficiency.

These are four very different types, yet even a surface observation, if only accurate enough, shows that they nevertheless have trends in common: insecurity regarding their female self-confidence, conflictful or antagonistic attitude toward men, and incapacity to "love"—whatever this term may mean. If they do not dodge the female role altogether, they rebel against it or exaggerate it in a distorted manner. In all these cases much more guilt is connected with sexuality than they admit. "Not all are free who ridicule their chains."[1]

Psychoanalytic observation shows a still more striking similarity, so much so that for a while one is apt to forget about the differences shown in their attitudes toward life:

All of them feel a general antagonism against everyone, men and women, yet there is a difference in their attitude to men and women. While the antagonism toward men varies in intensity and motivation and is elicited comparatively easily, toward women there is an absolutely destructive hostility and consequently it is deeply hidden. They may be vaguely aware of its existence, but never realize its real scope, its violence and ruthlessness, and its further implications.

All of them have a strongly defensive attitude toward masturbation. At most they may remember having masturbated as small children or they even deny its ever having played a role. They are quite honest about it on a conscious level. They really do not practice it or do so only in a very disguised form, and they feel no conscious desire to do so. As is shown later, powerful impulses of this sort exist but are completely dissociated from the rest of their personality and are concealed in this way because they are mixed up with enormous feelings of guilt and fear.

What accounts for the extreme hostility against women? Only part of it is understandable from their life history. Certain reproaches against the mother come up: lack of warmth, protection, understanding, preference for a brother, over-strict demands as to sexual purity. All of this is more or less supported by facts, but they themselves feel that the hostility is out of proportion to

1. *"Es sind nicht alle frei, die ihrer Ketten spotten."* (Schiller)

the amount of existing suspicion, defiance, and hatred.

The real implications become apparent, however, in their attitudes toward a woman analyst. Omitting technical details and omitting not only individual differences but also the differences in the defenses, characteristic for the types under discussion, the following picture gradually develops: They are convinced of being disliked by the analyst; they suspect that the analyst is really malevolent toward the patient, that she resents their being happy and successful, particularly that she condemns their sexual life and interferes with it or wants to do so.

While this is being disclosed as a reaction to feelings of guilt, and as an expression of fears, one gradually sees that they have some reason to be apprehensive, because their actual behavior toward the analyst in the analytic situation is dictated by an enormous defiance and by the tendency to defeat the analyst no matter if they defeat their own ends at the same time.

The actual behavior, however, still is only an expression of the existing hostility on the reality level. Its entire scope is revealed only if one descends into the fantasy life as it appears in dreams and daydreams. Here the hostility is lived out in the most cruel, archaic forms.

These crude primitive impulses lived out in fantasies, allow an understanding of the depth of the guilt feelings toward the mother and mother images. Furthermore they eventually allow an understanding of why masturbation has been entirely repressed and is still, at the present time, tinged with horror. The fantasies have accompanied masturbation and therefore have aroused guilt feelings about it. Guilt feelings, in other words, have not concerned the physical process of masturbation but the fantasies. Yet only the physical process and the desire for it could be repressed. The fantasies have kept on living in the depths, and having been repressed at an early age, have kept their infantile character. Though not aware of their existence, the individual keeps on responding with guilt feelings.

Yet the physical part of masturbation is not unimportant either. Intense fears have issued from it, the essence of which is the fear of being damaged, of being injured beyond repair. The content of this fear has not been conscious, but it has found numerous disguised expressions in all sorts of hypochondriac fears concerning all organs from the brain down to the feet—fears that something is wrong with them as women—fears that they will never be able to marry and have children—and finally, common to all cases, fears of being unattractive. Though these fears go back directly to the physical masturbation they, too, are understandable only from the psychic implications of masturbation.

The fear really implies: "Because I have cruel, destructive fantasies toward my mother and other women I ought to be afraid that they want to destroy me in the same way. 'An eye for an eye and a tooth for a tooth.'"

The very same fear of retaliation is responsible for their not feeling at ease with the analyst. In spite of consciously existing confidence in her fairness and dependability, they cannot help feeling deeply concerned that the sword hanging over them is bound to fall. They cannot help feeling that the analyst maliciously and intentionally wants to torment them. They have to choose a narrow path between the danger of displeasing her and the danger of revealing their hostile impulses.

Since they are constantly in fear of a fatal attack, it is easy enough to understand why they feel the vital necessity to defend themselves. And they do, by being evasive and trying to defeat the analyst. Their hostility, therefore, in an upper layer, has the connotation of a defense. Similarly, most of their hatred toward the mother has the same connotation of feeling guilty in reference to her and of warding off the fear connected with this guilt by turning against her.

When this has been worked through, the primary sources of the antagonism toward the mother are emotionally accessible. Their traces have been visible from the beginning in this fact: that with the exception of Group 2—which goes in for competition with other girls, though with an enormous apprehensiveness —all of them carefully avoid competition with other girls. Wherever another woman is in the field, they retreat immediately. Being convinced of their own lack of attractiveness, they feel inferior to any other girls who are around. In this fight, they may be observed to carry out with the analyst the same tendencies to avoid a competitive appearance. The actually existing

competitive struggle is hidden behind their feeling hopelessly
inferior to her. Even if eventually they cannot but admit their
competitive intentions they do so only with reference to intelligence and capability in work, while they shun comparisons that
would indicate competition on the female level. For instance,
they consistently repress disparaging thoughts about the analyst's
appearance and dress and are in deadly embarrassment if thoughts
of this kind come to the surface.

Competition has to be avoided because there has been a particularly strong rivalry with the mother or with an older sister
in childhood. Usually one or the other of the following factors
has greatly intensified the natural competition of the daughter
with the mother or an older sister: premature sexual development
and sex-consciousness; early intimidations that prevented them
from feeling self-confident; marital conflicts between the parents,
which forced the daughter to side with one or the other parent;
open or disguised rejection on the part of the mother; demon-
strations of an over-affectionate attitude on the part of the father
to the little girl, which may range from singling her out with
attentions to overt sexual approaches. Schematically summarizing
the facts, we find that this vicious circle has been set up: jealousy
and rivalry toward mother or sister; hostile impulses lived out in
fantasies; guilt and fear of being attacked and punished; defensive
hostility; reinforced fear and guilt.

The guilt and fear from these sources is, as I said, most firmly
anchored in the masturbatory fantasies. They do not, however,
remain restricted to these fantasies, but spread in a major or
minor degree to all sexual desires and sexual relations. They are
carried over to sexual relations with men and surround them
with a guilty and apprehensive atmosphere. They are responsible,
to a great extent, for the fact that relations with men remain
unsatisfactory.

There are other reasons, too, accounting for this result, which
have to do more directly with their attitude toward men themselves. I mention them only briefly because they have little bearing on the points I want to stress in this paper. They may have
an old resentment against men, issuing from old disappointments
and resulting in a secret desire for revenge. Moreover, on the

basis of feeling unlikable, they anticipate rejection from men and react antagonistically toward them. Insofar as they have turned away from their female role, because of its being too full of conflict, they often develop masculine strivings and carry over their competitive tendencies into their relations with men, competing now with men in masculine fields instead of with women. If this masculine role is highly desirable to them, they may develop a strong envy toward men with the tendency to disparage their faculties.

What happens when a girl with this structure enters puberty? At the time of puberty there is an increase of libidinal tension; sexual desires become more demanding and necessarily encounter the barrier of guilt and fear reactions. These are reinforced by the possibility of actual sexual experiences. The onset of menstruation at this time, for the girl who has a fear of being damaged by masturbation, emotionally means a definite proof that this damage has in fact occurred. Intellectual knowledge about menstruation does not make any difference, because the understanding is on a superficial level and the fears are deep and so they do not reach each other. The situation is getting acute. Desires and temptations are strong, and fears are strong.

It seems that we cannot long bear to live under the stress of a conscious anxiety—"I would rather die than have a real attack of anxiety," patients say. Therefore, in situations like these, vital necessity compels us to search for means of protection, i.e., we try automatically to change our attitude toward life in such a way that we either avoid anxiety or establish safeguards against it.

Regarding the basic conflicts present in all of the four types under discussion, they represent various ways of warding off anxiety. The fact that various ways are chosen accounts for the differences in the types. They develop opposite characteristics and opposite trends although they have the common aim of warding off the same sort of anxiety. The girl in Group I protects herself against fears by avoiding competition with women altogether and by almost completely dodging the female role. Her competitive urge becomes uprooted from its original soil and transplanted to some mental field. Competing for having the best character, the highest ideals, or for being the best student is so far removed from the competition for a man that her fears also are greatly attenuated. Her striving for perfection at the same time helps her to overcome guilt feelings.

The solution, being quite radical, has great temporary advantages. For years she may feel quite contented. The reverse side only appears if eventually she comes in contact with men, and particularly if she marries. One may then observe that here contentment and self-assurance break down rather suddenly and the contented, gay, capable, independent girl changes into a discontented woman greatly troubled with inferiority feelings, easily depressed, and refraining from taking an active share in the responsibilities of marriage. She is frigid sexually, and instead of a loving attitude toward her husband, a competitive attitude toward him prevails.

The girl in Group 2 does not resign her competitive attitude toward other women. Her wide-awake protest against other females drives her to beat them whenever an opportunity arises, with the result that she has, in contrast to the girl of Group 1, a rather free-floating anxiety. Her way of warding off this anxiety is to cling to men. While the first-mentioned girls retreat from the battlefield, these latter seek allies. Their insatiable thirst for the admiration of men is no indication whatever of their being constitutionally in greater need of sexual gratification. In fact they, too, prove to be frigid if they enter into actual sexual relations. The fact that men have for them the function of serving as a reassurance becomes apparent as soon as they fail to have one or several boy friends; their anxiety then comes near the surface and they feel desolate, insecure, and lost. Winning the admiration of men also serves as a reassurance for them in reference to their fear of not being "normal," which as I have indicated is an outcome of the fear of being damaged by masturbation. There is far too much guilt and fear connected with sexuality to allow them to have a satisfactory relation with men. Therefore only the ever-renewed conquest of men may serve the purpose of reassurance.[2]

2. A more exact description of the mechanisms at work in this type of woman is given in the paper, "Overvaluation of Love," which is to be published in the *Psychoanalytic Quarterly*. Editor's note: See "Overvaluation of Love" in this volume.

The fourth group, the potential homosexuals, try to solve the problem by overcompensation for their destructive hostility toward women. "I don't hate you, I love you." One might describe the change as a complete, blind denial of the hatred. How far they succeed with it depends on individual factors. Their dreams usually show an extreme degree of violence and cruelty toward the girl to whom they feel consciously attracted. A failure in their relations with girls throws them into spasms of despair and often brings them near to suicide, which indicates a turning of the aggression against themselves.

Like Group 1, they dodge their own female role completely, with the one difference that they more definitely develop the fiction of being a man. On a nonsexual level their relations with men often are devoid of conflicts. Furthermore, while Group 1 resigns from sexuality altogether, these girls resign from their heterosexual interests only.

The solution toward which Group 3 is driven is fundamentally different from the others. While all the others aim at reassurance by emotionally clinging to something—to accomplishment, to men, to women—their main way is that of stunting their emotional life and thereby diminishing their fears. "Don't become emotionally involved, then you won't get hurt." This principle of detachment is perhaps the most effective, lasting protection against anxiety, but the price paid for it seems to be very high too, insofar as it usually means attenuation of vitality and spontaneity and a considerable deterioration in the amount of available energy.

No one familiar with the intricate complexity of psychic dynamics that leads to a *seemingly* simple result will mistake these statements about the four types of personality changes for a complete revelation of their dynamics. The intention was not to give an "explanation" of the phenomenon of homosexuality or of detachment, for instance, but to regard them from one point of view only, as representing different solutions or pseudo-solutions for similar underlying conflicts. Which solution is chosen does not depend on the free volition of the girls, as the term "chosen" might imply, but is strictly determined by the concatenation of events in childhood and the girls' reactions to them.

The effect of circumstances may be so compelling that only one solution is possible. Then one will encounter the type in its pure, clearly delineated form. Others are driven by their experiences during or after adolescence to abandon one way and try another. The girl who is a female Don Juan type for a period, for instance, may develop ascetic tendencies later on. Furthermore one may find different attempts at solution tried simultaneously, as for instance the boy-crazy girl may show trends of detachment, though never in the pronounced way of Group 3. Or there may be imperceptible transitions between Group 1 and 4. The changes in the picture and the mixture of typical trends do not offer any particular difficulty to our understanding, provided we have understood the basic function of the various attitudes as presented in the clear-cut types.

Still a few remarks about prophylaxis and treatment: It is evident I hope, even from this rough outline, that any prophylactic effort made at puberty, such as a sensible enlightenment about menstruation, comes too late. Enlightenment is received on the intellectual level and does not reach the deeply barricaded infantile fears. The prophylaxis can only be effective if it starts from the first days of life. I think one may be justified in formulating its aim in this way: to educate children in courage and endurance instead of filling them with fears. All such general formulae may, however, be more misleading than helpful, because their value depends entirely on the special and exact implications one derives from them, which should be discussed in detail.

Concerning treatment: Difficulties of minor nature may be cured by favorable life circumstances. I doubt whether clear-cut personality changes of this kind are accessible to any psychotherapist working with a less delicate instrument than psychoanalysis, for in contrast to any single neurotic symptom, these disturbances indicate an insecure foundation in the whole personality. We must not forget, however, that even so, life may be the better therapist.

THE NEUROTIC NEED FOR LOVE*

oooooooooooooooooooooooooooooooooooooooooooooooooo

THE TOPIC THAT I WANT TO DISCUSS TODAY is the neurotic need for love. I will probably not present you with new observations, since you are acquainted with the clinical material, which in one form or another has been described many times. The subject matter is vast and so complicated that I must limit myself to a few points. I will be as brief as possible in describing the pertinent phenomena, but rather explicit in discussing their meaning.

I understand in this connection the term "neurosis" not to mean situational neurosis but character neurosis, which starts in early childhood and encompasses more or less the total personality.

When I speak of the neurotic need for love, I mean that phenomenon found in different forms and degrees of awareness in almost every neurosis of our time, which appears as an increased need of the neurotic to be loved, esteemed, and recognized, to be helped, advised, and supported, as well as an increased sensitivity to the frustration of these needs.

What is the difference between the normal and the neurotic need for love? I call normal that which is usual in a given culture. We all want to and enjoy being loved. It enriches our lives and gives us a feeling of happiness. To that extent, the need for love —or more accurately, the need to be loved—is not a neurotic phenomenon. In the neurotic, the need for love is increased. If a waiter or a newspaper vendor are less friendly than usual, it may spoil his mood. This may also happen when at a party everybody is not friendly. I do not need to give more examples, because

* Lecture given at the meeting of the Deutsche Psychoanalytische Gesellschaft, December 23, 1936. "Das neurotische Liebesbedürfnis," *Zentralbl. f. Psychother.*, 10 (1937), pp. 69-82. Reprinted in translation with the permission of the Karen Horney Estate.

these phenomena are well-known. The difference between the normal and the neurotic need for love may be formulated as follows:

While it is important to the healthy person to be loved, honored, and esteemed by those whom he esteems or on whom he is dependent, the neurotic need for love is compulsive and indiscriminate.

These reactions can best be observed in analysis, since there is one characteristic in the patient-analyst relationship that distinguishes it from other human relationships. In analysis the doctor's relative lack of emotional involvement and the patient's free associating make it possible to observe these reactions more easily than in everyday life. However neuroses may differ, we can observe time and again how much the analysand is willing to sacrifice to gain the analyst's acceptance and how sensitive he is to anything that might cause the analyst's displeasure.

Among all the manifestations of the neurotic need for love, I want to emphasize one that is very common in our culture. It is the overvaluation of love. I refer particularly to a type of neurotic women who feel unhappy, insecure, and depressed as long as they do not have someone devoted to them, who loves them or somehow cares for them. I also refer to women for whom the wish to get married has taken on a compulsive quality. They keep staring at this one point in life—getting married—as if hypnotized, even though they themselves are absolutely incapable of loving and their relations to men are notoriously poor. Such women are incapable of developing their creative potentials and talents.

An important characteristic of the neurotic need for love is its insatiability, which shows itself as an extreme jealousy: "You must love only me!" We can observe this phenomenon in many marriages, love affairs, and friendships. Jealousy, as I understand it here, is not a reaction based on rational factors, but is insatiable and demands that they be loved exclusively.

Another expression of the insatiability of the neurotic need for love is the need for unconditional love, which is expressed as "You must love me, no matter how I behave." This is an important factor, particularly at the beginning of the analysis. We may then get the impression that patients behave in a provocative manner, not out of primary aggression, but rather to plead "Will you still accept me, even if I behave abominably?" These patients take exception to the slightest nuances of the analyst's voice, as if to say, "You see, you can't stand me after all." The need for unconditional love shows itself also in their demand to be loved without having to give anything, as if to say: "It is simple to love someone who reciprocates, but let's see if you love me, if you don't get anything in return." Even the fact that the patient has to pay the analyst is proof to him that the doctor's primary intention is not to help; otherwise he would not derive any benefit from treating the patient. It can go so far that even in their sex life they may feel, "You love me only because you get your sexual satisfaction from me." The partner must prove his real love by making sacrifices in his moral values, reputation, money, time, etc. Anything that falls short of this absolute demand is taken as a rejection.

Observing the insatiability of the neurotic need for love I asked myself whether it is really affection that the neurotic person craves, or whether he is not actually out for material gain. Is the demand for love, perhaps, only a façade for the secret wish to get something from another person, be it a favor, sacrifice of time, money, gifts, etc.?

This question cannot be answered in general terms. There is a wide range of individual differences from people who indeed crave affection, esteem, help, etc., to neurotics who do not seem interested at all in affection, but who want to exploit and take all they can get. And between these two extremes there are all kinds of transitions and shadings.

At this point the following comment may be appropriate. Those people who consciously have completely repudiated love will say, "This talk about love is a lot of nonsense. Give me something real!" These people have been deeply embittered early in life and they are convinced that there is no such thing as love. They have blotted it out completely from their lives. The truth of my assumption seems confirmed by the analyses of these individuals. If they stay in analysis long enough, they begin to believe that kindness, friendship, and affection really exist. Then, like in a system of communicating tubes or scales, their insatiable desires and cravings for material things disappear. An honest desire to be loved comes to the fore, at first subtly, then more and more forcefully. There are cases in which the connection between the insatiable desire for love and general greed can be clearly observed. When these people who present the neurotic character trait of insatiability develop love relationships, and when subsequently these relationships break up for inner reasons, these people may start to eat insatiably and may gain twenty pounds or more. They lose this excess weight when they begin a new love relationship, and the cycle may be repeated a number of times.

Another sign of the neurotic need for love is the extreme sensitivity to rejection, which is so frequent among persons with hysterical characteristics. They perceive all kinds of things as rejections and react with intense hate. One of my patients has a cat that occasionally would not react to his show of affection. Once, in a rage, he threw the cat against the wall. This is a typical example of the rage that can be triggered by rejection, whatever its form.

The reaction to real or imagined rejection is not always obvious; more often it is hidden. In analysis the hidden hate may appear as a lack of productiveness, as doubts about the value of analysis, or in some other form of resistance. The patient may become resistant because he takes an interpretation as a rejection. While we believe that we are giving him some realistic insight, he reads into it nothing but criticism and contempt.

Patients in whom one finds an unshakable, though unconscious, conviction that there is no such thing as love, usually have suffered severe disappointments in childhood, which made them blot out of their lives love, affection, and friendship once and for all. Such conviction serves at the same time as a protection against the actual experiencing of rejection. Here is an example: I have in my consultation room a sculpture of my daughter. A patient once asked me—and she admitted that she had wanted to ask me this question for a long time—whether I liked the sculpture. I said, "Since it represents my daughter, I like it." The patient was shaken by my reply since—without being aware of it—love and affection had been only empty words for her in which she never had believed.

While these patients protect themselves against the actual experiencing of rejection through the pre-established assumption that they cannot be liked, others protect themselves against disappointment by overcompensating. They distort the actual rejection into an expression of esteem. Recently I had the following experience with three of my patients: One patient had applied half-heartedly for a position and was told that the job was not for him—a typical courteous American way of saying no. He interpreted this to mean that he was too good for the job. Another patient had fantasies that after the sessions I would go to the window to see her leave. She later admitted to a strong fear of being rejected by me. The third patient was one of those few whom I do not respect as a human being. While he had dreams that clearly showed his conviction of my contempt for him, he succeeded in convincing himself consciously that I liked him very much.

If we realize how great this neurotic need for love is, how many sacrifices a neurotic person is willing to accept, and how far he will go in his irrational behavior in order to be loved and esteemed and to receive kindness, advice, and help, we must ask ourselves why it is so difficult for him to get these things.

For he does not succeed in obtaining the degree and measure of love that he needs. One reason is the insatiability of his need for love, whereby—with rare exceptions—nothing is ever enough. If we go deeper, we recognize another reason, implicit in the first one. It is the incapacity of the neurotic person to love.

It is very difficult to define love. Here we can content ourselves with describing it in very general and nonscientific terms as the capacity to give spontaneously of oneself either to people or to a cause or to an idea, instead of retaining everything for oneself in an egocentric way. The neurotic person is generally not capable of this, because of the anxiety and the many latent and open hostilities that he usually acquired early in life, since he himself was treated badly. These hostilities have considerably increased in the course of his development. However, he has repressed them again and again out of fear. As a consequence, either because of his fears or because of his hostility, he is unable to give of himself, to surrender. For the same reasons, he is incapable of real consideration for others. He hardly takes into account how much love, time, and help another person can give or wants to give. He therefore takes it as an injurious rejection if someone needs to be alone sometimes or has time and interest for other goals or other people.

The neurotic person is generally not aware of his inability to love. He does not know that he cannot love. There are, however, all degrees of awareness. Some neurotics say openly, "No, I cannot love." However, much more commonly, a neurotic lives under the illusion that he is a great lover and that he has a particularly strong capacity for giving of himself. He will assure us, "It is easy enough for me to get things for other people, but I cannot do it for myself." This is not because of a motherly, caring attitude for others, as he believes, but is due to other factors. It may be caused by his craving for power or by his fear that he will not be acceptable to others unless he is useful to them. Furthermore, he has a deeply ingrained inhibition against consciously desiring anything for himself and against wishing to be happy. These taboos, together with the fact that for the above-mentioned reasons the neurotic person occasionally can do something for other people, strengthen his illusion that he can love and actually does love deeply. He holds onto this self-deception, since it has the important function of justifying his own claim for love. It would be untenable to demand that much love from others, if he were aware that basically he does not care for others at all.

These thoughts help us understand the illusion of the "great love," a problem that I cannot go into today.

We had begun to discuss the reasons why it is so difficult for the neurotic to obtain the affection, help, love, etc., that he craves so much. So far we have found two reasons: his insatiability and his incapacity to love. The third reason is his enormous fear of rejection. This fear can be so great as to prevent him from approaching people either with a question or even a kind gesture, because he lives in constant fear that the other person might reject him. He may even be afraid to give a present, out of fear of rejection.

As we have seen, a real or imagined rejection produces intense hostility in a neurotic person of this type. The fear of rejection and his hostile reaction to rejection cause him to withdraw more and more. In less severe cases, kindness and friendliness may make the neurotic person feel better for a while. More severely neurotic persons cannot accept any degree of human warmth. They may be compared with someone who is starving but whose hands are tied behind his back. They are convinced that they cannot be loved—a conviction that is unshakable. Here is an example: One of my patients wanted to park his car in front of a hotel; the doorman came to help him. But when my patient saw the doorman approach, he became frightened, thinking, "Oh my God, I must have parked in the wrong spot!" Or if a girl were friendly, he would interpret her friendliness as sarcasm. You all know that when you pay such a patient an honest compliment—e.g., that he is intelligent—he will be convinced that you acted out of therapeutic considerations and therefore did not sincerely mean it. This distrust can be more or less conscious.

Friendliness can produce severe degrees of anxiety in cases that approach schizophrenia. A friend of mine who has a great deal of experience with schizophrenics told me of a patient who occasionally asked him for an extra session. My friend would make an annoyed face, look into his appointment book and finally grumble: "All right, if it has to be, come . . ." He acted this way because he was aware of the anxiety that friendliness may cause in these people. These reactions frequently occur in neuroses as well.

Please do not confuse love with sexuality. A female patient once told me: "I have no fear whatever of sex, but I am terribly afraid of love." In fact she could hardly pronounce the word "love" and she did everything in her power to keep inner distance from people. She entered easily into sexual relationships and even achieved complete orgasms. Emotionally, however, she remained very distant from men and spoke of them with the kind of objectivity one might use when talking about cars.

This fear of love in any form deserves its own detailed discussion. Essentially, these people protect themselves against their enormous fear of living, their basic anxiety, by keeping themselves all closed up and they maintain their feeling of security by withholding themselves.

Part of the problem is their fear of dependency. Since these people actually are dependent on the affection of others and since they need it as much as one needs oxygen to breathe, the danger of getting into a tormenting dependency relationship is indeed very great. They fear any form of dependency the more, since they are convinced that other people are hostile toward them.

We can frequently observe how the same person is utterly and helplessly dependent in one period of his life, and how in another period he fends off with all his might anything which slightly resembles dependency. One young girl, prior to entering analysis, had had several love affairs of a more or less sexual character, all of which had ended in great disappointment. At those times she had become profoundly unhappy, had wallowed in her misery and had felt that she could live only for this particular man, as if her whole life had no meaning without him. Actually, she was completely unrelated to these men and had no real feeling for any of them. After a few such experiences her attitude changed into the opposite, i.e., into an overanxious refusal of any possible dependency. To avoid any danger from this source, she shut off her feelings completely. All she wanted now was to have men in her power. To have feelings or to show them, became a weakness to her, and therefore contemptible. An expression of this fear is the following: She had started analysis with me in Chicago. Then I moved to New York. There was no reason for her not to come with me, since she could work there just as well. However, the fact of having gone to New York because of me disturbed her so much that she harassed me for three months, complaining of how hideous a place New York was. The motive was: Don't ever give in, don't do anything for anybody else, because this already means dependency and therefore is dangerous.

These are the most important reasons that make it so extremely difficult for the neurotic to find fulfillment. I should like to briefly mention what roads, nevertheless, are open to him to achieve it. I refer here to factors with which you are all familiar. The main means by which the neurotic tries to obtain fulfillment are: calling attention to his own love; his appeal for pity; and his threats.

The meaning of the first one can be expressed as, "I love you so much, therefore, you must love me, too." The forms this takes may differ, but the basic position is the same. This is a very common attitude in love relationships.

You are also familiar with the appeal to pity. This presupposes a complete disbelief in love and a conviction of the basic hostility in others. Under the circumstances, the neurotic feels that only by emphasizing his helplessness, weakness, and misfortune can he get anywhere.

The last way consists of threats. A Berlin saying expresses it well, "Love me or I'll kill you." We see this attitude often enough in analysis as well as in everyday life. There may be open threats to harm oneself or others; threats of suicide, of destroying a person's reputation, etc. They, however, may also be disguised—e.g., in the form of an illness—when some wish for love is not satisfied. There are innumerable ways in which completely unconscious threats may be expressed. We see them in all kinds of relationships: love affairs, marriages, and also in the doctor-patient relationship.

How can this neurotic need for love, with all its enormous intensity, compulsivity, and insatiability, be understood? There are a number of possible interpretations. It could be considered as nothing more than an infantile trait, but I do not think so. Compared with adults, children do have a greater need for support, help, protection, and warmth—Ferenczi has written some good papers on the subject. This is so, because children are more helpless than adults. A healthy child, growing up in an atmosphere where he is treated well and feels welcome, where there is actual warmth—such a child is not insatiable in his need for love. When he falls, he might go to his mother to be consoled. A child, however, who is tied to his mother's apron strings, is already neurotic.

One might also think that the neurotic need for love is an expression of a "mother fixation." This seems to be confirmed by dreams that express directly or symbolically the desire to suck on the mother's breasts or to return to the womb. The early history of these persons shows indeed that they did not get enough love and warmth from their mothers or that, already in child-hood, they were tied to their mothers by a similar compulsivity. It seems that in the first case, the neurotic need for love is the expression of a persistent longing for the love of a mother, which was not freely given in early life. This, however, does not explain why these children hold on so tenaciously to the claim for love, instead of looking for other possible solutions—e.g., a complete withdrawal from people. In the second case, one might think that it represents a direct repetition of the clinging to the mother. This interpretation, however, merely throws the problem back into an earlier phase without clarifying it. It still remains to be explained why these children needed to cling excessively to their mothers in the first place. In both cases the question remains unanswered. What are the dynamic factors that maintain, in later life, an atti-tude acquired in childhood, or that make it impossible to let go of this infantile attitude?

In many cases the obvious interpretation seems to be that the neurotic need for love is the expression of particularly strong narcissistic traits. As I have pointed out before, these people are actually unable to love others. They are indeed egocentric. I be-lieve, however, that one should be very careful in the way one uses the word "narcissistic." There is a great difference between self-love and the egocentricity based on anxiety. The neurotics I have in mind have anything but a good relationship with themselves. As a rule they treat themselves as their worst enemies and usually they have outright contempt for themselves. As I will show later on, they need to be loved in order to feel tolerably secure and to raise their disturbed self-esteem.

Another possible explanation is the fear of loss of love, which Freud considered to be specific for the female psyche. The fear of loss of love is very great indeed in these cases. I question, how-ever, whether this phenomenon in itself does not need to be explained. I believe that it can be understood only if we know what value a person places on being loved.

Finally we must ask whether the increased need for love actually is a libidinal phenomenon. Freud would certainly answer in the affirmative, because to him affection is in itself an aim-inhibited sexual desire. It seems to me, though, that this concept is unproven, to say the least. Ethnological research seems to indicate that the connection between tenderness and sexuality is a relatively late cultural acquisition. If one considers the neurotic need for love as a basically sexual phenomenon, it would be hard to understand why it occurs also in those neurotics who have a satisfactory sex life. Furthermore, this concept would necessarily lead us to consider as sexual phenomena not only the desire for affection, but also the desire for advice, protection, and recognition.

If one puts the emphasis on the insatiability of the neurotic need for love, the whole phenomenon could represent, in terms of the libido theory, an expression of an "oral erotic fixation" or a "regression." This concept presupposes a willingness to reduce very complex psychological phenomena to physiological factors. I believe that this assumption is not only untenable, but that it makes the understanding of psychological phenomena even more difficult.

Aside from the validity of these explanations, they all suffer from the fact that they focus only on one particular aspect of the phenomenon—that is, either on the desire for affection, or on the insatiability, the dependency, or the egocentricity. This made it difficult to see the phenomenon in its totality. My observations in the analytical situation have shown that all these manifold factors are only different manifestations and expressions of one phenomenon. It seems to me that we can understand the total phenomenon if we see it as one of the ways of protecting oneself against anxiety. Actually, these people suffer from an increased basic anxiety and their whole life shows that their unending search for love is but another attempt to assuage this anxiety.

Observations in the analytical situation clearly indicate that an increase of the need for love arises when the patient is pressured by some particular anxiety and that it disappears when he understands this connection. Since in analysis anxiety is necessarily stirred up, it is understandable that the patient tries again and again to cling to the analyst. We can observe, for example, that a patient who is under the pressure of his repressed hatred against the analyst and therefore is full of anxiety, begins to seek the analyst's friendship or love particularly in this situation. I believe that a large part of what is called a "positive transference" and what is interpreted as a repetition of an original attachment to the father or the mother, is in reality a desire to seek assurance and protection against anxiety. The motto is, "If you love me, you won't hurt me." Both the indiscriminateness of the choice of people and the compulsiveness and insatiability of the desire are understandable if one sees them as expressions of such need for assurance. I believe that a good deal of the dependency into which a patient in analysis falls so easily, can be avoided, if one recognizes these connections and uncovers them in all their details. It has been my experience that one gets into the core of the real anxiety problems much faster, if one analyzes the patient's need for love as an attempt to protect himself against anxiety.

Very often the neurotic need for love appears in the form of sexual seductiveness toward the analyst. The patient expresses either through his behavior or in his dreams that he is in love with the analyst and that he desires a sexual involvement of some kind. In some cases the need for love manifests itself mainly or even exclusively in the sexual area. To understand this phenomenon, one ought to remember that sexual desires do not necessarily express real sexual needs, but that sexuality may also represent a form of contact with another human being. My experience indicates that the neurotic need for love takes sexual forms the more readily, the more emotional relationships with other people have been disturbed. When sexual fantasies, dreams, etc., appear early in analysis, I take it as a signal that this person is full of anxiety and that his relationships with other people are basically poor. In such cases, sexuality is one of the few or maybe the only bridge to other people. Sexual desires toward the analyst readily disappear when they are interpreted as a need for contact, based on anxiety; this opens the road toward working through the anxieties that were meant to be assuaged.

Connections of this kind help us understand certain occurrences of increased sexual needs. To state the problem briefly: It is understandable that people whose neurotic need for love is expressed in sexual terms, will tend to start one sexual relationship after another, as if under a compulsion. This has to be so, because their relationship with other people is too disturbed to be conducted on a different plane. It is also understandable that these people do not tolerate sexual abstinence easily. What I have said so far about people with heterosexual leanings also holds true for people with homosexual or bisexual tendencies. A great deal of what appears as a homosexual tendency, or what is interpreted as such, is in reality an expression of the neurotic need for love.

Finally, the connection between anxiety and the increased need for love helps us to understand better the phenomenon of the Oedipus complex. In fact, all the manifestations of the neurotic need for love can be found in what Freud has described as the Oedipus complex: the clinging to one parent, the insatiability of the need for love, the jealousy, the sensitivity to rejection, and the intense hate following a rejection. As you know, Freud conceives of the Oedipus complex as a phenomenon that basically is phylogenetically determined. Our experience with adult patients, however, makes us wonder how many of these childhood reactions —so well observed by Freud—are already caused by anxiety in the same way as we see it later in life. Ethnological observations make it appear questionable that the Oedipus complex is a biologically determined phenomenon—a fact already pointed out by Böhm and others. The childhood histories of those neurotics who have a particularly strong tie with their father or mother always show a great number of such factors, known to arouse anxiety in children. Essentially, the following factors seem to work together in these cases—arousal of hostility, which is expressed because of coexisting intimidations and the coexisting lowering of self-esteem. I cannot at this point go into the detailed reasons why repressed hostility easily leads to anxiety. In a very general way it can be said that anxiety arises in the child because he senses that to express his hostile impulses would totally threaten the security of his existence.

With this last comment I do not mean to negate the existence and importance of the Oedipus complex. I mean only to question whether it is a general phenomenon and to what extent it is caused by the influence of neurotic parents.

Finally, I want to say briefly what I mean by increased basic anxiety. In the sense of "creature anxiety" (*Angst der Kreatur*), it is a general human phenomenon. In the neurotic this anxiety is increased. It can briefly be described as a feeling of helplessness in a hostile and overpowering world. For the most part the individual is not aware of this anxiety as such. He is only aware of a series of anxieties with very different contents: fear of thunderstorms, fear of streets, fear of blushing, fear of contagion, fear of examinations, fear of railroads, etc. It is, of course, strictly determined in each specific case why a person has this or that particular fear. If we look deeper we see, however, that all these fears derive their intensity from the underlying increased basic anxiety.

There are different ways to protect oneself against such basic anxiety. In our culture the following ways are most common. Firstly, the neurotic need for love, which carries the motto, "If you love me, you will not hurt me." Secondly, submissiveness—"If I give in, always do what people expect, never ask for anything, never resist—then nobody will hurt me." The third way has been described by Adler and particularly by Künkel. It is the compulsive drive for power, success, and possessions under the motto, "If I am the stronger, the more successful one, then you cannot hurt me." The fourth way consists of withdrawing from people emotionally in order to be safe and independent. One of the most important effects of this strategy is the attempt to repress feelings as such completely, so as to become invulnerable. Another way is the compulsive accumulation of possessions, which in this case is not subordinated to the drive for power, but rather to the desire to be independent of others.

One finds very frequently that the neurotic does not choose one of these ways exclusively, but that he attempts to achieve the goal of pacifying his anxiety by different, often quite opposite means. This is what leads him into unsolvable conflicts. In our culture the most important neurotic conflict is between a compulsive and inconsiderate desire to be the first under all circumstances and the simultaneous need to be loved by everybody.*

* This lecture is based upon the author's book, *The Neurotic Personality of Our Time* (New York, W. W. Norton & Co., Inc., 1937).

INDEX